The Lord's Prayer

A Collection of Historical Writings on the Lord's Prayer

Compiled and Edited By

Curtis Rose

reNEW Publications

Preface

The Lord's Prayer has become much more important in my life over the last few years. This has been especially true during times of deep wrestling and spiritual dryness. At times, this prayer became the substance of my prayers when I had no idea what else to pray. It has proven to be a foundation for prayer when I was afraid that I had no remaining foundations whatsoever.

In light of its significance to me, I began to search for and compile various writings about the Lord's Prayer from earlier times in church history. I wanted to better grasp the view of this prayer from church leaders and church teachings over the course of the church's history. That explains why this collection of writings includes six sections: first, the Scripture itself; second, several catechisms in church history; third, expositions on the Lord's Prayer; fourth, a section of sermons on the Lord's Prayer by well-known men in church history; fifth, other writings on the Lord's prayer; sixth, writings of some early church fathers.

Some of these writings are much more challenging to read than others. I would encourage you to push on as far as possible in reading them. Many treasures can be found here for those willing to press on through the material. I have tried to make these writings more readable by modernizing both the format and some of the wording. In some cases I have shortened sentences and divided long paragraphs into shorter paragraphs. I would encourage you to seek out the original sources if you are interested in seeing and reading exactly what these people said and wrote.

I have been conscious of over-editing that might make these writings unrecognizable. So, while you can expect some words and wording to have been edited for clarity, you can also expect that in many respects these writings will have most of their original flavor. This may make your reading a little more challenging, but it offers a better chance that the editor has not muddied the waters too much.

This search has been useful to me personally and my prayer is that it will be useful to you, as well. May these writings encourage you evermore to pray like this, "Our Father in heaven…"

Curtis Rose

reNEW Publications

Table of Contents

Section 1 – Scripture

Chapter 1 – The Scripture

(Matthew 6:9-13)

(c. 70-80 a.d.)

King James Version

After this manner therefore pray ye: Our Father which art in heaven, Hallowed be thy name. Thy kingdom come. Thy will be done in earth, as it is in heaven. Give us this day our daily bread. And forgive us our debts, as we forgive our debtors. And lead us not into temptation, but deliver us from evil: For thine is the kingdom, and the power, and the glory, forever. Amen.

English Standard Version

Pray then like this: "Our Father in heaven, hallowed be your name. Your kingdom come, your will be done, on earth as it is in heaven. Give us this day our daily bread, and forgive us our debts, as we also have forgiven our debtors. And lead us not into temptation, but deliver us from evil.

Williams New Testament

So this is the way you must pray: Our Father in heaven, Your name be revered. Your kingdom come. Your will be done on earth as it is done in heaven. Give us today our daily bread for the day. And forgive us our debts, as we have forgiven our debtors. And do not let us be subjected to temptation, but save us from the evil one.

Section 2 – The Teachings of the Church

Chapter 2 – Westminster Shorter Catechism

(England, 1646)

Q98: What is prayer?

A98: Prayer is an offering up of our desires unto God for things agreeable to his will, in the name of Christ, with confession of our sins, and thankful acknowledgement of his mercies.

Q99: What rule has God given for our direction in prayer?

A99: The whole Word of God is of use to direct us in prayer; but the special rule of direction is that form of prayer which Christ taught his disciples, commonly called The Lord's Prayer.

Q100: What does the preface of the Lord's prayer teach us?

A100: The preface of the Lord's prayer, which is, "Our Father which art in heaven," teaches us to draw near to God with all holy reverence and confidence, as children to a father, able and ready to help us; and that we should pray with and for others.

Q101: What do we pray for in the first petition?

A101: In the first petition, which is, "Hallowed be thy name," we pray, That God would enable us and others to glorify him in all that by which he makes himself known; and that he would dispose all things to his own glory.

Q102: What do we pray for in the second petition?

A102: In the second petition, which is, "Thy kingdom come," we pray, That Satan's kingdom may be destroyed; and that the kingdom of grace may be advanced, ourselves and others brought into it, and kept in it; and the kingdom of glory may be hastened.

Q103: What do we pray for in the third petition?

A103: In the third petition, which is, "Thy will be done in earth, as it is in heaven," we pray, That God, by his grace, would make us able and willing to know, obey, and submit to his will in all things, as the angels do in heaven.

Q104: What do we pray for in the fourth petition?

A104: In the fourth petition, which is, "Give us this day our daily bread," we pray, That of God's free gift we may receive a competent portion of the good things of this life, and enjoy his blessing with them.

Q105: What do we pray for in the fifth petition?

A105: In the fifth petition, which is, "And forgive us our debts, as we forgive our debtors," we pray, That God, for Christ's sake, would freely pardon all our sins; which we are able to be rather encouraged to ask, because by his grace we are enabled from the heart to forgive others.

Q106: What do we pray for in the sixth petition?

A106: In the sixth petition, which is, "And lead us not into temptation, but deliver us from evil," we pray, That God would either keep us from being tempted to sin, or support and deliver us when we are tempted.

Q107: What does the conclusion of the Lord's prayer teach us?

A107: The conclusion of the Lord's prayer, which is, "For thine is the kingdom, and the power, and the glory, forever, Amen." teaches us, to take our encouragement in prayer from God only, and in our prayers to praise him, ascribing kingdom, power and glory to him.

And, in testimony of our desire, and assurance to be heard, we say, Amen.

Chapter 3 - The Small Catechism – Martin Luther

(Germany, published in 1529 for the education of children)

Our Father who art in heaven.

What does this mean?

Answer - God would thereby [with this little introduction] tenderly urge us to believe that He is our true Father, and that we are His true children, so that we may ask Him confidently with all assurance, as dear children ask their dear father.

The First Petition. Hallowed be Thy name.

What does this mean?

Answer - God's name is indeed holy in itself; but we pray in this petition that it may become holy among us also.

How is this done?

Answer - When the Word of God is taught in its truth and purity, and we as the children of God also lead holy lives in accordance with it. To this end help us, dear Father in heaven. But he that teaches and lives otherwise than God's Word teaches profanes the name of God among us. From this preserve us, Heavenly Father.

The Second Petition. Thy kingdom come.

What does this mean?

Answer - The kingdom of God comes indeed without our prayer, of itself; but we pray in this petition that it may come unto us also.

How is this done?

Answer - When our heavenly Father gives us His Holy Spirit, so that by His grace we believe His holy Word and lead a godly life here in time and yonder in eternity.

The Third Petition. Thy will be done on earth as it is in heaven.

What does this mean?

Answer - The good and gracious will of God is done indeed without our prayer; but we pray in this petition that it may be done among us also.

How is this done?

Answer - When God breaks and hinders every evil counsel and will which would not let us hallow the name of God nor let His kingdom come, such as the will of the devil, the world, and our flesh; but strengthens and keeps us steadfast in His Word and in faith unto our end. This is His gracious and good will.

The Fourth Petition. Give us this day our daily bread.

What does this mean?

Answer - God gives daily bread, even without our prayer, to all wicked men; but we pray in this petition that He would lead us to know it, and to receive our daily bread with thanksgiving.

What is meant by daily bread?

Answer - Everything that belongs to the support and needs of the body, such as meat, drink, clothing, shoes, house, homestead, field, cattle, money, goods, a pious spouse, pious children, pious servants, pious and faithful magistrates, good government, good weather, peace, health, discipline, honor, good friends, faithful neighbors, and the like.

The Fifth Petition. And forgive us our trespasses, as we forgive those who trespass against us.

What does this mean?

Answer - We pray in this petition that our Father in heaven would not look upon our sins, nor deny such petitions on account of them; for we are worthy of none of the things for which we pray, neither have we deserved them; but that He would grant them all to us by grace; for we daily sin much, and indeed deserve nothing but punishment. So will we verily, on our part, also heartily forgive and also readily do good to those who sin against us.

The Sixth Petition. And lead us not into temptation.

What does this mean?

Answer - God, indeed, tempts no one; but we pray in this petition that God would guard and keep us, so that the devil, the world, and our flesh may not deceive us, nor seduce us into misbelief, despair, and other great shame and vice; and though we be assailed by them, that still we may finally overcome and gain the victory.

The Seventh Petition. But deliver us from evil.

What does this mean?

Answer - We pray in this petition, as in a summary, that our Father in heaven would deliver us from all manner of evil, of body and soul, property and honor, and at last, when our last hour shall come, grant us a blessed end, and graciously take us from this vale of tears to Himself into heaven.

Amen.

What does this mean?

Answer - That I should be certain that these petitions are acceptable to our Father in heaven and heard; for He Himself has commanded us so to pray, and has promised that He will hear us. Amen, Amen; that is, Yea, yea, it shall be so.

Chapter 4 - The Heidelberg Catechism

(Approved in 1563 by the Synod of Heidelberg)

116. Q. Why is prayer necessary for Christians?

A. Because prayer is the most important part of the thankfulness which God requires of us. Moreover, God will give His grace and the Holy Spirit only to those who constantly and with heartfelt longing ask Him for these gifts and thank Him for them.

117. Q. What belongs to a prayer which pleases God and is heard by Him?

A. First, we must from the heart call upon the one true God only, who has revealed Himself in His Word, for all that He has commanded us to pray. Second, we must thoroughly know our need and misery, so that we may humble ourselves before God. Third, we must rest on this firm foundation that, although we do not deserve it, God will certainly hear our prayer for the sake of Christ our Lord, as He has promised us in His Word.

118. Q. What has God commanded us to ask of Him?

A. All the things we need for body and soul, as included in the prayer which Christ our Lord Himself taught us.

119. Q. What is the Lord's prayer?

A. Our Father who art in heaven, Hallowed be Thy Name. Thy kingdom come, Thy will be done, On earth as it is in heaven. Give us this day our daily bread; And forgive us our debts, As we also have forgiven our debtors; And lead us not into temptation, But deliver us from the evil one. For Thine is the kingdom, and the power, and the glory, forever. Amen.

120. Q. Why has Christ commanded us to address God as Our Father?

A. To awaken in us at the very beginning of our prayer that childlike reverence and trust toward God which should be basic to our prayer: God has become our Father through Christ and will much less deny us what we ask of Him in faith than our fathers would refuse us earthly things.

121. Q. Why is there added, Who art in heaven?

A. These words teach us not to think of God's heavenly majesty in an earthly manner, and to expect from His almighty power all things we need for body and soul.

122. Q. What is the first petition?

A. Hallowed be Thy Name. That is: Grant us first of all that we may rightly know Thee, and sanctify, glorify, and praise Thee in all Thy works, in which shine forth Thy almighty power, wisdom, goodness, righteousness, mercy, and truth. Grant us also that we may so direct our whole life - our thoughts, words, and actions - that Thy Name is not blasphemed because of us but always honored and praised.

123. Q. What is the second petition?

A. Thy kingdom come. That is: So rule us by Thy Word and Spirit that more and more we submit to Thee. Preserve and increase Thy church. Destroy the works of the devil, every power that raises itself against Thee, and every conspiracy against Thy holy Word. Do all this until the fulness of Thy kingdom comes, wherein Thou shalt be all in all.

124. Q. What is the third petition?

A. Thy will be done, on earth as it is in heaven. That is: Grant that we and all men may deny our own will, and without any murmuring obey Thy will, for it alone is good. Grant also that everyone may carry out the duties of his office and calling as willingly and faithfully as the angels in heaven.

125. Q. What is the fourth petition?

A. Give us this day our daily bread. That is: Provide us with all our bodily needs so that we may acknowledge that Thou art the only fountain of all good, and that our care and labor, and also Thy gifts, cannot do us any good without Thy blessing. Grant therefore that we may withdraw our trust from all creatures, and place it only in Thee.

126. Q. What is the fifth petition?

A. And forgive us our debts, as we also have forgiven our debtors. That is: For the sake of Christ's blood, do not impute to us, wretched sinners; any of our transgressions, nor the evil which still clings to us, as we also find this evidence of Thy grace in us that we are fully determined wholeheartedly to forgive our neighbor.

127. Q. What is the sixth petition?

A. And lead us not into temptation, but deliver us from the evil one. That is: In ourselves we are so weak that we cannot stand even for a moment. Moreover, our sworn enemies-- the devil, the world, and our own flesh -- do not cease to attack us. Wilt Thou, therefore, uphold and strengthen us by the power of Thy Holy Spirit, so that in this spiritual war we may not go down to defeat, but always firmly resist our enemies, until we finally obtain the complete victory.

128. Q. How do you conclude your prayer?

A. For Thine is the kingdom, and the power, and the glory, forever. That is: All this we ask of Thee because, as our King, having power over all things, Thou art both willing and able to give us all that is good, and because not we but Thy holy Name should so receive all glory forever.

129. Q. What does the word Amen mean?

A. Amen means: It is true and certain. For God has much more certainly heard my prayer than I feel in my heart that I desire this of Him.

Section 3 - Expositions on the Lord's Prayer

Chapter 5 - J.C. Ryle on the Lord's Prayer

(John Charles Ryle, 1816-1900)

From 'The Gospel of Matthew'

Pray like this: 'Our Father in heaven, may your name be kept holy. Let your Kingdom come. Let your will be done, as in heaven, so on earth. Give us today our daily bread. Forgive us our debts, as we also forgive our debtors. Bring us not into temptation, but deliver us from the evil one. For yours is the Kingdom, the power, and the glory forever. Amen.'

"For if you forgive men their trespasses, your heavenly Father will also forgive you. But if you don't forgive men their trespasses, neither will your Father forgive your trespasses."

Perhaps no part of Scripture is so well known as this. Its words are familiar, wherever Christianity is found. Thousands, and tens of thousands, who never saw a Bible, or heard the pure Gospel, are acquainted with "Our Father," and "Paternoster." Happy would it be for the world, if this prayer was as well known in the spirit, as it is in the letter!

Perhaps no part of Scripture is so full and so simple at the same time, as this. It is the first prayer which we learn to offer up when we are little children. Here is its simplicity. It contains the germ of everything which the most advanced saint can desire. Here is its fullness. The more we ponder every word it contains, the more we shall feel, "this prayer is of God."

The Lord's Prayer consists of ten parts or sentences. There is one declaration of the Being to whom we pray. There are three prayers respecting His name, His kingdom, and His will. There are four prayers respecting our daily needs, our sins, our weakness, and our dangers. There is one profession of our feeling towards others. There is one concluding ascription of praise. In all these parts we are taught to say "we," and "our." We are to remember others, as well as ourselves. On each of these parts a volume might be written. We must content ourselves at present with taking up sentence by sentence, and marking out the direction in which each sentence points.

The first sentence declares to whom we are to pray, "**Our Father who is in heaven.**" We are not to cry to saints and angels, but to the everlasting Father, the Father of spirits, the Lord of heaven and earth. We call Him Father, in the lowest sense, as our Creator; as Paul told the Athenians, "in him we live, and move, and have our being--we are also his offspring" (Act 17:28). We call Him Father in the highest sense, as the Father of our Lord Jesus Christ, reconciling us to Himself, through the death of His Son (Col 1:20-22). We profess that which the Old Testament saints only saw dimly, if at all--we profess to be His children by faith in Christ, and to have "the Spirit of adoption by which we cry, Abba, Father" (Rom 8:15). This, we must never forget, is the sonship that we must desire if we would be saved. Without faith in Christ's blood, and union with Him, it is vain to talk of trusting in the Fatherhood of God.

The second sentence is a petition respecting God's name--"**May your name be kept holy.**" By the "name" of God we mean all those attributes under which He is revealed to us--His power, wisdom, holiness, justice, mercy, and truth. By asking that they may be "holy," we mean that they may be made known and glorified. The glory of God is the first thing that God's children should desire. It is the object of one of our Lord's own prayers--"Father, glorify your name." (John 12:28.) It is the purpose for which the world was created. It is the end for which the saints are called and converted. It is the chief thing we should seek, that "in all things God may be glorified" (1Pet 4:11).

The third sentence is a petition concerning God's kingdom. "**May your kingdom come.**" By His kingdom we mean first, the kingdom of grace which God sets up and maintains in the hearts of all living members of Christ, by His Spirit and word. But we mean chiefly, the kingdom of glory which shall one day be set up, when Jesus shall come the second time, and "all men shall know Him from the least to the greatest." This is the time when sin, and sorrow, and Satan shall be cast out of the world. It is the time when the Jews shall be converted, and the fullness of the Gentiles shall come in (Rom 11:25), and a time that is above all things to be desired. It therefore fills a foremost place in the Lord's prayer. We ask that which is expressed in the words of the Burial service, "that it may please you to hasten your kingdom."

The fourth sentence is a petition concerning God's will. **"May your will be done, as in heaven, so on earth."** We here pray that God's laws may be obeyed by men as perfectly, readily, and unceasingly, as they are by angels in heaven. We ask that those who now obey not His laws, may be taught to obey them, and that those who do obey them, may obey them better. Our truest happiness is perfect submission to God's will, and it is the highest charity to pray that all mankind may know it, obey it, and submit to it.

The fifth sentence is a petition respecting our own daily needs. **"Give us this day our daily bread."** We are here taught to acknowledge our entire dependence on God, for the supply of our daily necessities. As Israel required daily manna, so we require daily "bread." We confess that we are poor, weak, needy creatures, and beseech Him who is our Maker to take care of us. We ask for "bread," as the simplest of our needs, and in that word we include all that our bodies require.

The sixth sentence is a petition respecting our sins. **"Forgive us our debts."** We confess that we are sinners, and need daily grants of pardon and forgiveness. This is a part of the Lord's prayer which deserves especially to be remembered. It condemns all self-righteousness and self-justifying. We are instructed here to keep up a continual habit of confession at the throne of grace, and a continual habit of seeking mercy and remission. Let this never be forgotten. We need daily to "wash our feet" (John 13:10).

The seventh sentence is a profession respecting our own feelings towards others--we ask our Father to **"forgive us our debts, as we also forgive our debtors."** This is the only profession in the whole prayer, and the only part on which our Lord comments and dwells, when He has concluded the prayer. The plain object of it is, to remind us that we must not expect our prayers for forgiveness to be heard, if we pray with malice and spite in our hearts towards others. To pray in such a frame of mind is mere formality and hypocrisy. It is even worse than hypocrisy. It is as much as saying, "Do not forgive me at all." Our prayer is nothing without charity. We must not expect to be forgiven, if we cannot forgive.

The eighth sentence is a petition respecting our weakness. **"Bring us not into temptation."** It teaches us that we are liable, at all times, to be led astray, and fall. It instructs us to confess our infirmity, and beseech God to hold us up, and not allow us to run into sin. We ask Him, who orders all things in heaven and earth, to restrain us from going into that which would injure our souls, and never to allow us to be tempted above that which we are able to bear (1Co 10:13).

The ninth sentence is a petition respecting our dangers. **"Deliver us from evil."** We are here taught to ask God to deliver us from the evil that is in the world, the evil that is within our own hearts, and not least from that evil one, the devil. We confess that, so long as we are in the body, we are constantly seeing, hearing, and feeling the presence of evil. It is about us, and within us, and around us on every side. And we entreat Him, who alone can preserve us, to be continually delivering as from its power (John 17:15).

The last sentence is an ascription of praise. **"Yours is the kingdom, the power, and the glory."** We declare in these words our belief, that the kingdoms of this world are the rightful property of our Father - that to Him alone belongs all "power," - and that He alone deserves to receive all "glory." And we conclude by offering to Him the profession of our hearts, that we give Him all honor and praise, and rejoice that He is King of kings, and Lord of lords.

And now let us all examine ourselves, and see whether we really desire to have the things which we are taught to ask for in the Lord's Prayer. Thousands, it may be feared, repeat these words daily as a form, but never consider what they are saying. They care nothing for the "glory," the "kingdom," or the "will" of God. They have no sense of dependence, sinfulness, weakness, or danger. They have no love or charity towards their enemies. And yet they repeat the Lord's Prayer! These things ought not to be so. May we resolve that, by God's help, our hearts shall go together with our lips! Happy is he who can really call God his Father through Jesus Christ his Savior, and can therefore say a heartfelt "Amen" to all that the Lord's Prayer contains.

Chapter 6 - Matthew Henry on the Lord's Prayer

(Matthew Henry, 1662 – 1714)

From Matthew Henry's Commentary on the Whole Bible

When Christ had condemned what was amiss, he directs to do better; for his are reproofs of instruction. Because we know not what to pray for as we ought, he here helps our infirmities, by putting words into our mouths; after this manner therefore pray ye, Mat 6:9. So many were the corruptions that had crept into this duty of prayer among the Jews, that Christ saw it needful to give a new directory for prayer, to show his disciples what must ordinarily be the matter and method of their prayer, which he gives in words that may very well be used as a form; as the summary or contents of the several particulars of our prayers. Not that we are tied up to the use of this form only, or of this always, as if this were necessary to the consecrating of our other prayers; we are here bid to pray after this manner, with these words, or to this effect. That in Luke differs from this; we do not find it used by the apostles; we are not here taught to pray in the name of Christ, as we are afterward; we are here taught to pray that the kingdom might come which did come when the Spirit was poured out: yet, without doubt, it is very good to use it as a form, and it is a pledge of the communion of saints, it having been used by the church in all ages, at least (says Dr. Whitby) from the third century.

It is our Lord's prayer, it is of his composing, of his appointing; it is very compendious, yet very comprehensive, in compassion to our infirmities in praying. The matter is choice and necessary, the method instructive, and the expression very concise. It has much in a little, and it is requisite that we acquaint ourselves with the sense and meaning of it, for it is used acceptably no further than it is used with understanding and without vain repetition.

The Lord's prayer (as indeed every prayer) is a letter sent from earth to heaven. Here is the inscription of the letter, the person to whom it is directed, our Father; the where, in heaven; the contents of it in several errands of request; the close, for thine is the kingdom; the seal, Amen; and if you will, the date too, this day.

Plainly thus: there are three parts of the prayer.

I. The preface, **Our Father who art in heaven**. Before we come to our business, there must be a solemn address to him with whom our business lies; Our Father. Intimating, that we must pray, not only alone and for ourselves, but with and for others; for we are members one of another, and are called into fellowship with each other. We are here taught to whom to pray, to God only, and not to saints and angels, for they are ignorant of us, are not to have the high honors we give in prayer, nor can give favors we expect. We are taught how to address ourselves to God, and what title to give him, that which speaks him rather beneficent than magnificent, for we are to come boldly to the throne of grace.

1. We must address ourselves to him as our Father, and must call him so. He is a common Father to all mankind by creation, (Mal 2:10; Act 17:28). He is in a special manner a Father to the saints, by adoption and regeneration (Eph 1:5; Gal 4:6); and an unspeakable privilege it is. Thus we must eye him in prayer, keep up good thoughts of him, such as are encouraging and not [terrifying]; nothing more pleasing to God, nor pleasant to ourselves, than to call God Father. Christ in prayer mostly called God Father. If he is our Father, he will pity us under our weaknesses and infirmities (Psa 103:13), will spare us (Mal 3:17), will make the best of our performances, though very defective, will deny us nothing that is good for us, (Luke 11:11-13). We have access with boldness to him, as to a father, and have an advocate with the Father, and the Spirit of adoption. When we come repenting of our sins, we must eye God as a Father, as the prodigal did (Luke 15:18; Jer 3:19); when we come begging for grace, and peace, and the inheritance and blessing of sons, it is an encouragement that we come to God, not as an unreconciled, avenging Judge, but as a loving, gracious, reconciled Father in Christ, (Jer 3:4).

2. As our Father in heaven: so in heaven as to be everywhere else, for the heaven cannot contain him; yet so in heaven as there to manifest his glory, for it is his throne (Psa 103:19), and it is to believers a throne of grace: to that place we must direct our prayers, for Christ the Mediator is now in heaven,

(Heb 8:1). Heaven is out of sight and a world of spirits, therefore our converse with God in prayer must be spiritual. It is on high, therefore in prayer we must be raised above the world, and lift up our hearts, (Psa 5:1). Heaven is a place of perfect purity, and we must therefore lift up pure hands, must study to sanctify his name who is the Holy One, and dwells in that holy place, (Lev 10:3). From heaven God beholds the children of men, (Psa 33:13, 14). And we must in prayer see his eye upon us: [from there] he has a full and clear view of all our needs and burdens and desires, and all our infirmities. It is the firmament of his power likewise, as well as of his prospect, (Psa 150:1). He is not only, as a Father, able to help us, able to do great things for us, more than we can ask or think; he has with which to supply our needs, for every good gift is from above. He is a Father, and therefore we may come to him with boldness, but a Father in heaven, and therefore we must come with reverence, (Eccl 5:2). Thus all our prayers should correspond with that which is our great aim as Christians, and that is, to be with God in heaven. God and heaven, the end of our whole conversation, must be particularly eyed in every prayer; there is the center to which we are all tending. By prayer, we send before us [to that place] where we profess to be going.

II. The petitions, and there are six; the three first relating more immediately to God and his honor, the three last to our own concerns, both temporal and spiritual; as in the ten commandments, the four first teach us our duty toward God, and the last six our duty toward our neighbor. The method of this prayer teaches us to seek first the kingdom of God and his righteousness, and then to hope that other things shall be added.

1. **Hallowed be thy name**. It is the same word that in other places is translated 'sanctified.' But here the old word 'hallowed' is retained, only because people were used to it in the Lord's prayer. In these words,

(1.) We give glory to God; it may be taken not as a petition, but as an adoration; as that, the Lord be magnified, or glorified, for God's holiness is the greatness and glory of all his perfections. We must begin our prayers with praising God, and it is very fit that he should be first served, and that we should give glory to God before we expect to receive mercy and grace from him. Let him have praise of his perfections, and then let us have the benefit of them.

(2.) We fix our end, and it is the right end to be aimed at, and ought to be our chief and ultimate end in all our petitions, that God may be glorified. All our other requests must be in subordination to this and in pursuit of it. "Father, glorify thyself in giving me my daily bread and pardoning my sins," etc. Since all is of him and through him, all must be to him and for him. In prayer our thoughts and affections should be carried out most to the glory of God. The Pharisees made their own name the chief end of their prayers (Mat 6:5, to be seen of men), in opposition to which we are directed to make the name of God our chief end; let all our petitions centre in this and be regulated by it. "Do so and so for me, for the glory of thy name, and as far as is for the glory of it."

(3.) We desire and pray that the name of God, that is, God himself, in all that by which he has made himself known, may be sanctified and glorified both by us and others, and especially by himself. "Father, let thy name be glorified as a Father, and a Father in heaven; glorify thy goodness and thy highness, thy majesty and mercy. Let thy name be sanctified, for it is a holy name; no matter what becomes of our polluted names, but, Lord, what will you do to your great name?" When we pray that God's name may be glorified: [1.] We make a virtue of necessity; for God will sanctify his own name, whether we desire it or not; I will be exalted among the heathen, (Psa 46:10). [2.] We ask for that which we are sure shall be granted; for when our Savior prayed, Father glorify thy name, it was immediately answered, I have glorified it, and will glorify it again.

2. **Thy kingdom come**. This petition has plainly a reference to the doctrine which Christ preached at this time which John Baptist had preached before, and which he afterwards sent his apostles out to preach - the kingdom of heaven is at hand. The kingdom of your Father who is in heaven, the kingdom of the Messiah, this is at hand, pray that it may come. Note, we should turn the word we hear into prayer, our hearts should echo to it. Does Christ promise, surely I come quickly? Our hearts should answer, "Even so, come." Ministers should pray over the word: when they preach the kingdom of God is at hand, they should pray,

"Father, thy kingdom come." What God has promised we must pray for, for promises are given, not to supersede, but to quicken and encourage prayer; and when the accomplishment of a promise is near and at the door, when the kingdom of heaven is at hand, we should then pray for it the more earnestly. Thy kingdom come, as Daniel set his face to pray for the deliverance of Israel, when he understood that the time of it was at hand, (Dan 9:2). See Luke 19:11. It was the Jews' daily prayer to God, "Let him make his kingdom reign, let his redemption flourish, and let his Messiah come and deliver his people." (Dr. Whitby, ex Vitringa). "Let thy kingdom come, let the gospel be preached to all and embraced by all. Let all be brought to subscribe to the record God has given in his word concerning his Son, and to embrace him as their Savior and Sovereign. Let the bounds of the gospel-church be enlarged, the kingdom of the world be made Christ's kingdom, and all men become subjects to it, and live as becomes their character."

3. **Thy will be done in earth as it is in heaven**. We pray that God's kingdom being come, we and others may be brought into obedience to all the laws and ordinances of it. By this let it appear that Christ's kingdom is come, let God's will be done; and by this let it appear that it is come as a kingdom of heaven, let it introduce a heaven upon earth. We make Christ but an [honorary] Prince, if we call him King and do not do his will. Having prayed that he may rule us, we pray that we may in everything be ruled by him. Observe,

(1.) The thing prayed for, thy will be done; "Lord, do what you please with me and mine (1Sam 3:18). I refer myself to you, and am well satisfied that all your counsel concerning me should be performed." In this sense Christ prayed, not my will, but thine be done. "Enable me to do what is pleasing to you; give me that grace that is necessary to the right knowledge of your will, and an acceptable obedience to it. Let your will be done conscientiously by me and others, not our own will, the will of the flesh, or the mind, not the will of men (1Pet 4:2), much less Satan's will (John 8:44), that we may neither displease God in anything we do, nor be displeased at anything God does."

(2.) The pattern of it, that it might be done on earth, in this place of our trial and probation (where our work must be done, or

31

it never will be done), as it is done in heaven, that place of rest and joy. We pray that earth may be made more like heaven by the observance of God's will (this earth, which, through the prevalence of Satan's will, has become so near akin to hell), and that saints may be made more like the holy angels in their devotion and obedience. We are on earth, blessed be God, not yet under the earth; we pray for the living only, not for the dead that have gone down into silence.

4. **Give us this day our daily bread.** Because our natural being is necessary to our spiritual well-being in this world, therefore, after the things of God's glory, kingdom, and will, we pray for the necessary supports and comforts of this present life, which are the gifts of God, and must be asked of him - Bread for the day approaching, for all the remainder of our lives. Bread for the time to come, or bread for our being and subsistence, that which is agreeable to our condition in the world (Prov 30:8), food convenient for us and our families, according to our rank and station.

Every word here has a lesson in it: (1.) We ask for bread; that teaches us sobriety and temperance; we ask for bread, not dainties, not superfluities; that which is wholesome, though it be not nice.

(2.) We ask for our bread; that teaches us honesty and industry: we do not ask for the bread out of other people's mouths, not the bread of deceit (Prov 20:17), not the bread of idleness (Prov 31:27), but the bread honestly gotten.

(3.) We ask for our daily bread; which teaches us not to take thought for the morrow (Mat 6:34), but constantly to depend upon divine Providence, as those that live from hand to mouth.

(4.) We beg of God to give it us, not sell it us, nor lend it us, but give it. The greatest of men must be beholden to the mercy of God for their daily bread,

(5.) We pray, "Give it to us; not to me only, but to others in common with me." This teaches us charity, and a compassionate concern for the poor and needy. It intimates also, that we ought to pray with our families; we and our households eat together, and therefore ought to pray together.

(6.) We pray that God would give us this day; which teaches us to renew the desire of our souls toward God, as the needs of our bodies are renewed; as duly as the day comes, we must pray to our heavenly Father, and reckon we could as well go a day without meat, as without prayer.

5. **And forgive us our debts, as we forgive our debtors.** This is connected with the former; and forgive, intimating, that unless our sins are pardoned, we can have no comfort in life, or the supports of it. Our daily bread does but feed us as lambs for the slaughter if our sins are not pardoned. It intimates, likewise, that we must pray for daily pardon, as duly as we pray for daily bread. He that is washed, needs to wash his feet. Here we have,

(1.) A petition; Father in heaven forgive us our debts, our debts to thee. Note, [1.] Our sins are our debts; there is a debt of duty, which, as creatures, we owe to our Creator; we do not pray to be discharged from that, but upon the non-payment of that there arises a debt of punishment; in default of obedience to the will of God, we become obnoxious to the wrath of God; and for not observing the precept of the law, we stand obliged to the penalty. A debtor is liable to process, so are we; a malefactor is a debtor to the law, so are we. [2.] Our hearts' desire and prayer to our heavenly Father every day should be, that he would forgive us our debts; that the obligation to punishment may be cancelled and vacated, that we may not come into condemnation; that we may be discharged, and have the comfort of it. In suing out the pardon of our sins, the great plea we have to rely upon is the satisfaction that was made to the justice of God for the sin of man, by the dying of the Lord Jesus our Surety, or rather Bail to the action that undertook our discharge.

(2.) An argument to enforce this petition; as we forgive our debtors. This is not a plea of merit, but a plea of grace. Note, those who come to God for the forgiveness of their sins against him, must make conscience of forgiving those who have offended them, or else they curse themselves when they say the Lord's prayer. Our duty is to forgive our debtors; as to debts of money, we must not be rigorous and severe in exacting them from those that cannot pay them without ruining themselves and their families; but this means debt of injury; our debtors are those that trespass against us, that smite us (Mat 5:39, 40), and in strictness of law, might be prosecuted for it. We must forbear and forgive and forget the affronts put upon us, and the wrongs done to us; and this is a moral qualification for pardon and peace. It encourages [toward] hope, that God will forgive us; for if there is in us this gracious disposition, it is wrought of God, and therefore is a perfection eminently and transcendently in himself. It will be an evidence to us that he has forgiven us, having wrought in us the condition of forgiveness.

6. **And lead us not into temptation, but deliver us from evil.** This petition is expressed,

(1.) Negatively: **Lead us not into temptation**. Having prayed that the guilt of sin may be removed, we pray, as it is fit, that we may never return again to folly, that we may not be tempted to it. It is not as if God tempted any to sin; but, "Lord, do not let Satan loose upon us; chain up that roaring lion, for he is subtle and spiteful; Lord, do not leave us to ourselves (Psa 19:13), for we are very weak. Lord, do not lay stumbling-blocks and snares before us, nor put us into circumstances that may be an occasion of falling." Temptations are to be prayed against, both because of the discomfort and trouble of them, and because of the danger we are in of being overcome by them, and the guilt and grief that then follow.

(2.) Positively: **But deliver us from evil**; *apo tou ponērou* - from the evil one, the devil, the tempter. "Keep us, that either we may not be assaulted by him, or we may not be overcome by those assaults:" Or from the evil thing, sin, the worst of evils; an evil, an only evil; that evil thing which God hates, and which Satan tempts men to and destroys them by. "Lord, deliver us from the evil of the world, the corruption that is in the world through lust; from the evil of every condition in the world; from the evil of death; from the sting of death, which is sin: deliver us from ourselves, from our own evil hearts: deliver us from evil men, that they may not be a snare to us, nor we a prey to them."

III. The conclusion: **For thine is the kingdom, and the power and the glory, forever. Amen.** Some refer this to David's doxology, 1Ch 29:11. Thine, O Lord, is the greatness. It is,

1. A form of plea to enforce the foregoing petitions. It is our duty to plead with God in prayer, to fill our mouth with arguments (Job 23:4) not to move God, but to affect ourselves; to encourage the faith, to excite our fervency, and to evidence both. Now the best pleas in prayer are those that are taken from God himself, and from that which he has made known of himself. We must wrestle with God in his own strength, both as to the nature of our pleas and the urging of them. The plea here has special reference to the first three petitions; "Father in heaven, thy kingdom come, for thine is the kingdom; thy will be done, for thine is the power; hallowed be thy name, for thine is the glory." And as to our own particular errands, these are encouraging: "Thine is the kingdom; thou hast the government of the world, and the protection of the saints, thy willing subjects in it;" God gives and saves like a king. "Thine is the power, to maintain and support that kingdom, and to make good all thine engagements to thy people." Thine is the glory, as the end of all that which is given to, and done for, the saints, in answer to their prayers; for their praise waits for him. This is matter of comfort and holy confidence in prayer.

2. It is a form of praise and thanksgiving. The best pleading with God is praising of him. It is the way to obtain further mercy, as it qualifies us to receive it. In all our addresses to God, it is fit that praise should have a considerable share, for praise becomes the saints; they are to be our God for a name and for a praise. It is just and equal. We praise God, and give him glory, not because he needs it - he is praised by a world of angels, but because he deserves it; and it is our duty to give him glory, in compliance with his design in revealing himself to us. Praise is the work and happiness of heaven; and all who would go to heaven hereafter, must begin their heaven now. Observe, how full this doxology is, The kingdom, and the power, and the glory, it is all thine. Note, it becomes us to be copious in praising God. A true saint never thinks he can speak honorably enough of God: here there should be a gracious fluency, and this forever. Ascribing glory to God forever, intimates an acknowledgement that it is eternally due, and an earnest desire to be eternally doing it with angels and saints above, (Psa 71:14).

Lastly, To all this we are taught to affix our Amen, so be it. God's Amen is a grant. His fiat is, it shall be so; our Amen is only a summary desire. Our fiat is, let it be so: it is in the token of our desire and assurance to be heard, that we say 'Amen.' 'Amen' refers to every petition going before, and thus, in compassion to our infirmities, we are taught to knit up the whole in one word, and so to gather up, in the general, what we have lost and let slip in the particulars. It is good to conclude religious duties with some warmth and vigor that we may go from them with a sweet savor upon our spirits. It was of old the practice of good people to say, Amen, audibly at the end of every prayer and it is a commendable practice, provided it be done with understanding as the apostle directs (1Co 14:16), and uprightly, with life and liveliness, and inward expressions, answerable to that outward expression of desire and confidence.

Most of the petitions in the Lord's prayer had been commonly used by the Jews in their devotions, or words to the same effect: but that clause in the fifth petition, As we forgive our debtors, was perfectly new, and therefore our Savior here shows for what reason he added it, not with any personal reflection upon the peevishness, litigiousness, and ill nature of the men of that generation, though there was cause enough for it, but only from the necessity and importance of the thing itself. God, in forgiving us, has a peculiar respect to our forgiving those that have injured us. Therefore, when we pray for pardon, we must mention our making conscience of that duty, not only to remind ourselves of it, but to bind ourselves to it. See that parable in Mat 18:23-35. Selfish nature is loath to comply with this, and therefore it is here inculcated, (Mat 6:14, 15).

1. In a promise. If ye forgive, your heavenly Father will also forgive. Not as if this were the only condition required; there must be repentance and faith, and new obedience; but as where other graces are in truth, there will be this, so this will be a good evidence of the sincerity of our other graces. He that relents toward his brother, shows by it that he repents toward his God. Those which in the prayer are called debts, are here called trespasses, debts of injury, wrongs done to us in our bodies, goods, or reputation: trespasses is an extenuating term for offenses, *paraptōmata* - stumbles, slips, falls. Note, it is a good evidence, and a good help of our forgiving others, to call the injuries done us by a mollifying, excusing name. Call them not treasons, but trespasses; not willful injuries, but casual inadvertencies; peradventure it was an oversight

36

(Gen 43:12), therefore make the best of it. We must forgive, as we hope to be forgiven; and therefore must not only bear no malice, nor mediate revenge, but must not upbraid our brother with the injuries he has done us, nor rejoice in any hurt that befalls him, but must be ready to help him and do him good, and if he repent and desire to be friends again, we must be free and familiar with him, as before.

2. In a threatening. "But if you forgive not those that have injured you, that is a bad sign you have not the other requisite conditions, but are altogether unqualified for pardon: and therefore your Father, whom you call Father, and who, as a father, offers you his grace upon reasonable terms, will nevertheless not forgive you. And if other grace is sincere, and yet you are defective greatly in forgiving, you cannot expect the comfort of your pardon, but to have your spirit brought down by some affliction or other to comply with this duty." Note, those who would have found mercy with God must show mercy to their brethren. Nor can we expect that he should stretch out the hands of his favor to us, unless we lift up to him pure hands, without wrath, (1Tim 2:8). If we pray in anger, we have reason to fear God will answer in anger. It has been said, Prayers made in wrath are written in gall. What reason is it that God should forgive us the talents we are indebted to him, if we forgive not our brethren the pence they are indebted to us? Christ came into the world as the great Peace-Maker, and not only to reconcile us to God, but one to another, and in this we must comply with him. It is great presumption and of dangerous consequence, for any to make a light matter of that which Christ here lays such a stress upon. Men's passions shall not frustrate God's word.

Chapter 7 - John Wesley on the Lord's Prayer

(John Wesley, 1703-1791)

Taken from Wesley's Notes on the Bible

1. After having taught the true nature and ends of prayer, our Lord subjoins an example of it; even that divine form of prayer which seems in this place to be proposed by way of pattern chiefly, as the model and standard of all our prayers: "After this manner therefore pray ye." Whereas, elsewhere he enjoins the use of these very words: "He said unto them, When ye pray, say..." (Luke 11:2.)

2. We may observe, in general, concerning this divine prayer, First, that it contains all we can reasonably or innocently pray for. There is nothing which we have need to ask of God, nothing which we can ask without offending him, which is not included, either directly or indirectly, in this comprehensive form. Secondly, that it contains all we can reasonably or innocently desire; whatever is for the glory of God, whatever is needful or profitable, not only for ourselves, but for every creature in heaven and earth. And, indeed, our prayers are the proper test of our desires; nothing being fit to have a place in our desires which is not fit to have a place in our prayers: What we may not pray for, neither should we desire. Thirdly, that it contains all our duty to God and man; whatsoever things are pure and holy, whatsoever God requires of the children of men, whatsoever is acceptable in his sight, whatsoever it is by which we may profit our neighbor, being expressed or implied in this.

3. It consists of three parts, the preface, the petitions, and the doxology, or conclusion. The preface, "our Father which art in heaven," lays a general foundation for prayer; comprising what we must first know of God, before we can pray in confidence of being heard. It likewise points out to us all those tempers with which we are to approach to God, which are most essentially requisite, if we desire either our prayers or our lives should find acceptance with him.

4. **"our Father:"** If he is a Father, then he is good, then he is loving, to his children. And here is the first and great reason for prayer. God is willing to bless; let us ask for a blessing. "our Father;" our Creator; the Author of our being; He who raised us from the dust of the earth; who breathed into us the breath of life, and we became living souls. But if he made us, let us ask, and he will not withhold any good thing from the work of his own hands. "our Father;" our Preserver; who, day by day, sustains the life he has given; of whose continuing love we now and every moment receive life and breath and all things. So much the more boldly let us come to him, and we shall "obtain mercy, and grace to help in time of need." Above all, the Father of our Lord Jesus Christ, and of all that believe in him; who justifies us "freely by his grace, through the redemption that is in Jesus;" who has "blotted out all our sins, and healed all our infirmities;" who has received us for his own children, by adoption and grace; and, "because" we "are sons, has sent forth the Spirit of his Son into" our "hearts, crying, Abba, Father;" who "has begotten us again of incorruptible seed", and "created us anew in Christ Jesus." Therefore we know that he hears us always; therefore we pray to him without ceasing. We pray, because we love; and "we love him because he first loved us."

5 . **"our Father:"** Not mine only who now cry unto him, but ours in the most extensive sense. The God and "Father of the spirits of all flesh;" the Father of angels and men: So the very Heathens acknowledged him to be …The Father of the universe, of all the families both in heaven and earth. Therefore with him there is no respect of persons. He loves all that he has made. "He is loving unto every man, and his mercy is over all his works." And the Lord's delight is in them that fear him, and put their trust in his mercy; in them that trust in him through the Son of his love, knowing they are "accepted in the Beloved." But "if God so loved us, we ought also to love one another;" yea, all mankind; seeing "God so loved the world, that he gave his only-begotten Son", even to die the death, that they "might not perish, but have everlasting life"

6. **"Which art in heaven:"** High and lifted up; God over all, blessed forever: Who, sitting on the circle of the heavens, beholds all things both in heaven and earth; whose eye pervades the whole sphere of created being; yea, and of uncreated night; unto

whom "are known all his works", and all the works of every creature, not only "from the beginning of the world," (a poor, low, weak translation,) but… from all eternity, from everlasting to everlasting; who constrains the host of heaven, as well as the children of men, to cry out with wonder and amazement, O the depth! the depth of the riches, both of the wisdom and of the knowledge of God! Which art in heaven: The Lord and Ruler of all, superintending and disposing all things; who is the King of kings, and Lord of lords, the blessed and only Potentate; who is strong and girded about with power, doing whatsoever pleases you; the Almighty; for whenever you will, to do is present with you. In heaven: eminently there, heaven is thy throne, "the place where thine honor" particularly "dwells." But not there alone; for you fill heaven and earth, the whole expanse of space. "heaven and earth are full of thy glory. Glory be to thee, O Lord, most high!"

Therefore should we "serve the Lord with fear, and rejoice unto him with reverence." Therefore should we think, speak, and act, as continually under the eye, in the immediate presence, of the Lord, the King.

7. **"hallowed be thy name."** This is the first of the six petitions, whereof the prayer itself is composed. The name of God is God himself; the nature of God, so far as it can be discovered to man. It means, therefore, together with his existence, all his attributes or perfections; His eternity, particularly signified by his great and incommunicable name, Jehovah, as the Apostle John translates it: "the Alpha and Omega, the beginning and the end; He which is, and which was, and which is to come;" His Fullness of Being, denoted by his other great name, I AM THAT I AM! His omnipresence; His omnipotence; who is indeed the only Agent in the material world; all matter being essentially dull and inactive, and moving only as it is moved by the finger of God; and he is the spring of action in every creature, visible and invisible, which could neither act nor exist without the continual influx and agency of his almighty power; His wisdom, clearly deduced from the things that are seen, from the goodly order of the universe; His Trinity in Unity, and Unity in Trinity, discovered to us in the very first line of his written word; *bara Elohim,* literally, the Gods created, a plural noun joined with a verb of the singular number; as well as in every part of his subsequent revelations, given by the mouth of all his

holy Prophets and Apostles; His essential purity and holiness; and, above all, his love, which is the very brightness of his glory.

In praying that God, or his name, may "be hallowed" or glorified, we pray that he may be known, such as he is, by all that are capable thereof, by all intelligent beings, and with affections suitable to that knowledge; that he may be duly honored, and feared, and loved, by all in heaven above and in the earth beneath; by all angels and men, whom for that end he has made capable of knowing and loving him to eternity.

8. **"Thy kingdom come."** This has a close connection with the preceding petition. In order that the name of God might be hallowed, we pray that his kingdom, the kingdom of Christ, may come. This kingdom then comes to a particular person, when he "repents and believes the gospel;" when he is taught of God, not only to know himself, but to know Jesus Christ and him crucified. As "this is life eternal, to know the only true God, and Jesus Christ whom he has sent;" so it is the kingdom of God begun below, set up in the believers heart; "the Lord God Omnipotent" then "reigneth," when he is known through Christ Jesus. He takes unto himself his mighty power, that he may subdue all things unto himself. He goes on in the soul conquering and to conquer, till he has put all things under his feet, till "every thought is brought into captivity to the obedience of Christ."

When therefore God shall "give his Son the Heathen for his inheritance, and the uttermost parts of the earth for his possession;" when "all kingdoms shall bow before him, and all nations shall do him service;" when "the mountain of the Lord's house," the Church of Christ, "shall be established in the top of the mountains;" when "the fullness of the Gentiles shall come in, and all Israel shall be saved;" then shall it be seen, that "the Lord is King, and has put on glorious apparel," appearing to every soul of man as King of kings, and Lord of lords. And it is proper for all those who love his appearing to pray that he would hasten the time; that this his kingdom, the kingdom of grace, may come quickly, and swallow up all the kingdoms of the earth; that all mankind, receiving him for their King, truly believing in his name, may be filled with righteousness, and peace, and joy, with holiness and happiness, till they are removed from here into his heavenly kingdom, there to reign with him forever and ever.

For this also we pray in those words, "Thy kingdom come:" We pray for the coming of his everlasting kingdom, the kingdom of glory in heaven, which is the continuation and perfection of the kingdom of grace on earth. Consequently this, as well as the preceding petition, is offered up for the whole intelligent creation, who are all interested in this grand event, the final renovation of all things by God's putting an end to misery and sin, to infirmity and death, taking all things into his own hands, and setting up the kingdom which endure throughout all ages.

Exactly answerable to this are those awful words in the prayer at the burial of the dead: "Beseeching thee, that it may please thee of thy gracious goodness, shortly to accomplish the number of thine elect, and to hasten thy kingdom: That we, with all those that are departed in the true faith of thy holy name, may have our perfect consummation and bliss, both in body and soul, in thy everlasting glory."

9. **"Thy will be done in earth, as it is in heaven."** This is the necessary and immediate consequence wherever the kingdom of God is come; wherever God dwells in the soul by faith, and Christ reigns in the heart by love.

It is probable, many, perhaps the generality of men, at the first view of these words, are apt to imagine they are only an expression of, or petition for, resignation; for a readiness to suffer the will of God, whatsoever it be concerning us. And this is unquestionably a divine and excellent temper, a most precious gift of God. But this is not what we pray for in this petition; at least, not in the chief and primary sense of it. We pray, not so much for a passive, as for an active, conformity to the will of God, in saying, "Thy will be done in earth, as it is in heaven."

How is it done by the angels of God in heaven, those who now circle his throne rejoicing? They do it willingly; they love his commandments, and gladly hearken to his words. It is their meat and drink to do his will; it is their highest glory and joy. They do it continually; there is no interruption in their willing service. They rest not day nor night, but employ every hour (speaking after the manner of men; otherwise our measures of duration, days, and nights, and hours, have no place in eternity) in fulfilling his commands, in executing his designs, in performing the counsel of his will. And they do it perfectly. No sin, no defect belongs to angelic minds. It is true, "the stars are not pure in his sight," even the morning-stars that sing together before him. "In his sight," that is, in comparison of Him, the very angels are not pure. But this does not imply, that they are not pure in themselves. Doubtless they are; they are without spot and blameless. They are altogether devoted to his will, and perfectly obedient in all things.

If we view this in another light, we may observe, the angels of God in heaven do all the will of God. And they do nothing else, nothing but what they are absolutely assured is his will. Again they do all the will of God as he wills; in the manner which pleases him, and no other. Yea, and they do this, only because it is his will; for this end, and no other reason.

10. When therefore we pray, that the will of God may "be done in earth as it is in heaven," the meaning is, that all the inhabitants of the earth, even the whole race of mankind, may do the will of their Father which is in heaven, as willingly as the holy angels; that these may do it continually, even as they, without any interruption of their willing service; yea, and that they may do it perfectly, that "the God of peace, through the blood of the everlasting covenant, may make them perfect in every good work to do his will, and work in them all "which is well-pleasing in his sight."

In other words, we pray that we and all mankind may do the whole will of God in all things; and nothing else, not the least thing but what is the holy and acceptable will of God. We pray that we may do the whole will of God as he wills, in the manner that pleases him: And, lastly, that we may do it because it is his will; that this may be the sole reason and ground, the whole and only motive, of whatsoever we think, or whatsoever we speak or do.

11. **"Give us this day our daily bread."** In the three former petitions we have been praying for all mankind. We come now more particularly to desire a supply for our own needs. Not that we are directed, even here, to confine our prayer altogether to

ourselves; but this, and each of the following petitions, may be used for the whole Church of Christ upon earth.

By "bread" we may understand all things needful, whether for our souls or bodies, ...the things pertaining to life and godliness. We understand not just the outward bread, what our Lord terms the meat which perishes; but much more the spiritual bread, the grace of God, the food which endures unto everlasting life. It was the judgment of many of the ancient Fathers that we are here to understand the sacramental bread also; daily received in the beginning by the whole Church of Christ and highly esteemed, till the love of many waxed cold, as the grand channel by which the grace of his Spirit was conveyed to the souls of all the children of God.

Our daily bread. The word we render daily has been differently explained by different commentators. But the most plain and natural sense of it seems to be this, which is retained in almost all translations, as well ancient as modern - what is sufficient for this day; and so for each day as it succeeds.

12. "Give us:" For we claim nothing of right, but only of free mercy. We deserve not the air we breathe, the earth that bears, or the sun that shines upon us. All our desert we own is hell: But God loves us freely. Therefore, we ask him to give what we can no more procure for ourselves than we can merit it at his hands.

Not that either the goodness or the power of God is a reason for us to stand idle. It is his will that we should use all diligence in all things, that we should employ our utmost endeavors as much as if our success were the natural effect of our own wisdom and strength. And then, as though we had done nothing, we are to depend on him, the giver of every good and perfect gift.

"This day:" For we are to take no thought for the morrow. For this very end has our wise Creator divided life into these little portions of time, so clearly separated from each other, that we might look on every day as a fresh gift of God, another life, which we may devote to his glory; and that every evening may be as the close of life, beyond which we are to see nothing but eternity.

13. **"And forgive us our trespasses, as we forgive them that trespass against us."** As nothing but sin can hinder the

bounty of God from flowing forth upon every creature, so this petition naturally follows the former; that, all hindrances being removed, we may the more clearly trust in the God of love for every manner of thing which is good.

"Our trespasses:" The word properly signifies our debts. Thus our sins are frequently represented in Scripture. Every sin laying us under a fresh debt to God, to whom we already owe, as it were, ten thousand talents. What then can we answer when he shall say, "Pay me that you owe?" We are utterly insolvent. We have nothing to pay. We have wasted all our substance. Therefore, if he deals with us according to the rigor of his law, if he exacts what he justly may, he must command us to be "bound hand and foot, and delivered over to the tormentors."

Indeed we are already bound hand and foot by the chains of our own sins. These, considered with regard to ourselves, are chains of iron and fetters of brass. They are wounds with which the world, the flesh, and the devil, have gashed and mangled us all over. They are diseases that drink up our blood and spirits that bring us down to the chambers of the grave. But considered, as they are here, with regard to God, they are debts, immense and numberless. Well, therefore, seeing we have nothing to pay, may we cry unto him that he would "frankly forgive' us all!

The word translated *forgive* implies either to forgive a debt, or to unloose a chain. And if we attain the former, the latter follows of course: if our debts are forgiven, the chains fall off our hands. As soon as ever, through the free grace of God in Christ we "receive forgiveness of sins," we receive likewise "a lot among those which are sanctified, by faith which is in him." Sin has lost its power. It has no dominion over those who "are under grace," that is, in favor with God. As "there is now no condemnation for them that are in Christ Jesus," so they are freed from sin as well as from guilt. "The righteousness of the law is fulfilled in" them, and they "walk not after the flesh, but after the Spirit."

14. "As we forgive them that trespass against us." In these words our Lord clearly declares both on what condition, and in what degree or manner, we may look to be forgiven of God. All our trespasses and sins are forgiven us, if we forgive, and as we forgive others. [First, God forgives us if we forgive others.] This is a point

of the utmost importance. And our blessed Lord is so jealous lest at any time we should let it slip out of our thoughts, that he not only inserts it in the body of his prayer, but presently after repeats it twice over. "If," saith he, "ye forgive men their trespasses, your heavenly Father will also forgive you: But if ye forgive not men their trespasses, neither will your Father forgive your trespasses." (Matt. 6:14, 15.) Secondly, God forgives us as we forgive others. So that if any malice or bitterness, if any taint of unkindness or anger remains, if we do not clearly, fully, and from the heart, forgive all men their trespasses, we far cut short the forgiveness of our own. God cannot clearly and fully forgive us: he may show us some degree of mercy, but we will not suffer him to blot out all our sins, and forgive all our iniquities.

In the mean time, while we do not from our hearts forgive our neighbor his trespasses, what manner of prayer are we offering to God whenever we utter these words? We are indeed setting God at open defiance: we are daring him to do his worst. "Forgive us our trespasses, as we forgive them that trespass against us!" That is, in plain terms, "Do not thou forgive us at all; we desire no favor at thy hands. We pray that thou wilt keep our sins in remembrance, and that thy wrath may abide upon us." But can you seriously offer such a prayer to God? And has he not yet cast you quick into hell?' O tempt him no longer! Now, even now, by his grace, forgive as you would be forgiven! Now have compassion on your fellow servant, as God has had and will have pity on you!

15. **"And lead us not into temptation, but deliver us from evil."** And] lead us not into temptation." The word translated *temptation* means trial of any kind. And so the English word *temptation* was formerly taken in an indifferent sense, although now it is usually understood of solicitation to sin. St. James uses the word in both these senses; first, in its general, then in its restrained accepted meaning, he takes it in the former sense when he saith, "Blessed Blessed is the man who remains steadfast under trial, for when he has stood the test," or been approved of God, "he will receive the crown of life." (James 1:12, 13.) He immediately adds, taking the word in the latter sense, "Let no man say when he is tempted, I am tempted of God; for God cannot be tempted with evil, and he himself tempts no one. But every man is tempted, when he is drawn away of his own lust," or desire, …drawn out of God,

in whom alone he is safe. "And enticed;" caught as a fish with a bait. Then it is, when he is thus drawn away and enticed, that he properly "enters into temptation." Then temptation covers him as a cloud. It overspreads his whole soul. Then how hardly shall he escape out of the snare! Therefore, we beseech God "not to lead us into temptation," that is, (seeing God tempts no man,) not to suffer us to be led into it. "But deliver us from evil:" Rather "from the evil one"; *apo tou ponerou. ho Poneros* is unquestionably the wicked one, emphatically so called the prince and god of this world, who works with mighty power in the children of disobedience. But all those who are the children of God by faith are delivered out of his hands. He may fight against them; and so he will. But he cannot conquer, unless they betray their own souls. He may torment for a time, but he cannot destroy; for God is on their side, who will not fail in the end to "avenge his own elect, that cry unto him day and night." Lord, when we are tempted, suffer us not to enter into temptation! Do thou make a way for us to escape that the wicked one touch us not!

16. The conclusion of this divine prayer, commonly called the Doxology, is a solemn thanksgiving, a compendious acknowledgement of the attributes and works of God. "For thine is the kingdom" the sovereign right of all things that are or ever were created; yes, your kingdom is an everlasting kingdom, and your dominion endures throughout all ages. "The power" the executive power by which you govern all things in your everlasting kingdom, by which you do whatsoever pleases you in all places of your dominion. "And the glory" the praise due from every creature, for your power, and the mightiness of your kingdom, and for all your wondrous works which your work from everlasting, and shall do, world without end, "forever and ever! Amen!" So be it!

Chapter 8 – John Calvin on the Lord's Prayer

(John Calvin, 1509-1564)

From 'The Institutes of the Christian Religion'

34. We must now attend not only to a surer method, but also form of prayer, that, namely, which our heavenly Father has delivered to us by his beloved Son, and in which we may recognize his boundless goodness and condescension (Mt 6:9; Luke 11:2). Besides admonishing and exhorting us to seek him in our every necessity (as children are accustomed to betake themselves to the protection of their parents when oppressed with any anxiety), seeing that we were not fully aware how great our poverty was, or what was right or for our interest to ask, he has provided for this ignorance; that in which our capacity failed he has sufficiently supplied. For he has given us a form in which is set before us as in a picture everything which it is lawful to wish, everything which is conducive to our interest, everything which it is necessary to demand. From his goodness in this respect we derive the great comfort of knowing, that as we ask almost in his words, we ask nothing that is absurd, or foreign, or unseasonable; nothing, in short, that is not agreeable to him.

Plato, seeing the ignorance of men in presenting their desires to God, desires which if granted would often be most injurious to them, declares the best form of prayer to be that which an ancient poet has furnished: "O king Jupiter, give what is best, whether we wish it or wish it not; but avert from us what is evil even though we ask it," (Plato, Alcibiad. 2) This heathen shows his wisdom in discerning how dangerous it is to ask of God what our own passion dictates; while, at the same time, he reminds us of our unhappy condition in not being able to open our lips before God without dangers unless his Spirit instruct us how to pray aright (Rom 8:26). The higher value, therefore, ought we to set on the privilege, when the only begotten Son of God puts words into our lips, and thus relieves our minds of all hesitation.

35. This form or rule of prayer is composed of six petitions. For I am prevented from agreeing with those who divide it into seven by the adversative mode of diction used by the Evangelist, who appears to have intended to unite the two members together; as if he had said, "Do not allow us to be overcome by temptation, but rather bring assistance to our frailty, and deliver us that we may not fall."

Ancient writers also agree with us, that what is added by Matthew as a seventh head is to be considered as explanatory of the sixth petition. But though in every part of the prayer the first place is assigned to the glory of God, still this is more especially the object of the three first petitions in which we are to look to the glory of God alone, without any reference to what is called our own advantage. The three remaining petitions are devoted to our interest, and properly relate to things which it is useful for us to ask. When we ask that the name of God may be hallowed, as God wishes to prove whether we love and serve him freely, or from the hope of reward, we are not to think at all of our own interest; we must set his glory before our eyes, and keep them intent upon it alone. In the other similar petitions, this is the only manner in which we ought to be affected. It is true, that in this way our own interest is greatly promoted, because, when the name of God is hallowed in the way we ask, our own sanctification also is thereby promoted. But in regard to this advantage, we must, as I have said, shut our eyes, and be in a manner blind, so as not even to see it; and, thus, were all hope of our private advantage cut off, we still should never cease to wish and pray for this hallowing, and everything else which pertains to the glory of God.

We have examples in Moses and Paul, who did not count it grievous to turn away their eyes and minds from themselves, and with intense and fervent zeal long for death, if by their loss the kingdom and glory of God might be promoted (Exod 32:32; Rom 9:3). On the other hand, when we ask for daily bread, although we desire what is advantageous for ourselves, we ought also especially to seek the glory of God, so much so that we would not ask at all unless it were to turn to his glory. Let us now proceed to an exposition of the Prayer.

Our Father which are in heaven.

36. The first thing suggested at the very outset is, as we have already said (§ 17-19), that all our prayers to God ought only to be presented in the name of Christ, as there is no other name which can recommend them. In calling God our Father, we certainly plead the name of Christ. For with what confidence could any man call God his Father? Who would have the presumption to arrogate to himself the honor of a son of God were we not gratuitously adopted as his sons in Christ? He being the true Son has been given to us as a brother, so that that which he possesses as his own by nature becomes ours by adoption, if we embrace this great mercy with firm faith. As John says, "As many as received him, to them gave he power to become the sons of God, even to them that believe in his name," (John 1:12). Hence he both calls himself our Father, and is pleased to be so called by us, by this delightful name relieving us of all distrust, since nowhere can a stronger affection be found than in a father. Hence, too, he could not have given us a stronger testimony of his boundless love than in calling us his sons. But his love towards us is so much the greater and more excellent than that of earthly parents, the farther he surpasses all men in goodness and mercy (Isaiah 63:16). Earthly parents, laying aside all paternal affection, might abandon their offspring; he will never abandon us (Psa 27:10), seeing he cannot deny himself. For we have his promise, "If ye then, being evil, know how to give good gifts unto your children, how much more shall your Father which is in heaven give good things to them that ask him?" (Mt 7:11). In like manner in the prophet, "Can a woman forget her sucking child, that she should not have compassion on the son of her womb? Yea, they may forget, yet will not I forget thee," (Isaiah 49:15). But if we are his sons, then as a son cannot seek out the protection of a stranger and a foreigner without at the same time complaining of his father's cruelty or poverty, so we cannot ask assistance from any other quarter than from him, unless we would charge him with poverty, or need of means, or cruelty and excessive austerity.

37. Nor let us allege that we are justly rendered timid by a consciousness of sin, by which our Father, though mild and merciful, is daily offended. For if among men a son cannot have a better advocate to plead his cause with his father, and cannot employ a better intercessor to regain his lost favor, than if he come himself suppliant and downcast, acknowledging his fault, to implore

the mercy of his father, whose paternal feelings cannot but be moved by such entreaties, what will that "Father of all mercies, and God of all comfort," do? (2 Cor 1:3). Will he not rather listen to the tears and groans of his children, when supplicating for themselves (especially seeing he invites and exhorts us to do so), than to any advocacy of others to whom the timid have recourse, not without some semblance of despair, because they are distrustful of their father's mildness and clemency? The exuberance of his paternal kindness he sets before us in the parable (Luke 15:20), when the father with open arms receives the son who had gone away from him, wasted his substance in riotous living, and in all ways grievously sinned against him. He waits not till pardon is asked in words, but, anticipating the request, recognizes him afar off, runs to meet him, consoles him, and restores him to favor.

By setting before us this admirable example of mildness in a man, he designed to show in how much greater abundance we may expect it from him who is not only a Father, but the best and most merciful of all fathers, however ungrateful, rebellious, and wicked sons we may be, provided only we throw ourselves upon his mercy. And the better to assure us that he is such a Father if we are Christians, he has been pleased to be called not only a Father, but our Father, as if we were pleading with him after this manner, O Father, who art possessed of so much affection for thy children, and art so ready to forgive, we thy children approach thee and present our requests, fully persuaded that thou hast no other feelings towards us than those of a father, though we are unworthy of such a parent. But as our narrow hearts are incapable of comprehending such boundless favor, Christ is not only the earnest and pledge of our adoption, but also gives us the Spirit as a witness of this adoption, that through him we may freely cry aloud, Abba, Father. Whenever, therefore, we are restrained by any feeling of hesitation, let us remember to ask of him that he may correct our timidity, and placing us under the magnanimous guidance of the Spirit, enable us to pray boldly.

38. The instruction given us, however, is not that every individual in particular is to call him Father, but rather that we are all in common to call him Our Father. By this we are reminded how strong the feeling of brotherly love between us ought to be, since we are all alike, by the same mercy and free kindness, the children

of such a Father. For if He from whom we all obtain whatever is good is our common Father (Mt 23:9), everything which has been distributed to us we should be prepared to communicate to each other, as far as occasion demands. But if we are thus desirous as we ought, to stretch out our hands and give assistance to each other, there is nothing by which we can more benefit our brethren than by committing them to the care and protection of the best of parents, since if He is propitious and favorable nothing more can be desired. And, indeed, we owe this also to our Father. For as he who truly and from the heart loves the father of a family, extends the same love and good-will to all his household, so the zeal and affection which we feel for our heavenly Parent it becomes us to extend towards his people, his family, and, in fine, his heritage, which he has honored so highly as to give them the appellation of the "fulness" of his only begotten Son (Eph 1:23).

Let the Christian, then, so regulate his prayers as to make them common, and embrace all who are his brethren in Christ; not only those whom at present he sees and knows to be such, but all men who are alive upon the earth. What God has determined with regard to them is beyond our knowledge, but to wish and hope the best concerning them is both pious and humane. Still it becomes us to regard with special affection those who are of the household of faith, and whom the Apostle has in express terms recommended to our care in everything (Gal 6:10). In short, all our prayers ought to bear reference to that community which our Lord has established in his kingdom and family.

39. This, however, does not prevent us from praying specially for ourselves, and certain others, provided our mind is not withdrawn from the view of this community, does not deviate from it, but constantly refers to it. For prayers, though couched in special terms, keeping that object still in view, cease not to be common. All this may easily be understood by analogy. There is a general command from God to relieve the necessities of all the poor, and yet this command is obeyed by those who with that view give succor to all whom they see or know to be in distress, although they pass by many whose needs are not less urgent, either because they cannot know or are unable to give supply to all. In this way there is nothing repugnant to the will of God in those who, giving heed to this common society of the Church, yet offer up particular prayers,

in which, with a public mind, though in special terms, they commend to God themselves or others, with whose necessity he has been pleased to make them more familiarly acquainted. It is true that prayer and the giving of our substance are not in all respects alike. We can only bestow the kindness of our liberality on those of whose needs we are aware, whereas in prayer we can assist the greatest strangers, no matter how wide the space which may separate them from us. This is done by that general form of prayer which, including all the sons of God, includes them also. To this we may refer the exhortation which Paul gave to the believers of his age, to lift up "holy hands without wrath and doubting," (1 Tim 2:8). By reminding them that dissension is a bar to prayer, he shows it to be his wish that they should with one accord present their prayers in common.

40. The next words are, **which art in heaven**. From this we are not to infer that he is enclosed and confined within the circumference of heaven, as by a kind of boundaries. Hence Solomon confesses, "The heaven of heavens cannot contain thee," (1 Kings 8:27); and he himself says by the Prophet, "The heaven is my throne, and the earth is my footstool," (Isa 66:1); thereby intimating, that his presence, not confined to any region, is diffused over all space. But as our gross minds are unable to conceive of his ineffable glory, it is designated to us by heaven, nothing which our eyes can behold being so full of splendor and majesty. While, then, we are accustomed to regard every object as confined to the place where our senses discern it, no place can be assigned to God; and hence, if we would seek him, we must rise higher than all corporeal or mental discernment.

Again, this form of expression reminds us that he is far beyond the reach of change or corruption, that he holds the whole universe in his grasp, and rules it by his power. The effect of the expressions therefore, is the same as if it had been said, that he is of infinite majesty, incomprehensible essence, boundless power, and eternal duration. When we thus speak of God, our thoughts must be raised to their highest pitch; we must not ascribe to him anything of a terrestrial or carnal nature, must not measure him by our little standards, or suppose his will to be like ours. At the same time, we must put our confidence in him, understanding that heaven and earth are governed by his providence and power. In short, under the name of Father is set before us that God, who has appeared to us in his own image, that we may invoke him with sure faith; the familiar name of Father being given not only to inspire confidence, but also to curb our minds, and prevent them from going astray after doubtful or fictitious gods. We thus ascend from the only begotten Son to the supreme Father of angels and of the Church. Then when his throne is fixed in heaven, we are reminded that he governs the world, and, therefore, that it is not in vain to approach him whose present care we actually experience. "He that cometh to God," says the Apostle, "must believe that he is, and that he is a rewarder of them that diligently seek him," (Heb 11:6). Here Christ makes both claims for his Father, first, that we place our faith in him; and, secondly, that we feel assured that our salvation is not neglected by him, inasmuch as he condescends to extend his providence to us. By these elementary principles Paul prepares us to pray aright; for before enjoining us to make our requests known unto God, he premises in this way, "The Lord is at hand. Be careful for nothing," (Phil 4:5, 6). From this it appears that doubt and perplexity hang over the prayers of those in whose minds the belief is not firmly seated, that "the eyes of the Lord are upon the righteous," (Psa 34:15).

41. The first petition is, **hallowed be Thy name**. The necessity of presenting it bespeaks our great disgrace. For what can be more unbecoming than that our ingratitude and malice should impair, our audacity and petulance should as much as in them lies destroy, the glory of God? But though all the ungodly should burst with sacrilegious rage, the holiness of God's name still shines forth. Justly does the Psalmist exclaim, "According to thy name, O God, so is thy praise unto the ends of the earth," (Psa 48:10). For wherever God has made himself known, his perfections must be displayed, his power, goodness, wisdom, justice, mercy, and truth, which fill us with admiration, and incite us to show forth his praise. Therefore, as the name of God is not duly hallowed on the earth, and we are otherwise unable to assert it, it is at least our duty to make it the subject of our prayers. The sum of the whole is, It must be our desire that God may receive the honor which is his due: that men may never think or speak of him without the greatest reverence.

The opposite of this reverence is profanity, which has always been too common in the world, and is very prevalent in the present day. Hence the necessity of the petition, which, if piety had any proper existence among us, would be superfluous. But if the name of God is duly hallowed only when separated from all other names it alone is glorified, we are in the petition enjoined to ask not only that God would vindicate his sacred name from all contempt and insult, but also that he would compel the whole human race to reverence it. Then since God manifests himself to us partly by his word, and partly by his works, he is not sanctified unless in regard to both of these we ascribe to him what is due, and thus embrace whatever has proceeded from him, giving no less praise to his justice than to his mercy. On the manifold diversity of his works he has inscribed the marks of his glory, and these ought to call forth from every tongue an ascription of praise. Thus Scripture will obtain its due authority with us, and no event will hinder us from celebrating the praises of God, in regard to every part of his government. On the other hand, the petition implies a wish that all impiety which pollutes this sacred name may perish and be extinguished, that everything which obscures or impairs his glory, all detraction and insult, may cease; that all blasphemy being suppressed, the divine majesty may be more and more signally displayed.

42. The second petition is, **Thy kingdom come**. This contains nothing new, and yet there is good reason for distinguishing it from the first. For if we consider our lethargy in the greatest of all matters, we shall see how necessary it is that what ought to be in itself perfectly known should be inculcated at greater length. Therefore, after the injunction to pray that God would reduce to order, and at length completely efface every stain which is thrown on his sacred name, another petition, containing almost the same wish, is added—viz. Thy kingdom come. Although a definition of this kingdom has already been given, I now briefly repeat that God reigns when men, in denial of themselves and contempt of the world and this earthly life, devote themselves to righteousness and aspire to heaven (see Calvin, Harm. Mt 6) Thus this kingdom consists of two parts; the first is, when God by the agency of his Spirit corrects all the depraved lusts of the flesh,

which in bands war against Him; and the second, when he brings all our thoughts into obedience to his authority.

This petition, therefore, is duly presented only by those who begin with themselves; in other words, who pray that they may be purified from all the corruptions which disturb the tranquility and impair the purity of God's kingdom. Then as the word of God is like his royal scepter, we are here enjoined to pray that he would subdue all minds and hearts to voluntary obedience. This is done when by the secret inspiration of his Spirit he displays the efficacy of his word, and raises it to the place of honor which it deserves. We must next descend to the wicked, who perversely and with desperate madness resist his authority. God, therefore, sets up his kingdom, by humbling the whole world, though in different ways, taming the wantonness of some, and breaking the ungovernable pride of others. We should desire this to be done every day, in order that God may gather churches to himself from all quarters of the world, may extend and increase their numbers, enrich them with his gifts, establish due order among them; on the other hand, beat down all the enemies of pure doctrine and religion, dissipate their counsels, defeat their attempts. Hence it appears that there is good ground for the precept which enjoins daily progress, for human affairs are never so prosperous as when the impurities of vice are purged away, and integrity flourishes in full vigor. The completion, however, is deferred to the final advent of Christ, when, as Paul declares, "God will be all in all," (1 Cor 15:28).

This prayer, therefore, ought to withdraw us from the corruptions of the world which separate us from God, and prevent his kingdom from flourishing within us; secondly, it ought to inflame us with an ardent desire for the mortification of the flesh; and, lastly, it ought to train us to the endurance of the cross; since this is the way in which God would have his kingdom to be advanced. It ought not to grieve us that the outward man decays provided the inner man is renewed. For such is the nature of the kingdom of God, that while we submit to his righteousness he makes us partakers of his glory. This is the case when continually adding to his light and truth, by which the lies and the darkness of Satan and his kingdom are dissipated, extinguished, and destroyed, he protects his people, guides them aright by the agency of his Spirit, and confirms them in perseverance; while, on the other hand, he frustrates the impious conspiracies of his enemies, dissipates their wiles and frauds, prevents their malice and curbs their petulance, until at length he consume Antichrist "with the spirit of his mouth," and destroy all impiety "with the brightness of his coming," (2 Thess 2:8, Calv. Com).

43. The third petition is, **Thy will be done on earth as it is in heaven**. Though this depends on his kingdom, and cannot be disjoined from it, yet a separate place is not improperly given to it on account of our ignorance, which does not at once or easily apprehend what is meant by God reigning in the world. This, therefore, may not improperly be taken as the explanation, that God will be King in the world when all shall subject themselves to his will.

We are not here treating of that secret will by which he governs all things, and destines them to their end (see Chap. 24, § 17). For although devils and men rise in tumult against him, he is able by his incomprehensible counsel not only to turn aside their violence, but make it subservient to the execution of his decrees.

What we here speak of is another will of God, namely, that of which voluntary obedience is the counterpart; and, therefore, heaven is expressly contrasted with earth, because, as is said in The Psalms, the angels "do his commandments, hearkening unto the voice of his word," (Psa 103:20). We are, therefore, enjoined to pray that as everything done in heaven is at the command of God, and the angels are calmly disposed to do all that is right, so the earth may be brought under his authority, all rebellion and depravity having been extinguished. In presenting this request we renounce the desires of the flesh, because he who does not entirely resign his affections to God, does as much as in him lies to oppose the divine will, since everything which proceeds from us is vicious. Again, by this prayer we are taught to deny ourselves, that God may rule us according to his pleasure; and not only so, but also having annihilated our own may create new thoughts and new minds so that we shall have no desire save that of entire agreement with his will; in short, wish nothing of ourselves, but have our hearts governed by his Spirit, under whose inward teaching we may learn to love those things which please and hate those things which displease him. Hence also we must desire that he would nullify and suppress all affections which are repugnant to his will.

Such are the three first heads of the prayer, in presenting which we should have the glory of God only in view, taking no account of ourselves, and paying no respect to our own advantage, which, though it is thereby greatly promoted, is not here to be the subject of request. And though all the events prayed for must happen in their own time, without being either thought of, wished, or asked by us, it is still our duty to wish and ask for them. And it is of no slight importance to do so, that we may testify and profess that we are the servants and children of God, desirous by every means in our power to promote the honor due to him as our Lord and Father, and truly and thoroughly devoted to his service. Hence if men, in praying that the name of God may be hallowed, that his kingdom may come, and his will be done, are not influenced by this zeal for the promotion of his glory, they are not to be accounted among the servants and children of God; and as all these things will take place against their will, so they will turn out to their confusion and destruction.

44. Now comes the second part of the prayer, in which we descend to our own interests, not, indeed, that we are to lose sight of the glory of God (to which, as Paul declares, we must have respect even in meat and drink, 1 Cor 10:31), and ask only what is expedient for ourselves; but the distinction, as we have already observed, is this: God claiming the three first petitions as specially his own, carries us entirely to himself, that in this way he may prove our piety. Next he permits us to look to our own advantage, but still on the condition, that when we ask anything for ourselves it must be in order that all the benefits which he confers may show forth his glory, there being nothing more incumbent on us than to live and die to him.

By the first petition of the second part, **give us this day our daily bread**, we pray in general that God would give us all things which the body requires in this sublunary state, not only food and clothing, but everything which he knows will assist us to eat our bread in peace. In this way we briefly cast our care upon him, and commit ourselves to his providence, that he may feed, foster, and preserve us. For our heavenly Father disdains not to take our body under his charge and protection, that he may exercise our faith in those minute matters, while we look to him for everything, even to a morsel of bread and a drop of water. For since, owing to some strange inequality, we feel more concern for the body than for the soul, many who can trust the latter to God still continue anxious about the former, still hesitate as to what they are to eat, as to how they are to be clothed, and are in trepidation whenever their hands are not filled with corn, and wine, and oil, so much more value do we set on this shadowy, fleeting life, than on a blessed immortality. But those who, trusting to God, have once cast away that anxiety about the flesh, immediately look to him for greater gifts, even salvation and eternal life. It is no slight exercise of faith, therefore, to hope in God for things which would otherwise give us so much concern; nor have we made little progress when we get quit of this unbelief, which cleaves, as it were, to our very bones.

The speculations of some concerning supersubstantial bread seem to be very little accordant with our Savior's meaning; for our prayer would be defective were we not to ascribe to God the nourishment even of this fading life. The reason which they give is heathenish—viz. that it is inconsistent with the character of sons of God, who ought to be spiritual, not only to occupy their mind with earthly cares, but to suppose God also occupied with them. As if his blessing and paternal favor were not eminently displayed in giving us food, or as if there were nothing in the declaration that godliness has "the promise of the life that now is, and of that which is to come," (1 Tim 4:8). But although the forgiveness of sins is of far more importance than the nourishment of the body, yet Christ has set down the inferior in the prior place, in order that he might gradually raise us to the other two petitions, which properly belong to the heavenly life,—in this providing for our sluggishness. We are enjoined to ask our bread, that we may be contented with the measure which our heavenly Father is pleased to dispense, and not strive to make gain by illicit arts. Meanwhile, we must hold that the title by which it is ours is donation, because, as Moses says (Lev 26:20, Deut 8:17), neither our industry, nor labor, nor hands, acquire anything for us, unless the blessing of God be present; nay, not even would abundance of bread be of the least avail were it not divinely converted into nourishment. And hence this liberality of God is not less necessary to the rich than the poor, because, though their cellars and barns were full, they would be parched and pine with need did they not enjoy his favor along with their bread. The terms this day, or, as it is in another Evangelist, daily, and also the epithet daily, lay a restraint on our immoderate desire of fleeting good—a desire which we are extremely apt to indulge to excess, and from which other evils ensue: for when our supply is in richer abundance we ambitiously squander it in pleasure, luxury, ostentation, or other kinds of extravagance.

Wherefore, we are only enjoined to ask as much as our necessity requires, and as it were for each day, confiding that our heavenly Father, who gives us the supply of today, will not fail us on the morrow. How great soever our abundance may be, however well filled our cellars and granaries, we must still always ask for daily bread, for we must feel assured that all substance is nothing, unless in so far as the Lord, by pouring out his blessing, make it fruitful during its whole progress; for even that which is in our hand is not ours except in so far as he every hour portions it out, and permits us to use it. As nothing is more difficult to human pride than the admission of this truth, the Lord declares that he gave a special proof for all ages, when he fed his people with manna in the desert (Deut 8:3), that he might remind us that "man shall not live by bread alone, but by every word that proceeds out of the mouth of God," (Mt 4:4). It is thus intimated, that by his power alone our life and strength are sustained, though he ministers supply to us by bodily instruments. In like manner, whenever it so pleases, he gives us a proof of an opposite description, by breaking the strength, or, as he himself calls it, the staff of bread (Lev 26:26), and leaving us even while eating to pine with hunger, and while drinking to be parched with thirst. Those who, not contented with daily bread, indulge an unrestrained insatiable cupidity, or those who are full of their own abundance, and trust in their own riches, only mock God by offering up this prayer. For the former ask what they would be unwilling to obtain, nay, what they most of all abominate, namely, daily bread only, and as much as in them lies disguise their avarice from God, whereas true prayer should pour out the whole soul and every inward feeling before him.

The latter, again, ask what they do not at all expect to obtain, namely, what they imagine that they in themselves already possess. In its being called ours, God, as we have already said, gives a striking display of his kindness, making that to be ours to which we have no just claim. Nor must we reject the view to which I have already adverted—viz. that this name is given to what is obtained by just and honest labor, as contrasted with what is obtained by fraud and rapine, nothing being our own which we obtain with injury to others. When we ask God to give us, the meaning is, that the thing asked is simply and freely the gift of God, whatever be the quarter from which it comes to us, even when it seems to have been specially prepared by our own art and industry, and procured by our hands, since it is to his blessing alone that all our labors owe their success.

45. The next petition is, **forgive us our debts**. In this and the following petition our Savior has briefly comprehended whatever is conducive to the heavenly life, as these two members contain the spiritual covenant which God made for the salvation of his Church, "I will put my law in their inward parts, and write it on their hearts." "I will pardon all their iniquities," (Jer 31:33; 33:8). Here our Savior begins with the forgiveness of sins, and then adds the subsequent blessing—viz. that God would protect us by the power, and support us by the aid of his Spirit, so that we may stand invincible against all temptations.

To sins he gives the name of debts, because we owe the punishment due to them, a debt which we could not possibly pay were we not discharged by this remission, the result of his free mercy, when he freely expunges the debt, accepting nothing in return; but of his own mercy receiving satisfaction in Christ, who gave himself a ransom for us (Rom 3:24). Hence, those who expect to satisfy God by merits of their own or of others, or to compensate and purchase forgiveness by means of satisfactions, have no share in this free pardon, and while they address God in this petition, do nothing more than subscribe their own accusation, and seal their condemnation by their own testimony. For they confess that they are debtors, unless they are discharged by means of forgiveness. This forgiveness, however, they do not receive, but rather reject, when they obtrude their merits and satisfactions upon God, since by so doing they do not implore his mercy, but appeal to his justice.

Let those, again, who dream of a perfection which makes it unnecessary to seek pardon, find their disciples among those whose itching ears incline them to imposture (see Calv. on Dan 9:20); only let them understand that those whom they thus acquire have been carried away from Christ, since he, by instructing all to confess their guilt, receives none but sinners, not that he may soothe, and so encourage them in their sins, but because he knows that believers are never so divested of the sins of the flesh as not to remain subject to the justice of God. It is, indeed, to be wished, it ought even to be our strenuous endeavor, to perform all the parts of our duty, so as truly to congratulate ourselves before God as being pure from every stain; but as God is pleased to renew his image in us by degrees, so that to some extent there is always a residue of corruption in our flesh, we ought by no means to neglect the remedy. But if Christ, according to the authority given him by his Father, enjoins us, during the whole course of our lives, to implore pardon, who can tolerate those new teachers who, by the phantom of perfect innocence, endeavor to dazzle the simple, and make them believe that they can render themselves completely free from guilt? This, as John declares, is nothing else than to make God a liar (1 John 1:10).

In like manner, those foolish men mutilate the covenant in which we have seen that our salvation is contained by concealing one head of it, and so destroying it entirely; being guilty not only of profanity in that they separate things which ought to be indissolubly connected; but also of wickedness and cruelty in overwhelming wretched souls with despair—of treachery also to themselves and their followers, in that they encourage themselves in a carelessness diametrically opposed to the mercy of God. It is excessively childish to object, that when they long for the advent of the kingdom of God, they at the same time pray for the abolition of sin. In the former division of the prayer absolute perfection is set before us; but in the latter our own weakness. Thus the two fitly correspond to each other—we strive for the goal, and at the same time neglect not the remedies which our necessities require.

In the next part of the petition we pray to be forgiven, "as we forgive our debtors;" that is, as we spare and pardon all by whom we are in any way offended, either in deed by unjust, or in word by contumelious treatment. Not that we can forgive the guilt of a fault or offense; this belongs to God only; but we can forgive to this extent: we can voluntarily divest our minds of wrath, hatred, and revenge, and efface the remembrance of injuries by a voluntary oblivion. Wherefore, we are not to ask the forgiveness of our sins from God, unless we forgive the offenses of all who are or have been injurious to us. If we retain any hatred in our minds, if we meditate revenge, and devise the means of hurting; nay, if we do not return to a good understanding with our enemies, perform every kind of friendly office, and endeavor to effect a reconciliation with them, we by this petition beseech God not to grant us forgiveness. For we ask him to do to us as we do to others. This is the same as asking him not to do unless we do also. What, then, do such persons obtain by this petition but a heavier judgment?

Lastly, it is to be observed that the condition of being forgiven as we forgive our debtors, is not added because by forgiving others we deserve forgiveness, as if the cause of forgiveness were expressed; but by the use of this expression the Lord has been pleased partly to solace the weakness of our faith, using it as a sign to assure us that our sins are as certainly forgiven as we are certainly conscious of having forgiven others, when our mind is completely purged from all envy, hatred, and malice; and partly using as a badge by which he excludes from the number of his children all who, prone to revenge and reluctant to forgive, obstinately keep up their enmity, cherishing against others that indignation which they deprecate from themselves; so that they should not venture to invoke him as a Father. In the Gospel of Luke, we have this distinctly stated in the words of Christ.

46. The sixth petition corresponds (as we have observed) to the promise of writing the law upon our hearts; but because we do not obey God without a continual warfare, without sharp and arduous contests, we here pray that he would furnish us with armor, and defend us by his protection, that we may be able to obtain the victory. By this we are reminded that we not only have need of the gift of the Spirit inwardly to soften our hearts, and turn and direct them to the obedience of God, but also of his assistance, to render us invincible by all the wiles and violent assaults of Satan. The forms of temptation are many and various. The depraved conceptions of our minds provoking us to transgress the law— conceptions which our concupiscence suggests or the devil excites,

are temptations; and things which in their own nature are not evil, become temptations by the wiles of the devil, when they are presented to our eyes in such a way that the view of them makes us withdraw or decline from God. These temptations are both on the right hand and on the left. On the right, when riches, power, and honors, which by their glare, and the semblance of good which they present, generally dazzle the eyes of men, and so entice by their blandishments, that, caught by their snares, and intoxicated by their sweetness, they forget their God: on the left, when offended by the hardship and bitterness of poverty, disgrace, contempt, afflictions, and other things of that description, they despond, cast away their confidence and hope, and are at length totally estranged from God.

In regard to both kinds of temptation, which either enkindled in us by concupiscence) or presented by the craft of Satan's war against us, we pray God the Father not to allow us to be overcome, but rather to raise and support us by his hand, that strengthened by his mighty power we may stand firm against all the assaults of our malignant enemy, whatever be the thoughts which he sends into our minds; next we pray that whatever of either description is allotted us, we may turn to good, that is, may neither be inflated with prosperity, nor cast down by adversity.

Here, however, we do not ask to be altogether exempted from temptation, which is very necessary to excite, stimulate, and urge us on, that we may not become too lethargic. It was not without reason that David wished to be tried, nor is it without cause that the Lord daily tries his elect, chastising them by disgrace, poverty, tribulation, and other kinds of cross. But the temptations of God and Satan are very different: Satan tempts, that he may destroy, condemn, confound, throw headlong; God, that by proving his people he may make trial of their sincerity, and by exercising their strength confirm it; may mortify, tame, and cauterize their flesh, which, if not curbed in this manner, would wanton and exult above measure. Besides, Satan attacks those who are unarmed and unprepared, that he may destroy them unawares; whereas whatever God sends, he "will with the temptation also make a way to escape, that ye may be able to bear it."

Whether by the term evil we understand the devil or sin, is not of the least consequence. Satan is indeed the very enemy who lays snares for our life, but it is by sin that he is armed for our destruction. Our petition, therefore, is, that we may not be overcome or overwhelmed with temptation, but in the strength of the Lord may stand firm against all the powers by which we are assailed; in other words, may not fall under temptation: that being thus taken under his charge and protection, we may remain invincible by sin, death, the gates of hell, and the whole power of the devil; in other words, be delivered from evil.

Here it is carefully to be observed, that we have no strength to contend with such a combatant as the devil, or to sustain the violence of his assault. Were it otherwise, it would be mockery of God to ask of him what we already possess in ourselves. Assuredly those who in self-confidence prepare for such a fight, do not understand how bold and well-equipped the enemy is with whom they have to do. Now we ask to be delivered from his power, as from the mouth of some furious raging lion, who would instantly tear us with his teeth and claws, and swallow us up, did not the Lord rescue us from the midst of death; at the same time knowing that if the Lord is present and will fight for us while we stand by, through him "we shall do valiantly," (Psa 60:12). Let others if they will confide in the powers and resources of their free will which they think they possess; enough for us that we stand and are strong in the power of God alone.

But the prayer comprehends more than at first sight it seems to do. For if the Spirit of God is our strength in waging the contest with Satan, we cannot gain the victory unless we are filled with him, and thereby freed from all infirmity of the flesh. Therefore, when we pray to be delivered from sin and Satan, we at the same time desire to be enriched with new supplies of divine grace, until completely replenished with them, we triumph over every evil.

To some it seems rude and harsh to ask God not to lead us into temptation, since, as James declares (James 1:13), it is contrary to his nature to do so. This difficulty has already been partly solved by the fact that our concupiscence is the cause, and therefore properly bears the blame of all the temptations by which we are overcome. All that James means is, that it is vain and unjust to ascribe to God vices which our own consciousness compels us to impute to ourselves. But this is no reason why God may not when he sees it proper bring us into bondage to Satan, give us up to a reprobate mind and shameful lusts, and so by a just, indeed, but often hidden judgment, lead us into temptation. Though the cause is often concealed from men, it is well known to him. Hence we may see that the expression is not improper, if we are persuaded that it is not without cause he so often threatens to give sure signs of his vengeance, by blinding the reprobate, and hardening their hearts.

47. These three petitions, in which we specially commend ourselves and all that we have to God, clearly show what we formerly observed (§ 38, 39), that the prayers of Christians should be public, and have respect to the public edification of the Church and the advancement of believers in spiritual communion. For no one requests that anything should be given to him as an individual, but we all ask in common for daily bread and the forgiveness of sins, not to be led into temptation, but delivered from evil.

Moreover, there is subjoined the reason for our great boldness in asking and confidence of obtaining (§ 11, 36). Although this does not exist in the Latin copies, yet as it accords so well with the whole, we cannot think of omitting it. The words are, **Thine is the kingdom, and the power, and the glory, forever**. Here is the calm and firm assurance of our faith. For were our prayers to be commended to God by our own worth, who would venture even to whisper before him? Now, however wretched we may be, however unworthy, however devoid of commendation, we shall never lack a reason for prayer, nor a ground of confidence, since the kingdom, power, and glory, can never be wrested from our Father.

The last word is **Amen**, by which is expressed the eagerness of our desire to obtain the things which we ask, while our hope is confirmed, that all things have already been obtained and will assuredly be granted to us, seeing they have been promised by God, who cannot deceive. This accords with the form of expression to which we have already adverted: "Grant, O Lord, for thy name's sake, not on account of us or of our righteousness." By this the saints not only express the end of their prayers, but confess that they are unworthy of obtaining did not God find the cause in himself and were not their confidence founded entirely on his nature.

48. All things that we ought, indeed all that we are able, to ask of God, are contained in this formula, and as it were rule, of prayer delivered by Christ, our divine Master, whom the Father has appointed to be our teacher, and to whom alone he would have us to listen (Mt 17:5). For he ever was the eternal wisdom of the Father, and being made man, was manifested as the Wonderful, the Counselor (Isa 11:2).

Accordingly, this prayer is complete in all its parts, so complete, that whatever is extraneous and foreign to it, whatever cannot be referred to it, is impious and unworthy of the approbation of God. For he has here summarily prescribed what is worthy of him, what is acceptable to him, and what is necessary for us; in short, whatever he is pleased to grant.

Those, therefore, who presume to go further and ask something more from God, first seek to add of their own to the wisdom of God (this it is insane blasphemy to do); secondly, refusing to confine themselves within the will of God, and despising it, they wander as their cupidity directs; lastly, they will never obtain anything, seeing they pray without faith. For there cannot be a doubt that all such prayers are made without faith, because at variance with the word of God, on which if faith do not always lean it cannot possibly stand. Those who, disregarding the Master's rule, indulge their own wishes, not only have not the word of God, but as much as in them lies oppose it. Hence Tertullian… has not less truly than elegantly termed it Lawful Prayer, tacitly intimating that all other prayers are lawless and illicit.

49. By this, however, we would not have it understood that we are so restricted to this form of prayer as to make it unlawful to change a word or syllable of it. For in Scripture we meet with many prayers differing greatly from it in word, yet written by the same Spirit, and capable of being used by us with the greatest advantage. Many prayers also are continually suggested to believers by the same Spirit, though in expression they bear no great resemblance to it. All we mean to say is, that no man should wish, expect, or ask anything which is not summarily comprehended in this prayer. Though the words may be very different, there must be no difference in the

sense. In this way, all prayers, both those which are contained in the Scripture, and those which come forth from pious breasts, must be referred to it, certainly none can ever equal it, far less surpass it in perfection. It omits nothing which we can conceive in praise of God, nothing which we can imagine advantageous to man, and the whole is so exact that all hope of improving it may well be renounced. In short, let us remember that we have here the doctrine of heavenly wisdom. God has taught what he willed; he willed what was necessary.

Chapter 9 - Charles Simeon on the Lord's Prayer

(Charles Simeon, 1759-1836)

From 'Horae homileticae', a commentary on the whole Bible

DISCOURSE: 1313 - HALLOWING GOD'S NAME

Mat 6:9. **After this manner therefore pray ye: Our Father which art in heaven, Hallowed be thy name.**

IT is of the utmost importance to every human being to know how he shall approach his God with acceptance. Hence some even of the heathen philosophers endeavored to instruct their disciples how to pray. Plato, in his Dialogue on Prayer, represents Socrates as teaching Alcibiades how to pray. We do not find indeed any form of prayer provided for the Jews, with the exception of some short passages which may be regarded in that light (Num 6:22-26; Num 10:35-36 and Hos 14:2-3). But in the New Testament we are informed that John the Baptist gave special instructions to his disciples respecting prayer; and our blessed Lord composed a prayer which should be used by his followers and should serve also as a pattern for prayer to his Church in all ages. If it is thought that it was intended only for his disciples in their infantine state, previous to the outpouring of the Spirit upon them, let it be remembered, that it was recorded by the Evangelists a great many years after the full establishment of Christianity, without any hint of its use having been superseded. And consequently, we have the same reason to use it as the form and pattern of our supplications as the Apostles themselves had. The only difference is that as our Lord more clearly taught them afterwards to offer their petitions in his name, we must avail ourselves of that further information to render our prayers more acceptable to God.

With our intention to enter at large into the consideration of this prayer, we shall confine ourselves at present to that portion of it which we have read; in which are two things to be noticed:

I.   The invocation—

It is to God alone and not to creatures, whether angels or men, that we are to address our prayers: "God is a jealous God, and will not give his glory to another." But to him we are invited to draw near; and are taught to regard him,

1.   As a loving Father—

Under this title God was known to his people of old. Indeed it was the appellation, which, in their eyes, was the surest pledge of his love (Isa 63:16): the designation too in which he himself appeared peculiarly to delight (Jer 3:4, 3:19). And well may it be a comfort to us to be permitted to address him by this endearing name: for, if he is a Father, he will pity our weakness (Psa 103:13), and pardon our sins (Luke 15:20), and supply our every need (Luke 11:11-13). True, if we have no nearer connection with him than the ungodly world and are his children only by creation, we can derive comparatively but little comfort from it because we are in rebellion against him. But, if we are his children by adoption and grace what may we not expect at his hands? When we come to him as members of that great family, pleading for ourselves individually, and for the whole collectively, and addressing him in the name of all as "our Father," it would seem he cannot turn away his ear from us: "We may ask what we will, and it shall be done unto us." Only let us come with "a spirit of adoption, crying, Abba, Father!" and, however "wide we may open our mouths, he will fill them."

2.   As an almighty Friend—

When we are taught to address God as our Father "which is in heaven," we are not to understand it as distinguishing him from our earthly parents, but as intended to impress our minds with a sense of his majesty: to remind us that he sees everything which passes upon earth, and that he has all power to relieve us to the utmost extent of our necessities. The consideration that he is our Father encourages us to come "with boldness and with confidence." But the thought that he is that "high and lofty One who inhabits eternity," and dwells in the light which no man can approach unto; the thought that he knows even the most secret motions of our hearts and is alike able to save or to destroy; these considerations, I say, are calculated to bring about a holy fear in our minds and to temper our boldness with reverential awe.

Such are the feelings which should be blended in our hearts whenever we draw near to a throne of grace. We should go to God as our Father; but, remembering that "he is in heaven and we upon earth, we should address him in words select and few" (Eccl 5:2).

Let us now turn our attention to,

II.   The address—

In this prayer there are six different petitions; three for the advancement of God's honor, and three for the promotion of our happiness. The former having the precedence may fitly teach us that a regard for God's honor ought to be first in our intention and desire. Yet it may well be doubted whether the address which is presented to God in our text is a petition or a thankful acknowledgment. Perhaps, in so concise a form as this, both may be properly included. Agreeably to this idea we shall consider the address,

1.   As eucharistic—

Though not generally regarded in this light it seems naturally enough to bear this construction, inasmuch as it accords exactly with the feelings of a devout soul when impressed and animated with a sense of God's paternal love. Suppose a person to have been meditating on the perfections of his God, the stupendous display of his love and mercy in Christ Jesus, his covenant engagements to his believing people, and the innumerable benefits conferred upon them. Suppose him also to be warmed with the thought that this God is his God, his Father, and "his eternal great reward;" what would be the first effusions of his soul? Would he not burst forth into praises and adorations, and even labor for words by which to express his love and gratitude towards him? Thus it was with David on many occasions (Psa 9:1-2; 103:1-5); and thus it will be with all who truly delight themselves in God. Sometimes, no doubt, the believer's mind will be led to dwell rather on other subjects, whether of confession or petition, as circumstances may require: but where nothing extraordinary has occurred to distract his attention, I am sure that the language of adoration is most expressive of his feelings, and most suited to his state.

2.　　　As supplicatory—

The Christian will not be satisfied with his own personal endeavors to honor God. But will wish and pray that the whole universe may render him the honor due unto his name. So, he will beg of God to banish from the world all ignorance and error; and so to reveal himself to mankind that all may be constrained to show forth his praise. This, I say, is near to the heart of the believer: he will long to promote it to the utmost of his power (Psa 57:7-11). He will pant after it, as an object of his most anxious desires (Psa 67:2-5): and he would be glad if every creature, rational and irrational, animate and inanimate, could unite in this as their one blest employ (Psa 148:1-11).

Hence we may learn,

1.　　　How glorious is the liberty of God's praying people—

They are rescued from the dominion of slavish fears and selfish desires. "Happy art thou, O Israel, O people saved by the Lord!" Inexpressibly happy are all whose hearts accord with the language of our text! It seems to me they resemble as nearly as such imperfect creatures can the inhabitants of the realms of light. The cherubim around the throne veil their faces and their feet, in token of that reverential awe which they feel in the presence of the Deity: and the glorified saints cast down their crowns before the footstool of their Lord to express their sense of their unworthiness of the mercies vouchsafed unto them; while the whole united choir vie with each other in hallelujahs to God and to the Lamb. Thus it is with the saints on earth, both in their secret chambers and in the house of God: they are filled with adoring thoughts of God their Savior, and "rejoice in him with joy unspeakable and glorified." Doubtless they experience changes in their frame, and seem at times almost to have forgotten their high privileges: but in their better seasons they show forth the power of divine grace, and enjoy a foretaste of heaven. O that all of us might know their blessedness, by sweet experience!

2.　　　What losers are they who neglect prayer—

The generality of people account prayer a drudgery, but they are bitter enemies to their own souls. What loss do they suffer in having God for an enemy when they might have him for their Friend and Father! As for God, he suffers no loss. If they refuse to glorify him willingly, he will glorify himself upon them against their will. Reflect then, brethren, what sufferers you are, while you are turning your back on God! You have no Father to go to in the time of trouble; no sweet assurance that Almighty wisdom and power are exercised for your support; no anticipations of the blessedness of heaven. On the contrary, all your enjoyments are empty, all your prospects dark. In this world you have little happiness above the beasts; and in the world to come, an eternity of unavailing sorrows. O that you would now begin to pray! O that God might say of you this day, as he did of Saul immediately after his conversion, "Behold, he prayeth!" Then, however desperate your case may now appear, you should soon be received into the family of your God and be partakers of his inheritance forevermore.

DISCOURSE: 1314 - THE LORD'S PRAYER

Mat 6:10. **Thy kingdom come. Thy will be done in earth, as it is in heaven.**

HIGHLY as the Lord's Prayer is esteemed among us, and frequently as it is used, there is scarcely any part of Scripture less considered. We are contented with repeating the words, without ever attending to its true meaning. The fact is that though it is written for the use of all, none can use it aright but the true Christian. It is the Christian only whose heart can embrace the subjects contained in it.

The first petition which we are taught to offer is that God's "name may be hallowed" and adored. The two next petitions (which now come under our consideration) are intimately connected with it; they have respect to,

I. The universal establishment of his kingdom—

The kingdom, for the establishment of which we pray, is that of the Messiah—

The dominion which God exercises by his providence cannot be more universal than it is: "his kingdom rules over all."

But the government which he maintains over the souls of men has in every age been extremely limited and partial. That is the kingdom which God has determined to erect: of that the prophets have distinctly prophesied (Dan 2:44), and declared that it should be subjected to "Messiah the Prince (Dan 7:13-14)." Its extent is to be universal, and its duration to the end of time (1Co 15:24-25).

The time was now at hand when the foundations of this kingdom were to be laid: and there was a general expectation, both among the godly (Luke 2:38; Mar 15:43) and the ungodly (Luke 17:20-21), that measures for its establishment would speedily be adopted. True it is, that few, if any, sufficiently advert to the spiritual nature of this kingdom. But our Lord gradually rectified the apprehensions of his followers with respect to it and taught them to expect the long-wished-for period, and to pray that nothing might be able to retard its arrival. Some have thought that since the establishment of Christianity in the world, there is no further occasion for this petition. But there is, in fact, the same occasion for it now as there was at the first moment it was suggested to the disciples. The only difference between their use of it and ours is that they prayed for the commencement of this kingdom, and we for its progressive and final establishment. Indeed, the kingdom itself will never have attained its utmost bounds until every enemy of it be put under the Messiah's feet and every subject of it be perfected in glory.

Nor can this event have too prominent a place in our prayers—

After the general petition that God's name may be glorified we are taught immediately to desire the advent of the Messiah's kingdom. Nor is this without reason: for it is by the establishment of this kingdom, and by that alone, that God's name can ever be sanctified in the earth. Look at the Heathen world who are worshipping devils, or bowing down to stocks and stones. What glory has the Lord from them? Look at those who are carried away by the Mahometan (Muslim) delusion, or hardened by Jewish infidelity. These profess indeed to acknowledge the one true God, but they cast his word behind them and are avowed enemies to his only-begotten Son. Look at the Christian world, by whom he is dishonored no less than by any of those whom we have before mentioned. With the exception of a little remnant whom he has renewed by his grace, there is not one on earth that truly loves him or cordially adores him. All have some idol in their hearts which they prefer to him, some darling lust which they will not sacrifice for his sake. Here surely is abundant reason why we should entreat him to put forth his almighty power for the conversion of the world.

Let this petition then be offered by us with constancy, and with an earnestness proportioned to its importance. Let us pray that "the word of the Lord may have free course and be glorified amongst us:" that he would "gird his sword upon his thigh, and ride on in the cause of meekness and truth and righteousness;" until "all the kingdoms of the world become the kingdom of the Lord and of his Christ."

God requires this at our hands; no more, the creation itself demands it of us. "The whole creation are represented as groaning and travailing in pain together" in expectation of this event (Rom 8:21-23); and therefore may well be considered as calling on us to exert ourselves in every possible way for their complete deliverance. Whenever then we contemplate the state of those around us or extend our views to the Heathen world, let us lift up our hearts to God and pray, "Thy kingdom come."

Closely connected with this petition is that which next occurs, for,

II.   The unlimited execution of his will—

This will flow from the former as an effect inseparable from it. We cannot approve ourselves subjects of the Redeemer's kingdom in any other way than by our obedience to his will. Hence we are taught to pray that God's will may be done by ourselves and all mankind, even as it is done in heaven: and that too,

1.   In a way of cheerful acquiescence—

The angels, notwithstanding they dwell immediately in the presence of their God, and behold "the works which he doeth for the children of men," are yet not privy to his ultimate designs. Nor do they understand the full scope of all that they behold. As, under the Mosaic dispensation, the cherubim upon the mercy-seat were formed in a bending posture, looking down upon the ark in order, as it were, to search out the mysteries contained in it, so are the angels represented by St. Peter as "desiring to look into" the Gospel salvation (1Pe 1:12). And St. Paul says that the revelation which God has with progressive clearness made of himself unto the Church is no less instructive to them than to us (Eph 3:10). But we are well assured that they never for a moment doubt either the wisdom or goodness of God in any of his dispensations (Rev 16:5-7; Rev 19:1-4).

In this they are a fit pattern for our imitation. We know not the secret purposes of God in anything that he does. His ways are in the great deep and his footsteps are not known. But we should be satisfied in our minds, that "he does, and will do all things well;" and that, though "clouds and darkness are round about him, righteousness and judgment are the basis of his throne." However mysterious his ways may appear, we should at all times solace ourselves with this, that "what we know not now, we shall know hereafter." Were this spirit universally prevalent, discontent would be utterly banished from the world. Under the most afflictive dispensations we should maintain a humble composure and a thankful frame (Isa 39:8. 1Sa 3:18. 2Sa 15:25-26). What a desirable state! How honorable to God and what a source of happiness to man!

2.   In a way of active obedience—

Here also are the angels a pattern for us: they are "ministers of God, to do his pleasure; and they do his commandments, hearkening unto the voice of his word (Psa 103:20-21)." The very first intimation of the Divine will is quite sufficient for them. Whatever the office is, whether to deliver Lot from Sodom, or to destroy a hundred and eighty-five thousand Assyrians, they execute it with equal readiness and equal pleasure. Thus should we engage in the service of our God. It should be "our meat and our drink to do his will." We should hearken diligently to his word in order to learn what we have to do; and then we should do it without hesitation, without weariness, without reserve. Nor should we be satisfied with having our own souls brought into this state. We should long to see every sinner upon earth and "every thought of his heart, captivated in like manner to the obedience of Christ." The

Apostle's prayer should be the language both of our hearts and lips (Heb 13:20-21).

But who can effect this change? Who can subdue the unruly wills and affections of sinful men? None but God. He must "make them willing in the day of his power, or they will continue in their rebellion even to the end. To him therefore we should look; and to him should we make our supplication, that he would "reveal his arm," and subdue the nations to the obedience of faith.

From this directory for prayer we cannot but observe,

1.   What elevation of mind religion inspires—

Statesmen and philosophers, however enlarged their minds, are occupied solely about the things of time and sense, whereas the Christian, even though he is poor and illiterate, "separates himself" for the pursuit of higher objects, and seeks out heavenly wisdom (Pro 18:1). The universal establishment of the Messiah's kingdom, and the unlimited execution of the Divine will, the bringing down of heaven to earth, and the assimilating of earth to heaven, these are the subjects of his daily meditation. These are the objects of his most ardent desire. The men of science justly value themselves on having enjoyed the blessings of education. They know and feel the benefit of having their thoughts raised to the contemplation of objects that are out of the reach of vulgar and illiterate minds. But the Christian surpasses them incomparably more than they surpass the lowest of mankind. His meditations are more noble, his mind is more enlarged. Let us learn then to form a proper estimate of religion and to regard it with the veneration it deserves.

2.   What happiness it is calculated to produce—

Let these petitions be answered; let this state of things prevail; let the Messiah reign in the hearts of all mankind; let the example of angels be emulated by every human being. Will anyone say that this would lessen the happiness of the world? Will anyone say that he even feels a doubt upon the subject? No. We are all convinced in our consciences that in proportion as we approximated to the holiness of angels we should also participate their bliss. See what it is that occasions by far the greater part of misery in the world: "What causes quarrels and what causes fights among you? Is it not this, that your passions are at war within you?"

It is to the same source that we must trace the greater part of our bodily disorders and our mental troubles. Sin is the parent of misery in ten thousand different forms, and it is religion alone that can heal the wounds which sin has made. If any who profess religion are not happy the fault is not in religion, but in them. They have either erroneous notions of God's kingdom or a partial regard for his will. Let them only possess the dispositions implied in these prayers, and they will have a very heaven upon earth (See Isa 60:19-20).

DISCOURSE: 1315 - THE LORD'S PRAYER

Mat 6:11. **Give us this day our daily bread.**

In those petitions which relate to the glory of God, that occurs first which is the most comprehensive and the most important: in these which relate to the welfare of man, a different order is observed. The comfortable support of our bodies, instead of being of chief importance is, when compared with spiritual blessings, quite insignificant. Yet is a petition respecting that with great propriety placed first, because, unless our bodies be preserved in life there will be no further scope for the communication of grace on God's part, or the exercise of it on ours. The subject of this petition indeed is such, as many would think scarcely worthy of a place in so short a summary of prayer as that before us:\. But our Lord did not account it so and therefore we should not.

That we may form a right judgment concerning it, let us consider,

I.   The import of this petition—

There are two things in it which call for explanation:

1.   The general scope of it—

Some have thought that because Christ is represented as "the bread of life" which everyone must eat we are here taught to pray for the knowledge and enjoyment of Him. Others have thought that the prayer referred to the sacramental bread, which in the primitive Church was partaken of daily by the whole body of believers. But neither of these interpretations accords with the terms in which the petition is conveyed. The plain and literal sense of the words seems to be that which was intended by our Lord. It may be thought strange indeed that when three petitions only are

78

suggested for the welfare of man, one of them should be confined to his bodily concerns. But it must be remembered that those are the concerns in which we are most apt to overlook the interpositions of Heaven, and consequently, that we particularly need to have this very direction given us. Nor is it a small matter to acknowledge the agency of God in things of such apparently inferior moment: for it leads us to realize the thought of an overruling Providence in everything, even in the death of a sparrow, or the falling of a hair of our head.

 2. The particular limitations contained in it—

The thing which we pray for is limited to the necessaries of life. This is the generally accepted meaning of the term "bread" in Scripture. It comprehends all the things which are needful for the body, but not any luxuries or superfluities. Doubtless those necessaries will vary according to our rank and situation in life, and according to the numbers we have dependent on us for support. And what would be a abundance under some circumstances would be no more than absolutely necessary under other circumstances: but, due respect being had to these things, this must be the limit of our requests. If we ask for anything, "to consume it upon our lusts, we ask amiss (Jam 4:3)."

The measure also of these necessaries is limited. We are not to ask for a store on which we may subsist for a time independent of God; but simply for such things as are requisite for our present subsistence. The term that is used in our text is indeed variously interpreted: but, when compared with the corresponding passage in St. Luke (Luke 11:3), its meaning will evidently appear to be that which our translators have affixed to it: we pray from day to day, that God will give us what is necessary for the day. We are not even to "take thought for the morrow;" at least, not so as to feel any anxious care respecting it (ver. 34): for we know not that we shall be alive on the morrow; or, if we be spared, we know that He who provided for us yesterday and today, can do the same tomorrow: on Him therefore we should "cast our care, believing that he cares for us," and that he will provide whatever in his wisdom he shall see good for us. In every place, in every event, in everything, we should see, as it were, that name inscribed, "Jehovah-jireh," The Lord will provide (Gen 22:8; Gen 22:14).

Now this petition will be found extremely important, if we consider,

II.   The instruction to be derived from it—

We need not put any forced interpretation on our text in order to render it instructive; for,

It teaches us many practical lessons that are of great importance:

1.   That we should be moderate in our desires of earthly things—

Our hearts are naturally set on earthly things. Our Lord tells us that the Gentiles think of little except what they shall eat, and drink, and wear (ver. 32). And it is precisely thus with the great mass of those who bear the Christian name. The heathen themselves do not exceed us in an eager pursuit after the good things of this life. Nor is perfect contentment known even among those who possess the largest fortunes. There is always something beyond their present attainments which they are aspiring after and anxious to possess. But it should not, nor indeed can it, be like this with any true Christian. The man who sees the worth and excellence of heavenly things can no longer pant after the worthless things of time and sense. He is like a man who, having looked at the sun, sees a dark spot upon every earthly object. From that moment, Agur's wish is his (Pro 30:8-9). In his addresses to his heavenly Father he can ask for nothing more than food and raiment (Gen 28:20): possessing that, he is content (1Tim 6:8). Or even if he does not possess it he "knows how to suffer need as well as to abound (Php 4:11-12);" and, when "having nothing, feels that he possesses all things (2Co 6:10)."

Let this lesson then be learned by us, and let everyone of us apply to himself that solemn caution, "And do you seek great things for yourself? Seek them not (Jer 45:5)."

2.   That we should depend on God's providence for the supply of them—

God is the true source of temporal, no less than of spiritual blessings. It is he who causes the earth to bring forth (Psa 104:14-15), and instructs men how to cultivate it to advantage (Deut 8:17-

18): and, without his blessing all our labors would terminate in disappointment (Hag 1:6). The whole creation subsists upon his kind and bounteous provision (Psa 104:27-28). Now because we have so long been in the habit of receiving the productions of the earth, either spontaneously presenting themselves to us or rewarding the labors of our hands, we are very apt to overlook the Donor and to forget our dependence upon God.

But we are in fact as dependent on him as "the fowls of the air, which neither sow, nor reap, nor gather into barns:" and we should in the habit of our minds live upon his providence, precisely as the Israelites did in the wilderness and receive "our daily bread" at his hands, as much as if it were daily given to us from the clouds. We are indeed to labor for the things which are necessary for the body, as well as for those which pertain to the soul. The prohibition which our Lord gave respecting this is not absolute, but only comparative (John 6:27). If we will not labor for ourselves we have no claim for assistance either from God or man (2Th 3:12). Nevertheless, when we have labored with ever so much skill and diligence we must bear in mind that "our daily bread is as truly the gift" of God as if we had not labored for it at all. And our hope for the future must be in him alone as much as if we were, like Elijah, subsisting daily on provision brought to us by ravens.

3.   That, whatever be the portion which God sees fit to give us, we should be content with it—

A person who forms his judgment by outward appearances would think that there is an exceeding great difference between the comforts of the rich and of the poor. But there is really far less difference than we are apt to imagine. The richest man has no security for his possessions. Experience proves that kings may be hurled from their thrones and nobles be reduced to subsist on charity. Moreover, while men possess their wealth they may, by disease of body or perturbation of mind, be deprived of all comfort and be made to envy the poorest man who is in the enjoyment of health and peace.

But the pious poor have necessaries secured to them on the most inviolable of all tenures, the promise of a faithful God (Mat 6:33. Psa 34:10). Besides, the rich have very little conception of the happiness that is derived from seeing the hand of God in their daily provision. This happiness is reserved for the poor. They are constrained to feel their dependence on God and, when they receive their supplies they often behold such peculiar circumstances attending them, as mark in the strongest manner the interposition of the Deity in their behalf. Can anyone doubt whether provision sent in such a way be enjoyed with a greater zest than that which is supplied out of our own store? Surely the thoughts which arise in the mind of a poor man on such occasions that fill his eyes with tears of gratitude and his mouth with songs of praise, are an infinitely richer feast than all the luxuries which even royal wealth could procure. Let not any then be discontented with their lot. "The rich and the poor meet together" far more nearly than is generally supposed (Pro 22:2). "A man's life does not consist in the abundance of the things that he possesses," but in the blessing which he enjoys along with it. "The blessing of the Lord, it makes rich; and he adds no sorrow with it (Pro 10:22)."

Our blessed Lord, who often lacked bread to eat and "a place where to lay his head," has sanctified a state of need and shown that the Father's love is not to be judged of by his external dispensations, or his children's happiness materially affected by them. Are any of you then under circumstances of trial? Be of good cheer. It is a small matter. It is a small matter for your bodies to be in need provided "your souls are satisfied with the plenteousness of your Father's house." Only "eat abundantly" of "the living bread," "which is meat indeed;" and then the scantiest pittance that you can subsist upon shall be sweet as honey or the honeycomb. Feed richly, I say, on that and "you shall never hunger," as long as the world shall stand (John 6:35, 55). As it respects your body, "your bread shall be given you, and your water shall be sure;" and, as it respects your soul, you shall evermore "delight yourself in fatness (Isa 33:16; 55:2)."

DISCOURSE: 1316 - THE LORD'S PRAYER

Mat 6:12. **And forgive us our debts, as we forgive our debtors.**

The petitions of men to the Supreme Being will be presented in a different order according to the general state of their minds, or according to the particular circumstances in which they are placed. A person just awakened to a sense of his guilt and danger would most probably assign the first place in his petitions to that which, at such a season, would press most forcibly upon his mind—the obtaining of reconciliation with an offended God. But when he has obtained peace with God and is enabled to come to him as a child unto his father, his slavish fear gives way to an ingenuous concern for his father's honor and his own personal safety occupies a less prominent situation in his prayers.

Not that he is less interested in the welfare of his soul than before; but he is more interested in other concerns, which at first had no place in his thoughts. Accordingly we find this order is observed in that form of prayer which our Lord himself has prescribed as the most perfect. The devout soul is first led to express its concern for the universal establishment of the Redeemer's kingdom. Then, after one petition for the preservation of its existence in the body, it is taught to implore the pardon of all its multiplied transgressions. This is the portion of that prayer which we are at this time to consider and in it we shall notice,

I.   The petition itself—

To pray for the forgiveness of our sins is,

1.   Universally necessary—

Sins are here spoken of under the notion of debts, for as by the preceptive part of the law we are bound to obedience, so by the sanctions of the law there is laid upon us an obligation to suffer punishment in case of disobedience. Our sins therefore are debts which we owe to divine justice for our violations of the laws of God. And who is there among the children of men that has not many debts to be forgiven? That there is a great difference between different persons in respect to the guilt they have contracted we readily acknowledge. But "there is no man that lives and sins not;" "in many things we all offend." "If any say that they have not sinned, they make God a liar, and his word is not in them," for his testimony respecting the whole race of mankind is that "all have sinned and come short of the glory of God," and, consequently, that "every mouth must be stopped, and all the world become guilty before him."

What then must be done? Can anyone discharge his own debt? If any will attempt it what method will he pursue? If he will obey the law in future that will no more satisfy its demands for past disobedience than the ceasing to increase a debt will discharge a debt that is already contracted. If he will endeavor to atone for his sins by tears of penitence, rivers of tears will never suffice to wash away one sin. There is but one possible remedy remaining for him, and that is to cast himself upon the mercy of God and to implore forgiveness for the Redeemer's sake. In this respect all are upon a level. Whether our sins have been greater or less, this is the only way in which we can return to God with any hope of acceptance. The proud self-justifying Pharisee will be dismissed with abhorrence and those only who come in the spirit of the self-abasing publican will obtain mercy at his hands.

There are two sorts of persons, indeed, who are apt to indulge very erroneous conceptions on this subject. Some suppose that they are so completely justified as not to need any renewed applications for pardon, and others that they are so perfectly sanctified as not to have any fresh occasion for pardon. But as David, after God by Nathan had sealed his pardon, still implored mercy at the hands of God (Compare 2 Sa 12:13. with Psalms 51), so must we. And they who fancy themselves living in a sinless state are proud deceivers of their own souls (1 Jn 1:8. Jam 3:2). There is not a day or an hour in which any human being has not just occasion to offer the petition in our text. The corruption of his nature, the transgressions of his former life, and the imperfections of his very best services, all require it of him (See John 13:10. As they who have walked in a bath yet need to wash their feet on account of the defilement contracted in coming from it, so, &c).

2.   Infinitely important—

Consider the state of a man whose iniquities are not forgiven. God, the Almighty God, is his enemy (Psa 7:11-13); He is every moment in danger of dropping into hell (Luke 12:20); He neither has, nor can have, any solid peace in his mind (Isa 57:20-21); He lives but to aggravate his guilt, and augment his condemnation (Rom 2:5). Can anyone reflect on this and not see the importance of urging the petition in our text? The only wonder is that any person in an unforgiven state can close his eyes in sleep, or give attention to any of the concerns of time or sense, until he has implored mercy at the hands of his offended God.

But while the general importance of this petition is obvious, there certainly is some obscurity in,

II.   The limitation or condition annexed to it—

To understand this part of the Lord's Prayer aright we must compare the expressions as recorded by St. Luke, with those which are used in the text. St. Luke says, "Forgive us, for we forgive others (Luke 11:4):" but in the text we pray, "Forgive us, as we forgive others." Now we cannot doubt but that both the Evangelists have given the prayer with accuracy, so far at least as not to comprehend in it anything which was not intended by our Lord. We, therefore, shall take the petition in both views and consider it as meaning,

1.   A profession of our readiness to forgive others—

This is a frame of mind which God requires in all who come to him for mercy, and he warns us not to expect mercy at his hands while we are indisposed to exercise it towards others (Jam 2:13). Such is the explanation which our Lord himself gives of his own words (ver. 14, 15): and, taken in this sense, they are a kind of plea with God to grant us our desire and an encouragement to ourselves to expect it. The duty of forgiving others being imposed upon us as a condition without the performance of which God will not forgive us, a consciousness of having performed the duty emboldens us to ask forgiveness at his hands.

Moreover, while we thus appeal to God respecting our endeavors to obey his commandments, we do in effect acknowledge the agency of his Spirit and the efficacy of his grace, without which we should have neither the ability nor inclination to fulfill his will (Php 2:13). In this view then it is also encouraging. For if God has already bestowed his grace upon us, and we have a clear evidence of it by its operation on our hearts and lives, we may reasonably hope that he will yet further extend his mercy to us in the pardon of all our sins. We may regard his past favors as a pledge and earnest of others yet to come and especially of those which our souls most need and which he himself is most ready to bestow.

2.   A consent that the mercy we show to others should be made the pattern of God's mercy to us—

We cannot with propriety request that the forgiveness which we exercise towards others may be the measure of that which we would receive from God; (because everything we do is so extremely imperfect) but the pattern it may and ought to be. Of course, as in the former case when we speak of a condition, we are not to be understood as if there were anything meritorious in forgiving others, or as if God bargained with us, as it were, and bartered away his mercies. So, in the present case we are not to be understood as if there were, or could be, anything in us that was worthy of God's imitation. There is a sense in which we are to be "pure, as God is pure," and "perfect, as he is perfect." And, in a similar sense, though not with equal strictness we may beg of God to forgive us our offenses as we forgive our offending fellow-creatures; that is, freely, fully, cordially, and forever.

True it is that, in offering this petition we need to speak "with fear and trembling;" lest there be in our hearts any root of bitterness unperceived by us, and lest, when praying for forgiveness we do in effect pray that we be not forgiven. And, that no doubt may exist respecting our sincerity in forgiving others, we ought to be rendering good for evil and "heaping thereby coals of fire on the heads" of our enemies to melt them into love. Then may we use this petition with safety, with confidence, and with comfort.

From this view of our subject, we learn,

1.   The temper of a Christian—

Knowing that his own debt to God is ten thousand talents and that his fellow-creature can at the utmost owe to him only a few pence, the Christian dares not take him by the throat unmercifully lest God should retaliate on him and require at his hands the debt, which the whole universe could never pay. Freely has he received remission, and freely does he grant it even to those who may have injured him in the highest degree. All bitterness, and wrath, and anger, and clamor, and evil speaking, are put away from him, with all malice: and he is kind, tender-hearted, and forgiving towards others even as God for Christ's sake has forgiven him (Eph 4:31-32).

Let us examine then whether this be indeed our character. Let us search whether our mode of speaking of others and of acting towards them accord with it. For if we bring our gift to the altar with an unforgiving spirit God bids us to "go our way," and not presume to expect any tokens of his favor until the most perfect reconciliation has been sought with our offending or offended brother (Mat 5:23-24 and especially 18:35).

2.   The privilege of a Christian—

Here God permits, encourages, commands us to ask of him the free and full pardon of all our sins. No consideration whatever is given to the number or greatness of them. The command is given to every human being and the fullest possible assurance that none shall ask in vain (Mat 7:7-8. Isa 1:18).

Some however have thought that because no mention is here made of Christ and his atonement we need not to have respect to him in our addresses at the throne of grace. But we must remember that our Lord had not yet declared the whole of what he was come to reveal. This sermon was delivered quite at the commencement of his ministry, and before the minds of his followers were sufficiently prepared for the clearer manifestation of divine truth. What therefore he afterwards declared respecting the intent of his death and resurrection, must direct us in our use of this prayer. He has told us, that he "shed his blood for the remission of sins," and that we must present our petitions to God in his name. Consequently we must have respect to the merit of his blood and to the efficacy of his intercession whenever we approach our God, whether in the use of this prayer or of any other, which we may think suited to our state. If the consideration of an atonement seem to detract from the freeness of the pardon, St. Paul saw no ground whatever for such an objection (Rom 3:24).

Be it known then to all, that a way of access unto the Father is opened to us through the crucifixion of the Son of God; and that, if only we ask forgiveness in the Redeemer's name our iniquities, whatever they may have been, shall be "blotted out as a morning cloud" and be irrecoverably "cast into the depths of the sea."

DISCOURSE: 1317 - THE LORD'S PRAYER

Mat 6:13. **And lead us not into temptation, but deliver us from evil.**

The obtaining of pardon would satisfy a person who was merely alarmed by the terrors of hell, but a truly regenerate person will desire deliverance from sin as much as from hell itself. He knows that he could not be happy even in heaven, if sin retained in any respect dominion over him. Therefore, having implored pardon for his past sins, he will with equal earnestness desire victory over his remaining corruptions. But how is this victory to be gained, seeing that we are encompassed with temptations and assaulted by all the powers of darkness? It must be gained by committing ourselves to the care of our heavenly Father and by seeking from him,

I.   The guidance of his providence—

Continually are we endangered by the temptations that surround us—

Temptations present themselves to us on every side. Everything that is agreeable to our senses or flattering to our minds has a tendency to draw us from God. Even the things which are the most innocent when moderately enjoyed often become snares to us. Our food, our raiment, our comforts of every kind, and even our dearest relatives are apt to engross our affections too much and to become the objects of an idolatrous regard. The cares and troubles of life also are frequently sources of unbelieving anxiety or murmuring discontent. Moreover, the contempt too generally poured upon religion has not infrequently a fatal influence on our minds to keep us from inquiring after God at all, or from confessing him openly before an ungodly world.

To these temptations incalculable force is given by the corruptions of our own hearts. We are of our own selves prone to evil. The heart is ready to catch fire from every spark; and all the appetites and passions are quickly brought into activity in the service of sin. In vain does reason remonstrate with us: "the law of sin that is in our members, wars against the law of our minds, and brings us into captivity (Rom 7:23)." Yes, even when the spiritual principle lusts and strives against the corruptions of the flesh, so strong is the corrupt principle within us that we cannot do the things that we would (Gal 5:17).

Well therefore may we pray to be kept from their power—

We are not to suppose that God is active in tempting us to sin: St. James expressly says, that it is our own lust, and not God, that is the occasion of sin (Jam 1:13-15). But God may in his providence give scope for the exercise of our corruptions, as he did when he raised up Pharaoh to the throne of Egypt and opened the Red Sea before him for the purpose of making him a more signal monument of his displeasure (Rom 9:17). On the other hand, he will often put an obstacle in the way of his people so as to keep them from executing the evil suggestions of their hearts. He will plant a "hedge," and, if that will not suffice, "he will build up a wall against them, that they may not find their former ways (Hos 2:6-7)." This he can do in ten thousand ways without at all infringing upon the liberty of the human will. Thus he diverted the patriarchs from destroying Joseph and David from wreaking his vengeance upon Nabal (1Sa 25:32-34).

Moreover, he has promised to do this in answer to our prayers. He will either make a way for us to escape from the temptations that assault us, or will moderate them so that they may not be too powerful for us, or increase our strength, that we may be able to overcome them (1Co 10:13. Isa 41:10). In a word, he will "order our goings," and "direct our paths." If we were to depend on our own wisdom we should only increase the difficulties which we designed to avoid (Amo_5:9). But if we make God our refuge we shall be preserved. He has bidden us "watch and pray that we enter not into temptation (Mat 26:41)," and he will never suffer us to use these means in vain (Psa 142:1-7; 138:3; 50:15).

But as we cannot hope to be kept from every temptation, we should also pray to God for,

II.   The assistance of his grace—

Besides our in-dwelling corruptions, we have in Satan a great and powerful enemy—

The words which in this and some other places are translated, "from evil," might properly be translated, "from the evil one." Satan is represented in Scripture as a most subtle and cruel adversary to man. He is called a serpent for his subtlety, a dragon for his fierceness, and a god for the dominion that he exercises over the children of men.

To withstand him in our own strength is impossible. He has wiles which we cannot discover and devices which we cannot fathom. If permitted, he could destroy the holiest of men. None are out of his reach. He not only instigated a wicked Judas to betray his Master and an hypocritical Ananias to lie unto his God, but an intrepid Peter to deny his Lord. And, if our Lord's intercession had not prevailed to secure the faith of this favored servant, Satan would have "sifted him as wheat," and brought him to everlasting destruction (Luke 22:31-32))

We should therefore pray to be delivered from him also—

God will deliver us from him, as well as from temptation. He has provided armor for us, which, if used aright, shall defend us against all his fiery darts. The head, the breast, the legs, have their several and appropriate means of protection. Every part is also doubly guarded by the shield of faith, and a sword of heavenly temper is put into the believer's hands (Eph 6:11-17); a sword which Satan is not able to withstand; a sword by which the Savior himself prevailed over him (Eph 6:17. with Mat 4:6-7, 4:10), and which, though in the weakest hands, shall vanquish all the powers of hell (Jam 4:7).

Does anyone ask, How shall I get this armor? We answer, pray to God to give it you. It is by prayer that it is obtained. By prayer it is put on. By prayer we are rendered expert in the use of it, and by prayer our heart is steeled with courage and our arm confirmed with strength (Eph 6:18). The petition that is taught us in the text will answer every end, and urged with frequency and faith, will soon make us more than conquerors. Would we see the whole exemplified? Behold the instance of St. Paul. In him the assault, defense, and victory, are all exhibited before our eyes. Satan assaulted him with the utmost violence. The Apostle instantly betook himself to prayer, and his triumph was speedy and complete. And in like manner shall "God's strength be perfected in our weakness," if only we rely on him for our deliverance: were we

90

a thousand times weaker than we are, his grace should assuredly be sufficient for us (2Co 12:7-9).

The petition, thus explained, is of use,

1. For caution—

When persons are urged to watch and pray, and to abstain from those things which are the occasions of sin, they are ready to complain that we are too strict, and that we abridge the liberties of men without necessity. But, what can be expected if we will frequent every scene of vanity and mix indiscriminately with all, whether godly or ungodly? What can be expected, but that we should drink into the spirit of the world and be drawn into many sinful compliances? Does not everyone find this to be the effect of associating with the world? Is not a conformity to its maxims and habits the almost necessary consequence of such conduct? Men, if on a field of battle, would not for their pleasure go and expose themselves where it was almost impossible to escape a wound; and yet, when their souls are in danger they will venture anywhere for the sake of conforming to the world or of obtaining some worthless gratification.

But how can such persons offer the prayer which our Lord has taught us? Is it not a mockery to beg of God "not to lead us into temptation," when we are rushing into it daily of our own accord? Know then, beloved, that your practice should correspond with your prayers. Know that to expose yourselves to sin is to tempt your God. Yes, it is to tempt the devil to tempt you. If you would be preserved by God you must "keep" yourselves, not your feet merely, but "your hearts also, and that with all diligence," avoiding not only sin itself, but also the means and occasions of sin.

2. For encouragement—

It may please God for wise and gracious ends to suffer you to be strongly tempted by the wicked one. Perhaps he may design to manifest and confirm the grace he has already given you (Job_1:8); or to discover to you some hidden evil in your own heart (2Ch 32:31). Or he may design to keep you from falling into sin (2Co 12:7. Mark the first and last words), or to make use of you for the strengthening of others by a contrasted exhibition of your own weakness and of his unbounded mercy in your recovery (Luke 22:32).

But, whatever his object is, and however painful your trial may be, remember that Satan is a vanquished enemy (John 16:11. Col 2:15), that he cannot go beyond the limits which God has assigned him, and that your God is ever at hand to hear and answer your petitions. Were you called to contend in your own strength, your situation would be tremendous. But you are commanded to "cast your care on God, who cares for you," and to "encourage yourselves in the Lord your God." Be strong then, and fear not. "Be strong in the Lord and in the power of his might," and know that he who has taught you to look to him for guidance and protection will "keep you from falling (Jude, ver. 24)," and "bruise Satan under your feet shortly (Rom 16:20)."

DISCOURSE: 1318 - THE LORD'S PRAYER

Mat 6:13. **For thine is the kingdom, and the power, and the glory, forever Amen.**

On a review of the Lord's Prayer, we cannot but be thankful that such a summary is here given us, not only because we are hereby instructed what to pray for, but are assured that, great as the petitions are, they shall all be granted, if we offer them up in faith. The conclusion of the prayer which we have now read is not contained in St. Luke's Gospel. But we must remember that the prayer was given to the disciples at two different times, and on different occasions: and that in the one it might be contained, though it might be omitted in the other. Doubts indeed have been suggested whether it originally formed any part of the prayer before us: but, while the Latin versions and fathers omit it, it is found in most of the Greek manuscripts, and is quoted by most of the Greek fathers: for this reason the translators of our Bible have admitted it as a part of the sacred text; as we also may safely do on their authority. Certain it is that there is in these words a perfect correspondence with the prayer itself, and that they admirably express the feelings of a devout soul. This may be understood in a twofold view:

I.   As a devout acknowledgment—

It is often called a doxology, or an ascription of praise to God. In this view we may observe concerning it,

1.   That it accords with many other passages of Holy Writ—

Such effusions of praise are frequent in the Holy Scriptures. Indeed, the very words appear to have been taken from that thanksgiving of David that he uttered when both he and his people had been consecrating their offerings to the Lord for the building of his temple (1Ch_29:10-13). In the New Testament such doxologies abound. The Apostles frequently interrupt the thread of their argument (if it can be called an interruption) by breaking forth into rapturous expressions of praise and thanksgiving (Gal 1:5. 1Ti 1:17), and more frequently conclude their epistles with such tokens of grateful adoration (Rom 16:27; 1Pe 5:11; Jude, ver. 24, 25). Sometimes also we find that after pouring out their souls before God in prayer the Apostles address their thanksgivings to him, just in the way that we are taught to do in the prayer before us (Eph 3:14; Eph 3:20-21). The propriety therefore of addressing God in this manner is evident, since it is sanctioned by the example of the saints in all ages.

2.   That it is well calculated for the use of the Christian Church—

Every work of God, whether animate or inanimate, renders unto him a tribute of praise. The beauty and order of the whole creation and the adaptation of everything to its proper end declares aloud the wisdom, the power, and the goodness of the Creator. But the people of God must be active in rendering praise to him, according to that distinction of the Psalmist. "All thy works praise thee, O God; and thy saints shall bless thee (Psa 145:10)." The redeemed of the Lord are called upon to testify their obligations to him in this manner day and night (Psa 107:1-2; 145:1-2; 146:1-2). It is "comely" for them so to do (Psa 147:1), and, "if they should hold their peace the very stones would cry out against them." And where shall we find words more proper for our use? They are so concise as to be easily remembered and so comprehensive as to include everything that we could wish to say. They are, in fact, an epitome of that song which saints and angels are singing in the realms above

(Rev 5:13), and if we offer them in a becoming manner we shall have an earnest and foretaste of the heavenly bliss.

Nor is there a small emphasis to be laid on the word with which the prayer concludes. "Amen," when annexed to praise and thanksgiving, denotes the full concurrence of the soul in all that has been uttered. In the fourth century, it was customary for the whole Church to utter this word aloud in order to express their cordial assent to everything that had been spoken. And at times, as St. Jerome tells us, the sound was like thunder. As far as respects their earnestness we approve of their custom. But we think that true devotion would be less clamorous and we far prefer that mode adopted by the Church in the days of Nehemiah, when the earnestness was equally, but more suitably, expressed, being chastened and tempered with ardent affection and reverential awe (Neh_8:6).

But we have observed that the words of our text may be also interpreted,

II.   As an humble plea—

Pleading with God is the very essence and perfection of prayer—

In all the more solemn addresses to the Deity recorded in the Scriptures pleading bears a very conspicuous part. We must not however imagine that such a mode of prayer was adopted with a view to prevail upon God to grant what he was otherwise averse to give. We mistake the nature of prayer altogether if we think that it has any such power, or is to be used for any such end. Prayer is rather intended to impress our own minds with a sense of our manifold necessities, and of our dependence upon God for a supply of them. In this way it prepares our souls for a grateful reception of the Divine favors, and consequently, the more urgent our prayers are the more will these ends be answered and God will be the more glorified by us when he has imparted to us the desired benefits. It was with such views that Moses (Exo 32:11-13), Jehoshaphat (2Ch 20:5-12), Hezekiah (Isa 37:15-20), and all the saints of old, presented their petitions, enforced and strengthened with the most urgent pleas (Isa 51:9-10; 63:15-19; and particularly Jer 14:21-22).

And it is impossible to feel our need of mercy, without following their example in this particular.

As a plea, this part of the prayer admirably enforces every petition in it—

Great are the things which we have asked in it and utterly unworthy are we to offer such petitions at the throne of grace. But God is a mighty Sovereign, who "may do what he will with his own," and therefore may hear and answer us, though we are the meanest and the vilest of the human race. It is this idea which we express when we say, "for thine is the kingdom." The word 'for' shows that it has respect to what goes before and that we urge this consideration as a plea to enforce the preceding petitions.

Next to the sovereign right of God to answer us we plead his power. Nothing short of omnipotence can affect the things which we desire of God in this prayer. But he is almighty and all-sufficient. "With him all things are possible," and we acknowledge our conviction that "there is nothing too hard for him." Lastly, we plead "the glory" which he will derive from granting all the things which we have prayed for. In the conversion and salvation of the world at large and in every mercy freely given to us in particular, whether in the supply of our bodily needs or in the pardon of our sins and the preservation of our souls. This sovereignty and this power are his immutable perfections, and this glory will result to him through all eternity, even "forever" and ever.

Such considerations may well animate us in our addresses at the throne of grace and encourage us in a further confirmation of our petitions by the word "Amen."

We have already mentioned one sense of the word "Amen." Namely, that it is a full assent to all that has been uttered. But it has another meaning also and imports a desire that the things which have been asked may be granted (Rev 22:20). In this latter sense it is often doubled in order to express more strongly the ardor of that desire (Psa 72:18-19). Would we understand its just importance? We may see it illustrated in the prayer of Daniel, where, having enforced his petitions by many urgent pleas he comes at last to renew them all with redoubled ardor, not indeed by the word "Amen," but in a more copious strain, expressive of the idea contained in it (Dan 9:17-19).

In the Apostolic age the use of this word was universal in the Church. While one person addressed the Lord in the name of the whole assembly, all who were present added their "Amen," and thereby made every petition and thanksgiving their own (1Co 14:16). Nor has the word lost its use and emphasis even in heaven, for the whole choir, both of saints and angels, are represented as using it in both the senses that we have mentioned, "saying, Amen: Blessing, and glory, and wisdom, and thanksgiving, and honor, and power, and might, be unto our God forever and ever. Amen (Rev 7:11-12)."

O that in adding our Amen to the prayer before us we might resemble them and so utter it now from our inmost souls that we may be counted worthy to utter it in full concert with them to all eternity!

Section 4 – Sermons on the Lord's Prayer

Chapter 10 - John Broadus on the Lord's Prayer

(John Broadus, 1827-1895)

Our Father which art in heaven, Hallowed he thy name. Matthew 6:9

The prayer which thus begins, which for many ages has been called among Christians "the Lord's Prayer," is above all eulogium for its sweetness. No wonder this is so! For our Lord presents it as a specimen, as a model of prayer. He said, "When ye pray, use not vain repetitions, as the heathen do: for they think that they shall be heard for their much speaking," saying over the same thing a thousand times. "Be ye not therefore like unto them: for your Father knoweth what things ye have need of, before ye ask him." Thus then do ye pray-this way and not with vain repetitions, not with much speaking, thus do ye pray! He gives it as a sample, as a model. So on a later occasion, recorded in the 11th Chapter of Luke - probably a long time after this, most likely in quite another part of the country, certainly on a later occasion-our Lord was praying himself, and when he ceased, the disciples asked him "Teach us to pray" and he said "When ye pray, say:" and then he gave them substantially the same prayer as the one here before us.

Now it very naturally occurs to many persons that our Lord has given this as a form of prayer; that when we pray we ought always to say these words. I do not object to using these words whenever anyone thinks them appropriate, that they express his sentiments; but it is very certain that our Lord did not give this as a form of prayer. If you will notice a moment I shall prove it. On the second occasion the prayer is very different from that which we here read. Even in the common text, it is different in several expressions; but if you will take any revised text as furnished by any competent scholar of the day, you will find that the prayer on that occasion is quite different. Allow me to repeat it as it is there. You all know the words as they occur here but on that second occasion this is what he said: "Father, Hallowed be thy name. Thy kingdom come. Give us day by day our daily bread. And forgive us our sins;

for we also forgive every one that is indebted to us. And bring us not into temptation."

Now you observe that I have omitted several phrases of the familiar prayer given here in the Sermon on the Mount. If you look a little closely you notice that nothing of essential importance, no distinctive idea, has been omitted here. Instead of "Our Father which art in heaven," you have simply "Father." You have lost some pleasing words, but you have really lost no part of the essential thought. When after the petition "Thy kingdom come," you find wanting the words "Thy will be done on earth as it is in heaven," you observe in a moment that although a pleasing expression has been expunged, it is involved in the preceding petition, "Thy kingdom come;" for when God's reign on earth is fully come, his will must of necessity be done on earth as in heaven. And so, when after the prayer "Bring us not into temptation," you miss the words "But deliver us from evil," you observe that they do, at most, but express the other side of the same truth; something that is implied in the words that remain.

On that second occasion then, our Lord has omitted no idea that belongs to the prayer. It is substantially the very same, but in form it is exceedingly different. Is not there the proof at once that he did not intend this as a form of prayer? If he did so intend, why in the world should he not have repeated his form correctly on the second occasion? No: he intended it not as a form of prayer, that precisely these words should be used, but as an example, "Thus do ye pray." Avoid the vain repetitions and much speaking of the heathen: Thus: thus comprehensively; thus simply. Oh, how much is included in these few, brief, simply expressed petitions! "Thus then do ye pray."

And my brethren, I venture to ask your special attention to this model in one respect. We have two good classes of petitions here, as is obvious at once, petitions with reference to God's glory, and petitions with reference to our own good. And my point is, that the petitions with reference to God's glory come first. Now you have noticed, and indeed it seems natural to us that when we pray, we pray first about ourselves, and a great deal about ourselves, and then if we do not forget, if there seems to be time left before we close the prayer, we may introduce some petitions as to God's glory.

But here the class of petitions which refer to God's glory come first. That is their rightful place. I do not feel they should always come first in order, that there ought to be any formality or stiffness in it, but that they should often be put in the place of priority, and regularly in the place of pre-eminence. Much more important is it that God's name should be hallowed, and God's kingdom come in the world, than that you and I, as individuals, should gain the blessings we desire.

And now I propose to you, that while of course we cannot bring out many of the thoughts involved in this comprehensive prayer, we shall try to get some practical lessons from it.

I. Observe first, the petitions which relate to God's glory.

1. "Hallowed be thy name." The words are so simple, we have known them so well from our childhood, that it is really difficult to stop and ask what they mean. Let thy name be made holy. God's name represents himself. It is a prayer that his name, and himself as represented by his name, may be regarded as holy-spoken of as holy-treated as holy. We have a model here in the picture given by Isaiah, the adoring Seraphs covering their faces in awe before the throne. What do they cry? Not, as often we do; great, majestic, glorious-not a word about his power, nor even about his wisdom-"Holy, Holy, Holy, Lord God of Hosts." That is the central thought, that ought to be our deepest desire, that God may be regarded, and spoken of, and treated, as holy.

Oh, what a contrast between that scene of the vision, and the sights and the souls of this world in which we live. Walk the streets anywhere; listen to the talk wherever you find it, especially when men grow excited. Hear them! Hear bow that high and holy name is bandied as a jest and polluted with profanity. It is enough to make a man shiver to hear the profanity that abounds everywhere. I have shivered, literally, sometimes as I listened. But my brethren, have we nothing to do but to look with horror at other men's profanity? There are some things important to our own life here. Have a care that while you may not use in vain the sacred name of God itself, you shall not fall into the practice of using other sacred expressions lightly and irreverently. I have heard even refined ladies use phrases in a light way, that were appropriate only in solemn prayer; and to a certain extent that was irreverence, that was profanity. Have a care about indulging wit that comes from profaning the language of Scripture, and allusions to God. Bluff old Dr. Johnson once said that "a man that has any respect for himself ought to be above that kind of wit, it is so cheap: any one can do that." Yes, anyone that has any respect for himself ought to be above that kind of wit, and a man that has any reverence for God ought to shrink from it. Have a care how you repeat the profanity of other men. You want to tell a good story and the point of it perhaps lies in a profane expression. Now is it that you should repeat that expression? Is it good for yourself to repeat it? Is it healthy?

Especially is it good for that boy there that is hearing, and may not make the nice distinction that you make, when you repeat other men's profanity? I would not inculcate scrupulosity about trifles, but perchance this is not a trifle, and it seems to me that we who pray this prayer, ought to lay such things to our hearts, and shrink with horror, and cultivate ourselves into shrinking with shuddering, from anything like profanity. Oh, that God's name might always be spoken with deepest reverence. Oh, that God himself might come to be everywhere thought of, and talked about, and obeyed, as holy. Anyhow, let us try to have it so in our hearts, on our lips, in our lives.

2. And the second petition, "Thy reign come." I am not going to explain all these simple words of course, but here is one that needs explaining. The Greek word which is rendered "kingdom" in the text requires three English words to convey its meaning. Primarily the word means "kingship," the condition of being a king, the possession of royal power. Then secondarily it means "reign," the exercise of royal power. As a final derivation it means what we call "kingdom," subjects or territory over whom or in which this royal power is exercised. Kingship, and reign, and kingdom.

There are many cases of that kind in translation, where several terms have to be used in one language to convey the meaning of a single word in another. Now the leading thought here is evidently that which we express by the word "reign." And the reference is to the Messianic reign which the prophets had long foretold; that Messianic reign of which David had sung; that

Messianic reign which John the Baptist bad declared was now near at hand, and Jesus at the beginning of his ministry in Galilee took up the same cry, "The kingdom of heaven is near at hand; repent therefore and believe the good tidings." Men had long prayed that that reign might come, and now there was all the more propriety in such a prayer, for it was near at hand.

Do you think there is no need of that prayer still? Do you think the reign, the Messianic reign of God in the world, has come? It has but begun. It was beginning when Jesus taught these teachings. It began still more when he rose triumphant from the grave and ascended glorious into the sky. It began still further, on the day of Pentecost. It began in another sense at the destruction of Jerusalem, which he spoke of beforehand as the time when he should come in his kingdom. It has begun on the earth, ah! it has not come yet. Alas, for the wide portions of the world where the very name of the King Messiah has not come. Alas, in the metropolis of one of the great Christian nations of today, the great mass of the men that surge around us, are utterly unsanctified by the gospel, utterly heedless of the reign of God. Stop any moment and think, between two heartbeats, of this great world you live in, of this great city you live in, and then you shall address yourself with new fervor to the prayer: "Thy reign come, O God! thy reign!" Anyhow, let it come in us; let it pervade our whole being; let it control our whole life; let it sanctify our home life; let it elevate our social life; let it purify our business life; let men feel, as they note our conduct, that we are subjects of the Lord God.

3. I shall not dwell, for lack of time, upon the third petition here, which is but an expansion of the preceding. For, as I have said, whenever God's reign has fully come, then his will must be done on earth. Many things occur now that are not according to God's will. The prayer is that God's will may take place; that everything may happen on earth in accordance with God's will, as in heaven everything does happen. Many times for us, I know it is hard even to consent that this shall be so. When it is plainly God's will that something should happen, which to us is painful, we shrink and with difficulty we say, "Thy will be done." No wonder: it has been so with better persons than we are. Certain disciples, when they besought Paul not to go up to Jerusalem and he would not be persuaded, ceased and said: "The will of the Lord be done." The

struggling Savior in Gethsemane as he strove in agony and prayer to nerve himself up for what he had to bear, said again and again- for it would not stay said: "nevertheless, not my will, but thine he done."

No wonder we find it hard sometimes to say that. The prayer teaches us not merely to submit to God's will, but to desire that God's will may take place in the world; that everything concerning us and concerning all around us may happen according to his will. And if he takes away our property, our health, our usefulness, our life, or someone we love better than our life, still we would say and we should rejoice when we say, "Thy will be done." Oh, if it could be so; if in the world, whether gaining or losing, in success or failure, it could be so, in us and about us, that God's will were done in all things-what a joy in the thought; what a springing gladness it puts into the heart, the very idea!

II. But perhaps we shall find, not more important but more practical lessons if we turn to the second part of the prayer, which contains petitions relating to ourselves.

1. First: "Give us this day our daily bread." Now I entreat you, don't listen to the commentaries, so many of which tell you that this means spiritual bread. I am weary of that everlasting spiritualizing. Spiritual things are far above temporal things, but there are many references in the Scriptures to our temporal and material needs, and why should we lose their meaning, and sustaining power, because we go on allegorizing everything. It is plainly a prayer for temporal good, as represented by that which is most essential, and thus stated in the simplest possible form; and a prayer with reference simply to day after day. A little child sees its meaning and feels its sweetness, and the wisest man can find no higher wisdom than to cry still: "Give us this day our daily bread."

My brethren, I should be inclined to think that above all the petitions of the prayer this needs to be enforced in our time. I have known some Christians who were very unwilling to realize that there was any human exertion in obtaining spiritual good. They say, if that be true, how is it the gift of God? And if it be the gift of God, how can it be the effort of our own labor? Yet if spiritual good is the gift of God, so is temporal good the gift of God, though it is obtained only by human effort. The truth is, we see, that both are the gift of God, and both are the result of our own exertions.

Especially with reference to one of the great tendencies of thought in our time is it important that we should cherish this petition for our daily bread. "Pshaw!" men say, "that depends upon physical forces and laws; upon material things; upon your own exertion, man; upon the climate and the weather." Now in the face of these notions it becomes all the more appropriate that we should pray to God to give us daily bread. Yes, and I tell you plainly and boldly, though I have not time to develop the thought, if it is not right and wise to ask God for daily bread, if as they tell you in the newspapers so often, there is no efficacy in prayer, there is no use in praying for rain, then there is no God at all. You are driven straight to it by absolute logical necessity.

If it is not proper to pray for daily bread and to pray for rain, there is no God; there is nothing in existence but matter, with its organization and its results. You cannot help it; there is no standing room, for the life of you, between those two positions. Alas, alas, how many in our time, one-sided or superficial, have gone into utter materialism. Never was there a time when it was more needful that the Christian world should realize in their experience the sentiment of this prayer. We work for daily bread, and we plan for years to come, but none the less are we to seek it as the daily gift of the daily goodness of our Father in heaven.

2. "And forgive us our debts, as we forgive our debtors." The simple prayer for temporal things all embraced in that one petition for what is most indispensable, and now in addition, a twofold prayer-forgiveness for past sin, and deliverance from sin in the future. That our God may be glorified; that our earthly needs may be supplied, and that we may be forgiven our sin, and delivered from evil-that is all there is to pray for.

You know that the term "debt" is used here as an Aramaic expression to denote sin-sin regarded as a debt, which we must pay to God, or in the kindred phrase of other languages, "pay the penalty." You notice that when our Lord repeats the thought a moment later he say trespasses, or transgressions. You remember that when he gives the prayer on a subsequent occasion it is: "Forgive us our sins; for we also forgive everyone that is indebted to us." "Forgive us our debts" means, forgive us our sins. My friends, does it ever occur to you that you are more anxious about the "give" than the "forgive"? Does it ever happen in your experience that you pray that God would give and forget to ask that God would forgive? And yet, is not this last as deep a need? Yea, a deeper need than the other? Ah! that a man should have all earthly things given him, and his sins not forgiven, would be a poor gift. Yet a man who should be deprived of all earthly things and go starving into the other world, yet with his sins forgiven, would be rich and might rejoice. Let us not forget as we go on praying for what God has to give, to ask still more earnestly that he would forgive us our sins.

I must beg you in connection with the prayer to dwell upon the condition which our Lord here presents. It is a matter of the utmost practical importance to all of us. "Forgive us our debts, as we forgive our debtors." You have noticed surely, that after completing this simple prayer, Jesus before going on to speak of other things, takes up again one of the thoughts of the prayer; and which one is it? Something about God's name being hallowed, or his reign coming? Something about daily bread? Something about temptation, or evil? Nay: it is this one; this one thought he repeats, repeats it positively and negatively. For if you forgive men their trespasses, your Heavenly Father will also forgive you, and if you forgive not, neither will your Heavenly Father forgive you. You know why - you know yourself but little if you do not well know why he dwells upon this. The disposition to be revengeful, or at any rate to be unforgiving, is one of the deepest rooted, one of the hardest to correct, one of the most hurtful and ruinous in its influence, of all the evil dispositions that belong to our sinful human nature.

So our Lord presents forgiving as the condition of being forgiven, the condition sine qua non-if we do not forgive men we cannot be forgiven. He does not mean that our forgiving in the meritorious ground of our being forgiven. It is an indispensable condition. Only if we do forgive men can we be forgiven, but then we are forgiven on the ground which the gospel provides-the merit which is not our own.

Now let us make a practical distinction. We use that word "forgive" in a somewhat ambiguous fashion. In the strict and proper sense it is not our duty to forgive a man unless he repents. God forgives in that sense no man but the penitent, and Jesus said, you remember: "If thy brother sin against you seven times in the day and seven times in the day turn saying, 'I repent,' thou shalt forgive him." It is not right that you should restore a man to the confidence he has forfeited, unless he shows himself worthy of it. It is not right that you should forgive a man, in the full sense of the term, unless he repents; not only is it not your duty, but it is not right.

"Love your enemies, that ye may be sons of your Father in heaven." God forgives only the penitent, and loves them as his friends, but even the impenitent God loves. "He makes his sun to rise on the evil and the good, and sends rain on the just and the unjust." He wishes his enemies no harm, but does them good. We need not, and really should not, forgive a man in the full sense while he remains impenitent, but we must in the other sense forgive him. We must bear him no malice. We must do him no harm. We must be glad to do him good, in anything that will not promote his evil designs against us. Thus shall we be the sons of our Father in heaven.

I think this distinction is practically important. The idea of forgiving a man who is impenitent does seem to be impracticable, and that is not what the Scriptures teach; but that we should bear no malice and yield to no revenge, that is what the Scriptures teach. Ah me, even this is hard enough for poor human nature! Let us strive to do that; let us lay it to heart. Who is there here today among us who has not sometimes thought himself to have been cruelly wronged? Who? We all have need then to exercise this forgiveness.

3. And finally, "bring us not into temptation." For it is not simply lead it is bring. Human agency is, for the moment, here left out of account. The thought is, of God's providence as bearing us on, and bringing us into certain situations, and the prayer is that God will not bring us into circumstances of temptation of trial. Why? Because we are afraid we cannot stand temptation. Ah, every

man that knows himself will most certainly feel an echo in his heart, "I am weak, O Lord bring me not into temptation."

A man advertised for a coachman, and when the applicants came, he asked each one, "How near would you undertake to run my carriage wheel to the edge of a precipice?" The first one said he would run within a foot of it. The second said he would run within six inches. The third was an Irishman, who said, "I would kape away as far as I could,"-and he got the place. Maybe you will remember that, if you forget my solemn injunction. O my Christian friends, pray that you may be kept away from temptation, for you are weak, and let him who thinks he stand, take heed lest he fall.

"Bring us not into temptation, but deliver us from evil." My brethren, this simple prayer ought as a model to control all our praying. Its spirit ought to strike into our blood, shaping our whole character, regulating our whole life. And as we pray it, oh, ought not our life's endeavor to accord with it? What folly to pray, "Thy reign come," and never a finger lifted to urge forward the progress of that reign; never a sacrifice made, never deed done, nor word spoken, [nothing] but idle prayer. What folly to pray for forgiveness of sin, and pray for deliverance from evil, if along with the prayer there be not the cherished desire after holiness, and the perpetual effort to abhor-to abhor-that which is evil, and cleave to that which is good.

Chapter 11 - John Henry Jowett on the Lord's Prayer

(John Henry Jowett, 1864-1923)

Bringing Heaven to Earth

"Thy will be done on earth as it is in heaven." MATT." 6:10.

I suppose that to the majority of people these familiar words suggest a funeral rather than a wedding. They recall experiences to which we were compelled to submit but in which we found no delight. They awaken memories of gathering clouds, and gloomy days, and blocked roads, and failing strength, and open graves. "Thy will be done!" They remind us of afflictions in the presence of which we were numb and dumb. And so we have a sort of negative and passive attitude toward the words. We have a feeling toward them as to some visitor we have to "put up with," rather than to a welcome friend whose corning fills the house with life and happy movement. They suggest the Cyprus and the yew tree, things sullen and gloomy, rather than the coronal attributes of the cedar and the palm.

And so it is that the graces and virtues which are most frequently associated with these words are of the dull and passive order. The grace of resignation is the plant which is most prolific in this bitter soil. Even many of the hymns which sing about the will of God are in the minor tone, and they dwell upon the gloomier aspects of Providence which call for the grace of resignation. I am not unmindful of the fields of sadness which often stretch around our homes like marshy fens. Our circumstances gather about us in stormy cloud and tempest, and the rains fall, and the floods cover our lot in dreary desolation. And we may reverently recall one black night in the days of the Son of Man when in Gethsemane the rains descended, and the floods came, and the winds blew, and the afflicted heart of the Savior submitted itself in strong resignation, crying, "Nevertheless, not My will but Thine be done."

And yet if resignation be our only attitude to the will of God our life will be sorely lacking in delightful strength and beauty, A Cyprus here and there is all very well, but not a woodland of them! A yew tree here and there is all very well, but not a whole forest of them! In one of his letters Robert Louis Stevenson has a paragraph which represents an imaginary conversation with his gardener about the black winter green known as Resignation:

"John, do you see that bed of Resignation?" "It's doing bravely, sir!'

"John, I will not have it in my garden; it flatters not the eye, and it is no comfort; root it out!' "Sir, I ha'e seen a' them that rose as high as nettles; gran' plants." "What then? Were they as tall as Alps, if still unsavory and bleak, what matters it? Out with it, then; and in its place put a bush of Flowering Piety but see it be the flowering sort the other species is no ornament to any gentleman's back garden!'

But then how are we going to get more of the flowering piety into our gardens? I think this is the answer. We shall get it by cultivating a more active and positive attitude toward the will of God. The will of God is not always something burdensome which we have to bear; it is something glorious which we have to do. And therefore we are not to stand before it as mourners only, humbly making our submission, but as keen and eager knights gladly receiving our commissions. The will of God is not always associated with deprivation; it is more commonly associated with a trust. It is not something withheld, it is something given. There is an active savor about it. There is a ringing challenge in it. It is a call to chivalry and crusade. And therefore the symbol of our relation to the will of God is not that of the bowed head, but that of the lit lamp and the girt loin, as of happy servants delighted with their tasks. It is in this positive relationship to the will of God that the will becomes our song, the song of ardent knights upon the road, riding abroad to express the will of their King in all the common inter- course and relationships of men. "Thy will be done on earth!" That is not merely the poignant cry of mourners surrendering their treasures; it is the cry of a jubilant host, with a King in their midst, consecrating the strength of their arms to the cause of His

Kingdom. The will of God is here not something to be endured, but something to be done.

How, then, are we to take our share in this commission? How are we to do the will of God on earth as it is done in heaven? First of all by finding out what life is like in heaven. "As it is done in heaven!" If our privileged commission is to make earth more like heaven it must surely be our first enquiry to find out what heaven is like. Well, what is heaven like? I will very frankly confess to you that I am in no wise helped to answer our question by the so-called spiritualistic revelations of these latter days.

These strange séances with the lights out and a trumpet on the table, and the rowdy singing, they bring me no authoritative word or vision. The character of the heavenly life that is revealed is so unsatisfying the glare of it, the garishness of it, its furnishings as of a cheap and tawdry theatre, the utter weakness and insipidity of its utterance they tell me nothing that I want to know. Its leaders assure me that their revelations are chasing away uncertainties, that they are transforming lean hypotheses into firm experiences, that they are proving the reality of the life beyond, that they are making immortality sure. ... I am waiting for a revelation of something which deserves to be immortal. I am reverently listening for some word which is both spirit and life. I am listening for something worthy of kinship with the word of the Apostle Paul; nay, worthy of the risen Lord; and what is offered to me is like cheap jewelry in contrast with precious stones and fine gold. Eternal life is to me not merely endless length of line; it is quality of line; it is height, and depth, and breadth; "This is life eternal, to know Thee and Jesus Christ whom Thou hast sent."

I therefore turn away from the so-called modern revelations if I wish to know what life is like in heaven. What is life like as it is lived in the immediate presence and fellowship of God? What are the habits of the heavenly community? What is the manner of their affections? What is the nature of their discernments? What are their standards of values? What are their ways of looking at things? What are their quests, and their labors, and their delights? What are their relationships one to another? Is there any answer to these questions? My brethren, if I wish to learn what life is like in heaven, I turn to Him who came from heaven. He made certain tremendous claims, and the very greatness of them arrests my soul and fills me with receptive awe.

Let us listen to Him: "No man has ascended into heaven but He that came down from heaven." . . . "He that cometh from above is above all; what He has seen and heard, of that He beareth witness." . . . "The bread of God is He which comes down out of heaven and gives life unto the world." ... "I am come down from heaven to do the will of Him that sent Me." . . . What is that last most wonderful word? It seems to come very near to the way of my quest. I am eagerly enquiring how God's will is done in heaven, and here is One who claims that He comes down from heaven to do the will of Him that sent Him. He brings heaven with Him. His speech is full of it. He talks about "Your Father in heaven," He talks about "the treasures in heaven," and about "the Kingdom of Heaven," and He uses simile after simile, and parable after parable, to tell us what it is like. "The Kingdom of Heaven is like unto ... is like unto ... is like unto . . ." The familiar words run like some lovely and inspiring refrain. ... If I would know what heaven is like I must listen to His word.

But the revelation in Christ Jesus is more than a revelation in words. The Word became flesh, and it was not only something we can hear, it was something we can see. He not only startled men's ears, as with a music which had never before been heard in their grey, unlovely streets, He startled men's eyes as with a light which had never before fallen on sea or land. He not only talked about the heavenly life, He lived it. His life on earth was just a transcript of the life in heaven.

As we reverently gaze upon Him we can watch the process of the incarnation. The heavenly is imaged forth in the earthly, and it is taking form in human life and story. Every movement of Jesus spells a word of the heavenly literature. Every feature in Jesus is a lineament of the invisible life. Every gesture tells a story. Every one of His earthly relationships unfolds the nature of the heavenly communion. His habits unveil their habits, His quests reveal their quests. The Eternal breaks through every moment, and the light is tempered to our mortal gaze. The revelation never ceases. It begins in Nazareth and it continues to Calvary, and beyond Calvary to Olivet. You can never catch our Lord in some moment when the divine afflatus has been withdrawn, when the inspiration ends, and when His life drops down to dull and un- suggestive commonplace. Everything in Jesus is a ministry of revelation. He is revelation; "I am the Truth." His earthly life reveals the landscape of the heavenly fields. If, therefore, I would know what heaven is like I must listen to the word of Jesus, and with eager, reverent eyes I must follow the Word made flesh.

But let me give this counsel about the quest. When we set about studying the words of Jesus do not let us become entangled in the letter. It is possible to be imprisoned in the words and so to miss the hidden treasure. We are in search of the spirit of the Kingdom of Heaven, we want to know its attitudes, its royal moods, its splendid manners, its principles, its life. We must not, therefore, be deterred and interred in the literalism of the letter. We must seek the hidden treasure in the earthen vessel. We must seek the heavenly wine in the earthly wine-skins. We must seek the beating heart of a simile, the secret vitality of a parable, the holy fire which burns on the innermost altar of the word. We are in search of heavenly principles, principles which we can apply to the humdrum life of earth and so transform it into heaven.

Go, then, in search of the principles of the heavenly life. And whenever you find a heavenly principle, something which controls and orders the life of heaven, write it down in your own words, and regard it as one of the controlling guides of humdrum life. Do the same with the Master's life. What a brief little record it is! I turn away my eyes to my study shelves and I see the life of Lincoln in five large volumes. I then turn to the biography of Jesus, and in the Bible which I am using it covers 107 pages, and in those 107 pages the story is told four times over? How marvelously brief it is and yet how marvelously pregnant! Go over it with the utmost slowness. You are in search of something more precious than gold, yea, than much fine gold. If our Savior moves, if He turns His face toward anybody, if He looks at a little child, or at someone who is near the Kingdom of Heaven, follow the movement, and watch Him, and challenge your judgment as to its significance. Is the movement a revelation? Is it an earthly segment suggesting a heavenly circle, and can you venture to reverently complete the circle? Thus must we go in search of the heavenly principles, and again when we have found one let us express it in our own words, and write it down as one of the fundamental controls of human life.

And when you have got your heavenly principles, when you have analyzed them, and have arranged them in some order, will you have many of them? I think not. Will your notebook be overflowing with entries? I think not. You will probably have just a little handful, perhaps not more than a dozen of them, perhaps only half-a-dozen; but they will be something you can handle, for not only are they the principles of heaven, they are the laws of heaven for our life on earth, they are the fundamental things in the ministry of transformation, and they are to make earth and heaven one. If, therefore, you would know what life in heaven is like, study Him who came from heaven, even the Son of Man Who is in heaven.

Well, now, having found out what life is like in heaven, we must now find out what life is like on earth. What are the facts about things on this planet of ours in which we pitch our moving tents for three-score years and ten? If we are to bring the principles of the heavenly life to mould and fashion our life upon earth we must know what we are about. Is our life on earth in any way like the life in heaven which is revealed in Jesus Christ, or is it very unlike it? We must go in search of the facts. What are the facts? And there you face the difficulty which only an unwearying perseverance can conquer. For, strangely enough, it is far more easy to discover the facts about the life in heaven than to discover the facts about the life on earth. Heaven yearns to reveal itself, to make itself known, to share its secrets, and it has done these things in Jesus Christ; but earth seeks to hide its facts, to obscure them, to skillfully camouflage them, until it is almost impossible to discover the simplicity of truth in all this elaborate paraphernalia of falsehood and disguise.

How intensely difficult it is to see a thing just as it is, in all the clear, vivid, untampered outlines of sheer veracity! Our newspapers do not really help us in the quest. Their vision is perverted in many ways it is perverted by political partisanship, by the spirit of class, by the narrowing mood of sect, by the proud domination of wealth, by the desire to please more than to inform. How hard it is to find the facts through the daily press! I take two morning papers, and I have chosen them on the ground of their being as absolutely unlike each other as can be well conceived. I look out upon the world through their two lenses in the fond hope that one may regulate the other, and that in their mutual correction I may arrive at something like the truth.

But through what a riot of confusion one has to fight his way if he is to find the fact of things in their simple and transparent order! For instance, the facts about the miners and the owners of the mines! The facts about Prohibition in the United States! The facts about the drinking customs of our people! Where are our working people assembling in vast multitudes to demonstrate their determination to have more drink? Where are the masses of people who are assembling to demand a brighter London, and who are going to secure it by extending the drinking facilities for an hour or two longer at night? What are the facts about things? The facts about the starving populations of Russia! The facts about India, about the inner currents of its thought and feeling, the secret aspirations of its countless multitudes, the sleepless activities of Islam! What a hunt it is, this hunting for facts! And yet, if the heavenly principles are to be brought to earth, to govern and regulate her life, if the crooked is to be made straight and the rough places plain, we must know where the dangerous crookedness is to be found on the road, and where the road is so rough that it breaks the feet of pilgrims and lames them for their honest and necessary journey.

I can well imagine that if the Church of Christ the whole Church of Christ, were united in life and purpose, if she were really what we sometimes sing she is a mighty army, not shuffling along any and every road in loose and bedraggled array, but marching under one plan of campaign and moving in invincible strength I can imagine she would have her own Intelligence Department, her own secret service, her own exploring eyes and ears, peering everywhere, listening everywhere, knowing the most hidden facts of the nation's life, and proclaiming them from ten thousand pulpits in every part of the land. But while we wait for the united Church of Christ we must not go to sleep. Young people must strenuously and untiringly seek to get at the facts. How is it with old mother-earth? Is she full of the glory of God? Or is she full of shameful things, crooked things, wasteful things, wicked things? Is her life really vital, or is it superficial, artificial, a poor withered, wrinkled thing hidden in powders and cosmetics? What are the facts? Knowing what life is like in heaven find out what life is like on earth. Get at the fact.

And now for a last thing. Having a firm grip of divine principles "as it is in heaven," and with a clear knowledge of earthly facts "as it is done on earth," then with fearless application bring your principles close to your facts, and make your facts bow to your principles, reshaping them by the heavenly standards so that the crooked becomes straight and the rough places plain. Bring the heavenly close to the earthly, and change every earthly thing into heavenly currency, stamping it with the divine image and superscription. "Thy will be done on earth as it is done in heaven!" That is gloriously positive work. It is challenging work. It is exhilarating work. It is work which is worthy of the knights of God. It is to bring heaven and earth together until the two become one. It is to bring the heavenly to the earthly, to bring divine principles into the region of economics, into the realm of business, it is to bring them into the thicket of politics, to the simplification of society and to the reconstruction of international relationships.

"It can't be done!" What is that? "It can't be done!" What can't be done? "You cannot mix the heavenly and the earthly; you cannot wed them into vital union. Religion is religion, and business is business, and never the twain shall meet. Religion is religion, and politics is politics, and to try to marry the two is to seek a covenant between oil and water. You cannot bring religion into commerce, and let the heavenly visitor settle the height of the tariff wall, or remove it altogether. No, religion is religion, and trade is trade! There was no chair for Religion in the Council Chamber at Versailles; she was not expected, she was not really invited. And if, by any chance, she had appeared and spoken she would have been pathetically out of place." "But why would she have been out of place?" "Oh, well, everything in its place; and Versailles was the place for the stern soldier, the astute and wily diplomatist, the subtle politician; it was no place for the saint! You cannot have a coalition between Christ and Caesar. It can't be done!"

"Thy will be done on earth as it is done in heaven," Jesus Christ said it could be done, and that is the end of it. Nothing is expected from the heavenly claim. God claims everything. There is no confusion at the heart of things. There is one Intelligence in the universe, one central Will, one great White Throne. God's decree runs through all things, and His holy will is best in everything. What is good religion can never be bad business. What is rotten religion can never be sound economics. What is morally right can never be politically wrong. "Thy will be done on earth!" That is the right road in everything. On that road alone can true life be found, the abiding secret of vital progress and happiness. Then let us firmly grasp the divine principles revealed to us in Christ, let us fearlessly apply them to every sort of earthly facts, let us mould the facts according to the pattern which we have found in the holy Mount. But let us remember this. These words of our Master are first of all a prayer before they become a commandment. Our hands are to be uplifted in supplication before our feet begin their journey. We are to fall to our knees before we take to the road. It is first a prayer, then a crusade, and then a victory* "Thy will is done on earth as it is done in heaven."

Chapter 12 – George Morrison on the Lord's Prayer

("Our Daily Bread," taken from Devotional Sermons by George H. Morrison)

(1866-1928)

Give us this day our daily bread--Mat 6:11

Every Harvest Is Prophecy

Once more in the kindly providence of God we have reached the season of the harvest. The reaper has been busy in the fields, and sower and reaper have rejoiced together. Many a day in the past summer season we wondered if the corn would ever ripen. There was such rain, so pitiless and ceaseless. There was such absence of sunshine and of warmth. Yet in spite of everything harvest has arrived, and the fields have been heavy with their happy burden, and in the teeth of clenched antagonisms the promises of God have been fulfilled. Every harvest is a prophecy. It is the shadow of an inward mystery. It cries to us, as with a golden trumpet, "With God all things are possible." And so in days when all the world is dreary, and excellence seems farther off than ever, the wise man will pluck up heart again, as not despairing of his harvest home. Well, now I want to take our text and set it in the light of harvest. I want to look upon our daily bread against the background of the harvest field. A thing seems very different, does it not, according to the light in which you view it? Suppose then that in this light we look for a little at these familiar words.

First then in that light let us think of what the answer to this prayer involves.

The Tiniest Petitions

Now when you read it unimaginatively, this seems an almost trifling petition. It almost looks like an intruder here, and men have often spoken of it so. On the one side of it there is the will of God, reaching out into the height of heaven. On the other side of it there

118

are our sins, reaching down into unfathomed depths. And then, between these two infinities, spanning the distance from cherubim to Satan, there is "Give us this day our daily bread." Our sin runs back to an uncharted past, but in this petition there is no thought of yesterday. The will of God shall be for evermore, but in this petition there is no tomorrow. Give us this day our daily bread - supply us with a little food today - feed us til we go to rest tonight. As if a tiny cockleshell should be sailing between two mighty galleons, as if some hill that a child could climb should be set down between two mighty Alps, so seems this prayer for our daily bread between the will of the eternal God and the cry for pardon for our sins whose roots go down into the depths of hell.

But now suppose you take this prayer and set it in the light of harvest. Give us this day our daily bread - can you tell me what is involved when it is answered? Why, if you but realized it, and caught the infinite range of its relationships, never again would it be insignificant. For all the ministry of spring is in it, and all the warmth and glory of the summer. And night and day, and heat and cold, and frost, and all the falling of the rain. And light that has come from distances unthinkable, and breezes that have blown from far away, and powers of nourishment that for a million years have been preparing in the mother earth. Give us this day our daily bread. Is it a little thing to get a piece of bread? Is it so little that it is out of place here where we are moving in the heights and depths? Not if you set it in the light of harvest, and think that not a crust can be bestowed unless the sun has shone and the rain fallen and the earth been quietly busy for millenniums.

I think then there is a lesson here about the greatness of the things we pray for. Our tiniest petitions might seem large, if we only knew what the answer would involve. There are things which you ask for which seem little things. They are peculiar and personal and private. They are not plainly vast like some petitions, as when we pray for the conversion of the world. Yet could you follow out that prayer of yours, that little private prayer, you might find it calling for the power of heaven as mightily as the conversion of the nations. "Thou art coming to a King, large petitions with thee bring." Only remember that a large petition is not always measured by the compass of it. It may be small and yet it may be large. It may be trifling and be tremendous, for all the days beyond recall may somehow be implicated in the answer. You are lonely, and you pray to God that He would send a friend into your life. And then some day to you there comes that friend, perhaps in the most casual of meetings. Yet who shall tell the countless prearrangements, before there was that footfall on the threshold which has made all the difference in the world to you? Give us this day our daily bread, and the sunshine and the storm are in the answer. Give us a friend, and perhaps there was no answer saving for omniscience and omnipotence. Now we know in part and see in part, but when we know even as we are known we shall discover all that was involved in the answer to our humblest prayers.

The Toil It Cost

In the second place, in the light of harvest think of the toil that lies behind the gift.

There are some gifts which we shall always value because of the love which has suggested them. There are others which mean much to us because of the thoughtfulness which they reveal. But now and then a gift is given us which touches us in a peculiar way, because we recognize the toil it cost. It may be given us by a child perhaps, or it may be given us by some poor woman. And it is not beautiful, nor is it costly, nor would it fetch a shilling in the market. And yet to us who know the story of it, and how the hands were busied in the making, it may be beautiful as any diadem. It was not purchased with an easy purse. The purses that I am thinking of are lean. It was not ordered from a foreign market. Love is not fond of trafficking in markets. In that small workshop where your boy is busy, in that small room where the poor sufferer lives, it was designed and fashioned and completed. Such gifts are often sorry to the eye. Such gifts are never sorry to the heart. Poor may they be and insignificant, yet never to us can they be insignificant. We know what they have cost, and knowing that we recognize an unsuspected value. We know the toil that is behind the gift.

I want you then to take that thought and to apply it to your daily bread. It is a gift, and yet behind that gift do you remember all the toil there is? I could understand a man despising manna, even though manna was the bread of angels. It came so easily, and was so lightly gotten, and was so lavishly and freely given. But daily bread is more divine than manna, for it like manna is the gift of heaven, and yet we get it not till arms are weary and sweat has broken on the human brow. I think of the ploughman with his steaming horses driving his furrow in the heavy field. I think of the sower going forth to sow. I think of the stir and movement of the harvest. I think of the clanking of the threshing mill, and of the dusty grinding of the corn, and of all those who in our bakeries are toiling in the night when we are sleeping. Give us this day our daily bread - then it is a gift, that daily bread. It comes to us from God, in His great bounty, and in His compassion for His hungry children. And yet it does not always come through an opened heaven. But more often than not, it comes through the sweat and labor of humanity, through men and women who are often weary after bearing the heat and burden of the day.

And is it not generally in such ways that our most precious gifts are given us? Every good and perfect gift is from above, yet is there something of heart-blood on them all. A noble painting is a precious gift. It is a thing of beauty and a joy forever. Look at it, how calm and beautiful it is. There is not a trace of struggle in its beauty. But had you lived in communion with the artist, and had you been with him when he was painting that, what strain and agony you would have seen! So is it with every noble poem; so with our civil and religious liberty. They are all gifts to us; they come from God; they are ours to cherish and enjoy. Yet every one of them is wet with tears, and charactered with human toil and pain, and oftentimes, like the Messiah's garment, dipped in the final ministry of blood. Into that fellowship of lofty gifts I want you, then, to put your daily bread. It is not little, nor is it insignificant when you remember all that lies behind it. And do you not wonder now to find it here between the will of God and our transgressions, though the one rises to the height of glory and the other tangles in the pit of hell.

By Lowly Hands

Lastly, in the light of harvest think of the hands through which the gift is given. Give us this day our daily bread we pray, and then through certain hands it is bestowed. Whose hands? Are they the hands of God? "No man hath seen God at any time." Are they, then, the hands of the illustrious, or of those whose names are famous in the world? All of you know as well as I do that it is not thus our bread is ministered; it reaches us by the hands of lowly men. Out of his cottage does the reaper come, and back to his cottage does he go at evening. And we halt a moment, and we watch him toiling under the autumn sunshine in the field. But what his name is, or where he had his birth, or what are his hopes and what his tragedies, of that we know absolutely nothing. So was it with the sower in the spring. So is it with the harvester in autumn. They have no chronicle, nor any luster, nor any greatness in the eyes of man. And what I want you to realize is this, that when God answers this universal prayer it is such hands as these that he employs. Once in Scotland we had a different case. We had a genius at the plough. And he saw visions there and he dreamed dreams until his field was as a lawn of paradise. But for that one, who has his crown of amaranth, are there not tens of thousands who are nameless, toiling, sorrowing, rejoicing, dying, and never raising a ripple on the sea? Give us this day our daily bread - it is by such hands that the prayer is answered. It is by these that the Almighty Father shows that He is hearkening to His children. It is His recognition of obscurity, and of lives that are un-cheered by human voices, and of days that pass in silence and in shadow into the silence and shadow of the grave.

Now have you ever quietly thought of what we owe to ministries like that? One of the deepest debts we owe is to those who are sleeping in un-regarded graves. It is not the rare flower which makes the meadow beautiful. It is the flower that blossoms by the thousand there. It is not the aurora which gives the sky its glory. It is the radiance of the common day. And so with life; perhaps we shall never know how it is beautified and raised and glorified by those who toil in undistinguished fashion. Such men may never write great poems, but it is they who make great poems possible. Such may never do heroic things, but they are the soil in which the seed is sown. Such men will not redeem the world. It takes the incarnate Son of God for that. But they - the peasants and the fishermen - will carry forth the music to humanity. Give us this day our daily bread. Are there not multitudes who are praying so? And you, you have no genius, no gifts? You are an obscure and ordinary person? But if there is any meaning in our text, set in the light of sowing and of harvest, it is that the answer to that daily prayer will be vouchsafed through lowly folk like you.

Chapter 13 - Charles Spurgeon on the Lord's Prayer

(Charles Haddon Spurgeon, 1834-1892)

"Lead Us Not Into Temptation"

(No. 1402)

DELIVERED BY C. H. SPURGEON,

AT THE METROPOLITAN TABERNACLE,
NEWINGTON.

"Lead us not into temptation." Matthew 6:13.

LOOKING over a book of addresses to young people the other day, I met with the outline of a discourse which struck me as being a perfect gem. I will give it to you. The text is the Lord's prayer and the exposition is divided into most instructive heads. "Our Father which are in Heaven"—a child away from home. "Hallowed be Your name"—a worshipper. "Your kingdom come"—a subject. "Your will be done in earth, as it is in Heaven"—a servant. "Give us this day our daily bread"—a beggar. "And forgive us our debts as we forgive our debtors"—a sinner. "And lead us not into temptation, but deliver us from evil"— a sinner in danger of being a still greater sinner.

The titles are, in every case, most appropriate and truthfully condense the petition. Now if you will remember the outline you will notice that the prayer is like a ladder. The petitions begin at the top and go downward. "Our Father which are in Heaven"—a child, a child of the heavenly Father. Now to be a child of God is the highest possible position of man. "Behold what manner of love the Father has bestowed upon us, that we should be called the sons of God." This is what Christ is—the Son of God—and "Our Father" is but a plural form of the very term which He uses in addressing

God, for Jesus says, "Father." It is a very high, gracious, exalted position which, by faith, we dare to occupy when we intelligently say, "Our Father which are in Heaven."

It is a step down to the next—"Hallowed be Your name." Here we have a worshipper adoring with lowly reverence the thrice holy God. A worshipper's place is a high one, but it attains not to the excellence of the child's position. Angels come as high as being worshippers, their incessant song hallows the name of God—but they cannot say, "Our Father," "for unto which of the angels has He said, 'you are My son'?" They must be content to be within one step of the highest, but they cannot reach the summit, for neither by adoption, regeneration, nor by union to Christ are they the children of God. "Abba, Father," is for men, not for angels and, therefore, the worshipping sentence of the prayer is one step lower than the opening, "Our Father."

The next petition is for us as subjects, "Your kingdom come." The subject comes lower than the worshipper, for worship is an elevated engagement wherein man exercises a priesthood and is seen in lowly but honorable estate. The child worships and then confesses the Great Father's royalty. Descending still, the next position is that of a servant, "Your will be done in earth, as it is in Heaven." That is another step lower than a subject, for Her Majesty the Queen has many subjects who are not her servants. They are not bound to wait upon her in the palace with personal service though they acknowledge her as their honored sovereign. Dukes and such like are her subjects, but not her servants. The servant is a grade below the subject.

Everyone will admit that the next petition is lower by far, for it is that of a beggar—"Give us this day our daily bread." A beggar for bread—an everyday beggar—one who has continually to appeal to charity, even for his livelihood. This is a fit place for us to occupy who owe our all to the charity of Heaven. But there is a step lower than the beggar's and that is the sinner's place. "Forgive" is lower than, "give." "Forgive us our debts as we forgive our debtors." Here, too, we may, each one, take up his position, for no word better befits our unworthy lips than the prayer, "Forgive." As long as we live and sin we ought to weep and cry, "Have mercy on us, O Lord."

And now, at the very bottom of the ladder stands a sinner afraid of yet greater sin. He is in extreme danger and in conscious weakness, sensible of past sin and fearful of it for the future. Hear him, as with trembling lip he cries in the words of our text, "Lead us not into temptation, but deliver us from evil." And yet, dear Friends, though I have thus described the prayer as a going downward—downward is, in matters of Divine Grace, much the same as upward—as we could readily show if time permitted. At any rate the going down process of the prayer might equally well illustrate the advance of the Divine life in the soul.

The last clause of the prayer contains in it a deeper inward experience than the earlier part of it. Every Believer is a child of God, a worshipper, a subject, a servant, a beggar and a sinner. But it is not every man who perceives the allurements which beset him, or his own tendency to yield to them. It is not every child of God, even when advanced in years, who knows the full meaning of being led into temptation—for some follow an easy path and are seldom buffeted—while others are such tender babes that they hardly know their own corruptions. To fully understand our text a man should have had sharp brushes in the wars and have done battle against the enemy within his soul for many a day.

He who has escaped as by the skin of his teeth offers this prayer with an emphasis of meaning. The man who has felt the fowler's net about him—the man who has been seized by the adversary and almost destroyed—he prays with hot eagerness, "Lead us not into temptation." I purpose at this time, in trying to commend this prayer to you, to notice, first of all, the spirit which suggests such a petition. Secondly, the trials which such a prayer deprecates. And then, thirdly, the lessons which it teaches.

I. WHAT SUGGESTS SUCH A PRAYER AS THIS?— "Lead us not into temptation." First, from the position of the clause, I gather, by a slight reasoning process, that it is suggested by watchfulness. This petition follows after the sentence, "Forgive us our debts." I will suppose the petition to have been answered and the man's sin is forgiven. What then? If you will look back upon your own lives, you will soon perceive what generally happens to a pardoned man, for "As in water face answers to face, so the heart of man to man." One believing man's inner experience is like another's and your own feelings are the same as his.

Very speedily after the penitent has received forgiveness and has the sense of it in his soul, he is tempted of the devil, for Satan cannot bear to lose his subjects—and when he sees them cross the border and escape out of his hand, he gathers up all his forces and exercises all his cunning if, perhaps, he may slay them at once. To meet this special assault the Lord makes the heart watchful. Perceiving the ferocity and subtlety of Satan's temptations, the new-born Believer, rejoicing in the perfect pardon he has received, cries to God, "Lead us not into temptation." It is the fear of losing the joy of pardoned sin which thus cries out to the good Lord—"Our Father, do not suffer us to lose the salvation we have so lately obtained. Do not even subject it to jeopardy! Do not permit Satan to break our newfound peace. We have but newly escaped—do not plunge us in the deeps again!

"Swimming to shore, some on boards and some on broken pieces of the ship, we have come safely to land—do not let us tempt the boisterous main again. Cast us not upon the rough billows any more. O God we see the enemy advancing— he is ready, if he can, to sift us as wheat! Do not allow us to be put into his sieve, but deliver us, we pray You." It is a prayer of watchfulness and mark you, though we have spoken of watchfulness as necessary at the commencement of the Christian life, it is equally needful even to the close! There is no hour in which a Believer can afford to slumber. Watch, I pray you, when you are alone, for temptation, like a creeping assassin, has its dagger for solitary hearts! You must bolt and bar the door well if you would keep out the devil.

Watch yourself in public, for temptations in troops cause their arrows to fly by day. The choicest companions you can select will not be without some evil influence upon you unless you are on your guard. Remember our blessed Master's words, "What I say unto you I say unto all, Watch," and as you watch, this prayer will often rise from your inmost heart—

"From dark temptation's power, From Satan's wiles defend. Deliver in the evil hour, And guide me to the end."

It is the prayer of watchfulness.

Next, it seems to me to be the natural prayer of holy horror at the very thought of falling into sin again. I remember the story of a pitman who, having been a gross blasphemer—a man of licentious life and everything that was bad—when converted by Divine Grace, was terribly afraid lest his old companions should lead him back again. He knew himself to be a man of strong passions and very apt to be led astray by others and, therefore, in his dread of being drawn into his old sins, he prayed most vehemently that sooner than ever he should go back to his old ways, he might die. He did die then and there. Perhaps it was the best answer to the best prayer that the poor man could have offered.

I am sure any man who has once lived an evil life, if the wondrous Grace of God has snatched him from it, will agree that the pitman's prayer was not one whit too enthusiastic. It were better for us to die at once than to live on and return to our first estate and bring dishonor upon the name of Jesus Christ our Lord! The prayer before us springs from the shrinking of the soul at the first approach of the tempter. The footstep of the fiend falls on the startled ear of the timid penitent—he quivers like an aspen leaf and cries out—"What? Is he coming again? And is it possible that I may fall again? And may I once more defile these garments with that loathsome murderous sin which slew my Lord? O my God," the prayer seems to say, "keep me from so dire an evil. Lead me, I pray You, where You will—yes, even through Death's dark valley, but do not lead me into temptation, lest I fall and dishonor You." The burnt child dreads the fire. He who has once been caught in the steel trap carries the scars in his flesh and is horribly afraid of being held, again, by its cruel teeth.

The third feeling, also, is very apparent, namely, overconfident personal strength. The man who feels himself strong enough for anything is daring and even invites the battle which will prove his power. "Oh," he says, "I don't care. They may gather about me who will—I am quite able to take care of myself and hold my own against any number." He is ready to be led into conflict. He courts the fray! Not so the man who has been taught of God and has learned his own weakness! He does not want to be tried, but seeks quiet places where he may be out of harm's way. Put him into the battle and he will play the man. Let him be tempted and you will see how steadfast he will be—but he does not ask for conflict, as, I think, few soldiers will, who know what fighting means. Surely it is only those who have never smelt gunpowder, or seen corpses heaped in bloody masses on each other, that are so eager for the shot and shell—but your veteran would rather enjoy the piping times of peace.

No experienced Believer ever desires spiritual conflict, though, perhaps, some raw recruits may challenge it. In the Christian a recollection of his previous weakness—his broken resolutions, his unkept promises—makes him pray that he may not be severely tested in the future. He does not dare to trust himself. He wants no fight with Satan or with the world—he asks that, if possible, he may be kept from those severe encounters. His prayer is, "Lead us not into temptation." The wise Believer shows a sacred fear—no, I think I may say an utter despair of himself—and even though he knows that the power of God is strong enough for anything, yet is the sense of his weakness so heavy upon him that he begs to be spared too much trial. Hence the cry, "Lead us not into temptation."

Nor have I quite exhausted, I think, the phases of the spirit which suggests this prayer, for it seems to me to arise somewhat out of charity. "Charity?" you say. "How so?" Well, the connection is always to be observed, and by reading the preceding sentence in connection with it, we get the words, "as we forgive our debtors, and lead us not into temptation." We should not be too severe with those persons who have done wrong and have offended us, but pray, "Lord, lead us not into temptation." Your maid servant, poor girl, did take a trifle from your property. I make no excuse for her theft, but I beseech you, pause awhile before you quite ruin her character for life. Ask yourself, "Might not I have done the same had I been in her position? Lord, lead me not into temptation."

It is true, it was very wrong of that young man to deal so dishonestly with your goods. Still, you know, he was under great pressure from a strong hand and only yielded from compulsion. Do not be too severe. Do not say, "I will push the matter through—I will call the law on him." No, but wait awhile. Let Pity speak! Let Mercy's silver voice plead with you. Remember yourself, lest you, also, be tempted, and pray, "Lead us not into temptation." I am afraid that badly as some behave under temptation, others of us might have done worse if we had been there. I like, if I can, to form a kind judgment of the erring—and it helps me to do so when I imagine myself to have been subject to their trials and to have looked at things from their point of view—and to have been in their circumstances and to have nothing of the Grace of God to help me.

Would not I have fallen as badly as they have done, or even gone beyond them in evil? May not the day come, to you who show no mercy, in which you may have to ask mercy for yourselves? Did I say, may it not come to you? No, it must come to you. When leaving all below you will have to take a retrospective view of your life and see much to mourn over. To what can you appeal, then, but to the mercy of God? And what if He should answer you, "An appeal was made to your mercy and you had none. As you rendered unto others, so will I render unto you." What answer would you have if God were to treat you so? Would not such an answer be just and right? Should not every man be paid in his own coin when he stands at the Judgment Seat? So I think that this prayer, "Lead us not into temptation," should often spring up from the heart through a charitable feeling towards others who have erred—who are of the same flesh and blood as ourselves.

Now, whenever you see the drunkard reel through the streets, do not glory over him, but say, "Lead us not into temptation." When you take down the papers and read that men of position have betrayed their trust for gold— condemn their conduct if you will, but do not exult in your own steadfastness— rather cry in all humility, "Lead us not into temptation." When the poor girl seduced from the paths of virtue comes across your way, look not on her with the scorn that would give her up to destruction, but say, "Lead us not into temptation." It would teach us milder and gentler ways with sinful men and women if this prayer were as often in our hearts as it is upon our lips.

Once more, do you not think that this prayer breathes the spirit of confidence—confidence in God? "Why," says one, "I do not see that." To me—I know not whether I shall be able to convey my thought—to me there is a degree of very tender familiarity and sacred boldness in this expression. Of course God will lead me, now that I am His child. Moreover, now that He has forgiven me, I know that He will not lead me where I can come to any harm. This my faith ought to know and believe—and yet for several reasons there rises to my mind a fear lest His Providence should conduct me where I shall be tempted.

Is that fear right or wrong? It burdens my mind. May I go with it to my God? May I express in prayer this misgiving of my soul? May I pour out this anxiety before the great, wise, loving God? Will it not be impertinent? No, it will not, for Jesus puts the words into my mouth and says, "After this manner pray." You are afraid that He may lead you into temptation, but He will not do so. Or should He see fit to try you, He will also afford you strength to hold out to the end. He will be pleased in His infinite mercy, to preserve you. Where He leads it will be perfectly safe for you to follow, for His Presence will make the deadliest air to become healthful! But since instinctively you have a dread lest you should be conducted where the fight will be too stern and the way too rough, tell it to your heavenly Father without reserve.

You know at home, if a child has any little complaint against his father, it is always better for him to tell it. If he thinks that his father overlooked him the other day, or half thinks that the task his father has given him is too severe, or fancies that his father is expecting too much of him—if he does not say anything at all about it, he may sulk and lose much of the loving tenderness which a child's heart should always feel. But when the child frankly says, "Father, I do not want you to think that I do not love you or that I cannot trust you, but I have a troublous thought in my mind and I will tell it right straight out"—that is the wisest course to follow and shows a filial trust.

That is the way to keep up love and confidence. So if you have a suspicion in your soul that perhaps your Father might put you into temptation too strong for you, tell Him! Tell Him though it seems taking a great liberty. Though the fear may be the fruit of unbelief, yet make it known to your Lord and do not harbor it sullenly. Remember, the Lord's prayer was not made for Him, but for you and, therefore, it reads matters from your standpoint and not from His. Our Lord's prayer is not for our Lord—it is for us, His children—and children say to their fathers ever so many things which it is quite proper for them to say, but which are not wise and accurate after the measure of their parents' knowledge. Their father knows what their hearts mean and yet there may be a good deal in what they say which is foolish or mistaken. So I look upon this prayer as exhibiting that blessed childlike confidence which tells its father a fear which grieves it whether that fear is altogether correct or not.

Beloved, we need not debate here the question whether God does lead into temptation or not, or whether we can fall from Grace or not. It is enough that we have a fear and are permitted to tell our Father in Heaven about it. Whenever you have a fear of any kind, hurry off with it to Him who loves His little ones and, like a father, pities them and soothes even their needless alarms. Thus have I shown that the spirit which suggests this prayer is that of watchfulness, of holy horror at the very thought of sin, of overconfidence of our own strength, of charity towards others and of confidence in God.

II. Secondly, let us ask, WHAT ARE THESE TEMPTATIONS WHICH THE PRAYER DEPRECATES? Or rather,

What are these trials which are so much feared? I do not think the prayer is intended at all to ask God to spare us from being afflicted for our good, or to save us from being made to suffer as a chastisement. Of course we should be glad to escape those things, but the prayer aims at another form of trial and may be paraphrased thus—"Save me, O Lord, from such trials and sufferings as may lead me into sin. Spare me from too great trials, lest I fall by their overcoming my patience, my faith, or my steadfastness."

Now, as briefly as I can, I will show you how men may be led into temptation by the hand of God. And the first is by the withdrawal of Divine Grace. Suppose for a moment—it is only a supposition—suppose the Lord were to leave us altogether? We would perish speedily. But suppose—and this is not a barren supposition—that He were in some measure to take away His strength from us—should we not be in an evil case? Suppose He did not support our faith— what unbelief we would exhibit! Suppose He refused to support us in the time of trial so that we no longer maintained our integrity, what would become of us? Ah, the most upright man would not be upright long, nor the most holy, holy any more. Suppose, dear Friends—you who walk in the light of God's Countenance and bear life's yoke so easily because He sustains you—suppose His Presence were withdrawn from you—what would your portion be?

We are all so like Samson in this matter that I must bring him in as the illustration, though he has often been used for that purpose by others. So long as the locks of our head are unshorn we can do anything and everything—we can tear lions apart, carry gates of Gaza and smite the armies of the alien. It is by the Divine consecrating mark that we are strong in the power of His might. But if the Lord is once withdrawn and we attempt the work alone, then are we weak as the tiniest insect! When the Lord has departed from you, O Samson, what are you more than another man? Then the cry, "the Philistines are upon you, Samson," is the end of all your glory. You do vainly shake those lusty limbs of yours! Now you will have your eyes put out and the Philistines will make sport of you.

In view of a like catastrophe we may well be in an agony of supplication. Pray then, "Lord, leave me not and lead me not into temptation by taking your Spirit from me."—

"Keep us, Lord, oh keep us ever, Vain our hope if left by Thee!

We are yours, oh leave us never,

Till your face in Heaven we see.

There to praise you

Through a bright eternity.

All our strength at once would fail us,

If deserted, Lord, by Thee.

Nothing then could anything avail us,

Certain our defeat would be.

Those who hate us

From then on their desire would see." Another set of temptations will be found in providential conditions. The words of Agur, the son of Jakeh, shall be my illustration here. "Remove far from me vanity and lies; give me neither poverty nor riches; feed me with food convenient for me; lest I be full and deny You, and say, Who is the Lord? Or lest I be poor and steal and take the name of my God in vain."

Some of us have never known what actual need means, but have, from our youth up, lived in social comfort. Ah, dear Friends, when we see what extreme poverty has made some men do, how do we know that we would not have behaved even worse if we had been as sorely pressed as they? We may well shudder and say, "Lord, when I see poor families crowded together in one little room where there is scarcely space to observe common decency. When I see hardly bread enough to keep the children from crying for hunger. When I see the man's garments wearing out upon his back and by far too thin to keep out the cold, I pray You subject me not to such trial, lest if I were in such a case I might put forth my hand and steal. Lead me not into the temptation of pining need."

And, on the other hand, look at the temptations of money when men have more to spend than they can possibly need and there is, around them, a society which tempts them into racing, gambling, whoredom and all manner of iniquities. The young man who has a fortune before he reaches years of discretion and is surrounded by flatterers and tempters all eager to plunder him—do you wonder that he is led into vice and becomes a ruined man morally? Like a rich galleon waylaid by pirates, he is never out of danger! Is it a marvel that he never reaches the port of safety? Women tempt him, men flatter him, vile messengers of the devil fawn upon him and the young simpleton goes after them like an ox to the slaughter, or as a bird hastens to the snare and knows not that it is for his life!

You may very well thank Heaven you never knew the temptation, for if it were put in your way you would also be in sore peril. If riches and honor allure you, follow not eagerly after them, but pray, "Lead us not into temptation." Providential positions often try men. There is a man very much pushed for ready money in business—how shall he meet that heavy bill? If he does not meet it, there will be desolation in his family—the mercantile concern from which he now draws his living will be broken up—everybody will be ashamed of him. His children will be outcasts and he will be ruined. He has only to use a sum of trust money—he has no right to risk a penny of it, for it is not his—but still, by its temporary use he may, perhaps, tide over the difficulty. The devil tells him he can put it back in a week! If he touches that money it will be a roguish action, but then he says, "Nobody will be hurt by it and it will be a wonderful accommodation," and so on. If he yields to the suggestion and the thing goes right, there are some who would say, "Well, after all, there was not much harm in it and it was a prudent step, for it saved him from ruin."

But if it goes wrong and he is found out, then everybody says, "It was a shameful robbery. The man ought to be put in prison!" But, Brothers and Sisters, the action was wrong in itself and the consequences neither make it better nor worse! Do not bitterly condemn, but pray again and again, "Lead us not into temptation. Lead us not into temptation." You see, God does put men into such positions in Providence at times that they are severely tried. It is for their good that they are tried—and when they can stand the trial they magnify His Grace—and they become stronger men. The test has beneficial uses when it can be borne and God, therefore, does not always screen His children from it. Our heavenly Father has never meant to cuddle us up and keep us out of temptation, for that is no part of the system which He has wisely arranged for our education.

He does not mean us to be babies in carriages all our lives. He made Adam and Eve in the garden and He did not put an iron fence round the Tree of Knowledge and say, "You cannot get at it." No, He warned them not to touch the fruit, but they could reach the tree if they would. He meant that they should have the possibility of attaining the dignity of voluntary fidelity if they remained steadfast. But they lost it by their sin and God means, in His new creation, not to shield His people from every kind of test and trial, for that were to breed hypocrites and to keep even the faithful weak and dwarfish! The Lord does, sometimes, put the chosen where they are tried, and we do right to pray, "Lead us not into temptation."

And there are temptations arising out of physical conditions. There are some men who are very moral in character because they are in good health. And there are other men who are very bad, who, I do not doubt, if we knew all about them, should have some little leniency shown them because of the unhappy conformation of their constitution. Why, there are many people to whom to be cheerful and to be generous is no effort whatever, while there are others who need to labor hard to keep themselves from despair and misanthropy. Diseased livers, palpitating hearts and injured brains are hard things to struggle against! Does that poor old lady complain? She has only had rheumatism 30 years and yet she now and then murmurs! How would you be if you felt her pains for 30 minutes?

I have heard of a man who complained of everybody. When He came to die and the doctors opened his skull they found a close fitting brain-box and that the man suffered from an irritable brain. Did not that account for a great many of his hard speeches? I do not mention these matters to excuse sin, but to make you and myself treat such people as gently as we can, and pray, "Lord, do not give me such a brain-box and do not let me have such rheumatisms or such pains, because upon such a rack I may be much worse than they. Lead us not into temptation."

So, again, mental conditions often furnish great temptations. When a man becomes depressed he becomes tempted. Those among us who rejoice much, often sink about as much as we rise. And when everything looks dark around us, Satan is sure to seize the occasion to suggest despondency. God forbid that we should excuse ourselves, but, dear Brother, pray that you are not led into this temptation. Perhaps if you were as much a subject of nervousness and sinking of spirit as the friend you blame for melancholy, you might be more blameworthy than he. Therefore pity rather than condemn. And, on the other hand, when the spirits are exhilarated and the heart is ready to dance for joy, it is very easy for levity to step in and for words to be spoken amiss. Pray the Lord not to let you rise so high nor sink so low as to be led into evil. "Lead us not into temptation," must be our hourly prayer.

Further than this, there are temptations arising out of personal associations which are formed for us in the order of

Providence. We are bound to shun evil company, but there are cases in which, without fault on their part, persons are made to associate with bad characters. I may bring up the pious child whose father is a swearer. And the godly woman, lately converted, whose husband remains a swearer and blasphemes the name of Christ. It is the same with workmen who have to labor in workshops where lewd fellows at every half-dozen words let fall an oath and pour forth that filthy language which shocks us each day more and more.

I think that in London our working people talk more filthily than they ever did—at least, I hear more of it as I pass along or pause in the street. Well, if persons are obliged to work in such shops, or to live in such families, there may come times when under the lash of jest and sneer and sarcasm the heart may be a little dismayed and the tongue may refuse to speak for Christ. Such a silence and cowardice are not to be excused, yet do not censure your Brother, but say, "Lord, lead me not into temptation." How do you know that you would be more bold? Peter quailed before a talkative maid, and you may be cowed by a woman's tongue! The worst temptation that I know of, for a young Christian, is to live with a hypocrite—a man so sanctified and demure that the young heart, deceived by appearances, fully trusts him while the wretch is false at heart and rotten in life.

And such wretches there are who, with the pretense and affectation of sanctimoniousness, will do deeds at which we might weep tears of blood! Young people are frightfully staggered and many of them become deformed for life in their spiritual characteristics through associating with such beings as these. When you see faults caused by such common but horrible causes, say to yourself, "Lord, lead me not into temptation. I thank You for godly parents and for Christian associations and for godly examples. But what might I have been if I had been subjected to the very reverse? If evil influences had touched me when, like a vessel I was upon the wheel, I might have exhibited even grosser failings than those which I now see in others."

Thus I might continue to urge you to pray, dear Friends, against various temptations. But let me say the Lord has, for some men, very special tests such as may be seen in the case of Abraham. He gives him a son in his old age and then says to him, "Take now your son, your only son, Isaac, whom you love, and offer him for a burnt-offering." You will do right to pray, "Lord, lead me not into such a temptation as that. I am not worthy to be so tried. Oh do not so test me." I have known some Christians sit down and calculate whether they could have acted as the Patriarch did. It is very foolish, dear Brothers and Sisters. When you are called upon to do it, you will be enabled to make the same sacrifice, by the Grace of God! But if you are not called upon to do it, why should the power be given? Shall God's Grace be left unused? Your strength shall be equal to your day, but it shall not exceed it. I would have you ask to be spared the sterner tests.

Another instance is to be seen in Job. God gave Job over to Satan within limits and you know how Satan tormented him and tried to overwhelm him. If any man were to pray, "Lord, try me like Job," it would be a very unwise prayer. "Oh, but I could be as patient as he," you say. You are the very man who would yield to bitterness and curse your God! The man who could best exhibit the patience of Job will be the first, according to his Lord's bidding, fervently to pray, "Lead us not into temptation." Dear Friends, we are to be prepared for trial if God wills it, but we are not to court it, but are rather to pray against it even as our Lord Jesus, though ready to drink the bitter cup, yet in agony, exclaimed, "If it is possible, let this cup pass from Me."

Trials sought after are not such as the Lord has promised to bless. No true child asks for the rod. To put my meaning in a way in which it will be clearly seen, let me tell an old story. I have read in history that two men were condemned to die as martyrs in the burning days of Queen Mary. One of them boasted very loudly to his companion of his confidence that he should play the man at the stake. He did not mind the suffering! He was so grounded in the Gospel that he knew he should never deny it. He said that he longed for the fatal morning even as a bride for the wedding. His companion in prison in the same chamber was a poor trembling soul who could not and would not deny his Master, but, he told his companion, he was very much afraid of the fire.

He said he had always been very sensitive of suffering and he was in great dread that when he began to burn, the pain might cause him to deny his Master. He begged his friend to pray for him and he spent his time very much in weeping over his weakness and crying to God for strength. The other continually rebuked him and chided him for being so unbelieving and weak. When they both came to the stake, he who had been so bold recanted at the sight of the fire and went back, ignominiously, to an apostate's life—while the poor trembling man whose prayer had been, "Lead me not into temptation," stood firm as a rock, praising and magnifying God as he was burnt to a cinder!

Weakness is our strength and our strength is weakness! Cry unto God that He try you not beyond your strength and in the shrinking tenderness of your conscious weakness, breathe out the prayer, "Lead us not into temptation." Then if He does lead you into the conflict, His Holy Spirit will strengthen you and you will be brave as a lion before the adversary! Though trembling and shrinking within yourself before the Throne of God, you could confront the very devil and all the hosts of Hell without one ounce of fear! It may seem strange, but so is the case.

III. And now I conclude with the last head—THE LESSONS WHICH THIS PRAYER TEACHES. I have not time to enlarge. I will just throw them out in the rough. The first lesson from the prayer, "Lead us not into temptation," is this—never boast of your own strength. Never say, "Oh, I shall never fall into such follies and sins. They may try me, but they will find more than a match in me." Let not him that puts on his harness boast as though he were taking it off! Never indulge one thought of congratulation as to your strength. You have no power of your own. You are as weak as water. The devil has only to touch you in the right place and you will run according to his will. Only let a loose stone or two be moved and you will soon see that the feeble building of your own natural virtue will come down at a run. Never court temptation by boasting your own capacity.

The next thing is, never desire trial. Does anybody ever do that? Yes. I heard one say, the other day, that God had so prospered him for years that he was afraid he was not a child of God, for he found that God's children were chastised and, therefore, he almost wished to be afflicted. Dear Brothers and Sisters, do not wish for that! You will meet with trouble soon enough. If I were a little boy at home, I do not think I should say to my brother, because he had been whipped, "I am afraid I am not my father's child, and fear that he does not love me because I am not smarting under the rod. I wish he would whip me just to let me know his love." No, no child would ever be so stupid! We must not for any reason desire to be afflicted or tried, but must pray, "Lead us not into temptation."

The next thought is, never go into temptation. The man who prays "Lead us not into temptation," and then goes into it, is a liar before God! What a hypocrite a man must be who utters this prayer and then goes off to the theater! How false is he who offers this prayer and then stands at the bar and drinks and talks with depraved men and bedizened women! "Lead us not into temptation," is shameful profanity when it comes from the lips of men who resort to places of amusement whose moral tone is bad. "Oh," you say, "you should not tell us of such things." Why not? Some of you do them and I am bold to rebuke evil wherever it is found and shall do so while this tongue can move! There is a world of cant about.

People go to Church and say, "Lead us not into temptation," and then they know where temptation is to be found and they go straight to it! You need not ask the Lord not to lead you there—He has nothing to do with you! The devil and you, between you, will go far enough without mocking God with your hypocritical prayers! The man who goes into sin willfully with his eyes open and then bends his knees and says half-a-dozen times over in his Church on Sunday morning "Lead us not into temptation," is a hypocrite without a mask! Let him take that home to himself and believe that I mean to be personal with him and to such barefaced hypocrites as he!

The last word is, if you pray God not to lead you into temptation, do not lead others there. Some seem to be singularly forgetful of the effect of their example, for they will do evil things in the presence of their children and those who look up to them. Now I pray you consider that by ill example you destroy others as well as yourself. Do nothing, my dear Brothers and Sisters, of which you have need to be ashamed, or which you would not wish others to imitate. Do the right thing at all times and do not let Satan make a "cat's paw" of you to destroy the souls of others!

Do you pray, "Lead us not into temptation"? Then do not lead your children there. They are invited, during the festive season, to such-and-such a family party where there will be everything but what will benefit their spiritual growth or even their good morals—do not allow them to go. Put your foot down. Be steadfast about it. Having once prayed, "Lead us not into temptation," be not the hypocrite by allowing your children to go into it.

God bless these words to us. May they sink into our souls and if any feel that they have sinned, oh that they may now ask forgiveness through the precious blood of Christ and find it by faith in Him! When they have obtained mercy, let their next desire be that they may be kept in the future from sinning as they did before and, therefore, let them pray, "Lead us not into temptation." God bless you.

Section 5 – Other Writings on the Lord's Prayer

Chapter 14 - Andrew Murray on the Lord's Prayer

(Andrew Murray, 1828 - 1917)

Taken from 'With Christ in the School of Prayer', Chapter 4--After this manner pray or The Model Prayer

After this manner therefore pray ye: Our Father, which art in heaven.-MATTHEW 6.9.

Every teacher knows the power of example. He not only tells the child what to do and how to do it, but shows him how it really can be done. In condescension to our weakness, our Heavenly Teacher has given us the very words we are to take with us as we draw near to our Father. We have in them a form of prayer in which there breathe the freshness and fullness of the Eternal Life. So simple that the child can lisp it, so divinely rich that it comprehends all that God can give. A form of prayer that becomes the model and inspiration for all other prayer, and yet always draws us back to itself as the deepest utterance of our souls before our God.

`**Our Father which art in heaven!**' To appreciate this word of adoration aright, I must remember that none of the saints had in Scripture ever ventured to address God as their Father. The invocation places us at once in the center of the wonderful revelation the Son came to make of His Father as our Father too. It comprehends the mystery of redemption - Christ delivering us from the curse that we might become the children of God. The mystery of regeneration - the Spirit in the new birth giving us the new life. And the mystery of faith - ere yet the redemption is accomplished or understood the word is given on the lips of the disciples to prepare them for the blessed experience still to come. The words are the key to the whole prayer, to all prayer. It takes time, it takes life to study them; it will take eternity to understand them fully.

The knowledge of God's Father-love is the first and simplest, but also the last and highest lesson in the school of prayer. It is in the personal relation to the living God, and the personal conscious fellowship of love with Himself, that prayer begins. It is in the knowledge of God's Fatherliness, revealed by the Holy Spirit, that the power of prayer will be found to root and grow. In the infinite tenderness and pity and patience of the infinite Father, in His loving readiness to hear and to help, the life of prayer has its joy. O let us take time, until the Spirit has made these words to us spirit and truth, filling heart and life: Our Father which art in heaven.' Then we are indeed within the veil, in the secret place of power where prayer always prevails.

'**Hallowed be your name.**' There is something here that strikes us at once. While we ordinarily first bring our own needs to God in prayer, and then think of what belongs to God and His interests, the Master reverses the order. First, your name, your kingdom, your will; then, give us, forgive us, lead us, deliver us. The lesson is of more importance than we think. In true worship the Father must be first, must be all. The sooner I learn to forget myself in the desire that HE may be glorified, the richer will the blessing be that prayer will bring to myself. No one ever loses by what he sacrifices for the Father.

This must influence all our prayer. There are two sorts of prayer: personal and intercessory. The latter ordinarily occupies the lesser part of our time and energy. This may not be. Christ has opened the school of prayer specially to train intercessors for the great work of bringing down, by their faith and prayer, the blessings of His work and love on the world around. There can be no deep growth in prayer unless this be made our aim. The little child may ask of the father only what it needs for itself; and yet it soon learns to say, give some for sister too. But the grownup son, who only lives for the father's interest and takes charge of the father's business, asks more largely, and gets all that is asked. And Jesus would train us to the blessed life of consecration and service, in which our interests are all subordinate to the Name, and the Kingdom, and the Will of the Father. O let us live for this and let, on each act of adoration, Our Father! there follow in the same breath, your Name, your Kingdom, your Will;-for this we look up and long.

Hallowed be your name.' What name? This new name of Father. The word Holy is the central word of the Old Testament; the name Father of the New. In this name of Love all the holiness and glory of God are now to be revealed. And how is the name to be hallowed? By God Himself: `I will hallow My great name which you have profaned.' Our prayer must be that in ourselves, in all God's children, in presence of the world, God Himself would reveal the holiness, the Divine power, the hidden glory of the name of Father. The Spirit of the Father is the Holy Spirit: it is only when we yield ourselves to be led of Him, that the name will be hallowed in our prayers and our lives. Let us learn the prayer: `Our Father, hallowed be your name.'

'Thy kingdom come.' The Father is a King and has a kingdom. The son and heir of a king has no higher ambition than the glory of his father's kingdom. In time of war or danger this becomes his passion; he can think of nothing else. The children of the Father are here in the enemy's territory, where the kingdom, which is in heaven, is not yet fully manifested. What more natural than that, when they learn to hallow the Father-name, they should long and cry with deep enthusiasm: 'Thy kingdom come. The coming of the kingdom is the one great event on which the revelation of the Father's glory, the blessedness of His children, the salvation of the world depends. On our prayers too the coming of the kingdom waits. Shall we not join in the deep longing cry of the redeemed: 'Thy kingdom come'? Let us learn it in the school of Jesus.

'Thy will be done, as in heaven, so on earth.' This petition is too frequently applied alone to the suffering of the will of God. In heaven God's will is done, and the Master teaches the child to ask that the will may be done on earth just as in heaven: in the spirit of adoring submission and ready obedience. Because the will of God is the glory of heaven the doing of it is the blessedness of heaven. As the will is done, the kingdom of heaven comes into the heart. And wherever faith has accepted the Father's love, obedience accepts the Father's will. The surrender to, and the prayer for a life of heaven-like obedience, is the spirit of childlike prayer.

`Give us this day our daily bread!' When first the child has yielded himself to the Father in the care for His Name, His

145

Kingdom, and His Will, he has full liberty to ask for his daily bread. A master cares for the food of his servant, a general of his soldiers, a father of his child. And will not the Father in heaven care for the child who has in prayer given himself up to His interests? We may indeed in full confidence say: Father, I live for your honor and your work; I know You care for me. Consecration to God and His will gives wonderful liberty in prayer for temporal things: the whole earthly life is given to the Father's loving care.

'**And forgive us our debts, as we also have forgiven our debtors.**' As bread is the first need of the body, so forgiveness for the soul. And the provision for the one is as sure as for the other. We are children, but sinners too; our right of access to the Father's presence we owe to the precious blood and the forgiveness it has won for us. Let us beware of the prayer for forgiveness becoming a formality: only what is really confessed is really forgiven. Let us in faith accept the forgiveness as promised: as a spiritual reality, an actual transaction between God and us, it is the entrance into all the Father's love and all the privileges of children. Such forgiveness, as a living experience, is impossible without a forgiving spirit to others: as forgiven expresses the heavenward, so forgiving the earthward, relation of God's child. In each prayer to the Father I must be able to say that I know of no one whom I do not heartily love.

'**And lead us not into temptation, but deliver us from the evil one.**' Our daily bread, the pardon of our sins, and then our being kept from all sin and the power of the evil one, in these three petitions all our personal need is comprehended. The prayer for bread and pardon must be accompanied by the surrender to live in all things in holy obedience to the Father's will, and the believing prayer in everything to be kept by the power of the indwelling Spirit from the power of the evil one.

Children of God! it is thus Jesus would have us to pray to the Father in heaven. O let His Name, and Kingdom, and Will, have the first place in our love; His providing, and pardoning, and keeping love will be our sure portion, So the prayer will lead us up to the true childlife: the Father all to the child, the Father all for the child. We shall understand how Father and child, the Your and the our, are all one, and how the heart that begins its prayer with the God-devoted Thine, will have the power in faith to speak out the

Our too. Such prayer will, indeed, be the fellowship and interchange of love, always bringing us back in trust and worship to Him who is not only the Beginning but the End:' For Yours is the Kingdom and the Power, and the Glory, forever Amen.' Son of the Father, teach us to pray, 'Our Father'.

O You who art the only-begotten Son, teach us, we beseech You, to pray, 'Our FATHER.' We thank You, Lord, for these Living Blessed Words which You have given us. We thank You for the millions who in them have learnt to know and worship the Father, and for what they have been to us. Lord! it is as if we needed days and weeks in your school with each separate petition; so deep and full are they. But we look to You to lead us deeper into their meaning: do it, we pray You, for your Name's sake; your name is Son of the Father.

Lord! You did once say: `No man knows the Father save the Son, and he to whom the Son wills to reveal Him.' And again: `I made known unto them your name, and will make it known, that the love with which You have loved Me may be in them.' Lord Jesus! reveal to us the Father. Let His name, His infinite Father-love, the love with which He loved You, according to your prayer, BE IN us. Then shall we say aright, `OUR Father!'

Then shall we apprehend your teaching and the first spontaneous breathing of our heart will be: `Our Father, your Name, your Kingdom, your Will.' And we shall bring our needs and our sins and our temptations to Him in the confidence that the love of such a Father cares for all.

Blessed Lord! we are your scholars, we trust You; do teach us to pray, 'Our Father.' Amen.

Chapter 15 - Thomas Watson on The Lord's Prayer

(Thomas Watson, c. 1620 – 1686)

First published as part of A Body of Practical Divinity, 1692

This selection by Thomas Watson forms just the first section of his book on the Lord's Prayer. The entire book is readily available.

The Preface to the Lord's Prayer

'Our Father which art in Heaven '

'After this manner therefore pray ye, Our Father which art in heaven hallowed,' Mt. 6: 9.

In this Scripture are two things observable: the introduction to the prayer, and the prayer itself.

The introduction to the Lord's prayer is, 'After this manner pray ye.' Our Lord Jesus, in these words, gave to his disciples and to us a directory for prayer. The ten commandments are the rule of our life, the creed is the sum of our faith, and the Lord's prayer is the pattern of our prayer. As God prescribed Moses a pattern of the tabernacle (Exod 25: 9), so Christ has here prescribed us a pattern of prayer. 'After this manner pray ye,' etc. The meaning is, let this be the rule and model according to which you frame your prayers. We ought to examine our prayers by this rule (Calvin). Not that we are tied to the words of the Lord's prayer. Christ says not, 'After these words, pray ye;' but 'After this manner:' that is, let all your petitions agree and symbolize with the things contained in the Lord's prayer; and well may we make all our prayers consonant and agreeable to this prayer. Tertullian calls it, 'a breviary and compendium of the gospel,' it is like a heap of massive gold.

The exactness of this prayer appears in the dignity of the Author. A piece of work has commendation from its artifices, and this prayer has commendation from its Author; it is the Lord's prayer. As the moral law was written with the finger of God, so this prayer was dropped from the lips of the Son of God. [The voice is not that of a man, but that of God]. The exactness of the prayer appears in the excellence of the matter. It is 'as silver tried in a furnace, purified seven times.' (Psa 12:6). Never was prayer so admirably and curiously composed as this. As Solomon's Song, for its excellence is called the 'Song of songs,' so may this be well called the 'Prayer of prayers.' The matter of it is admirable, 1. *For its comprehensiveness.* It is short and pithy, a great deal said in a few words. It requires most art to draw the two globes curiously in a little map. This short prayer is a system or body of divinity. 2. *For its clearness.* It is plain and intelligible to every capacity. Clearness is the grace of speech. 3. *For its completeness.* It contains the chief things that we have to ask, or God has to bestow.

Use. Let us have a great esteem of the Lord's prayer; let it be the model and pattern of all our prayers. There is a double benefit arising from framing our petitions suitably to this prayer. [By this] error in prayer is prevented. It is not easy to write wrong after this copy; we cannot easily err when we have our pattern before us. Hereby mercies requested are obtained; for the apostle assures us that God will hear us when we pray 'according to his will.' (1 John 5:14). And sure we pray according to his will when we pray according to the pattern he has set us. So much for the introduction to the Lord's prayer, 'After this manner pray ye.'

The prayer itself consists of three parts. 1. A Preface. 2. Petitions. 3. The Conclusion. The preface to the prayer includes, 'Our Father;' and, 'Which art in heaven.'

I. The first part of the preface is 'Our Father.' *Father* is sometimes taken personally, 'My Father is greater than I' (John 14:28); but Father in the text is taken essentially for the whole Deity. This title, Father, teaches us that we must address ourselves in prayer to God alone. There is no such thing in the Lord's prayer, as, 'O ye saints or angels that are in heaven, hear us'; but, 'Our Father which art in heaven.'

In what order must we direct our prayers to God? Here the Father only is named. May we not direct our prayers to the Son and Holy Ghost also?

Though the Father only is named in the Lord's prayer, yet the other two Persons are not excluded. The Father is mentioned because he is first in order; but the Son and Holy Ghost are included because they are the same in essence. As all the three Persons subsist in one Godhead, so, in our prayers, though we name but one Person, we must pray to all. To come more closely to the first words of the preface, 'Our Father.' Princes on earth give themselves titles expressing their greatness, as 'High and Mighty.' God might have done so and expressed himself thus, 'Our King of glory, our Judge:' but he gives himself another title, 'Our Father,' an expression of love and condescension. That he might encourage us to pray to him, he represents himself under the sweet notion of a Father. 'Our Father.' Sweet is the name of Father. The name Jehovah carries majesty in it: the name Father carries mercy in it.

In what sense is God a Father?

(1) By creation; it is he that has made us: 'We are also his offspring' (Acts 17:28). 'Have we not all one Father?' (Mal 2:10). Has not one God created us? But there is little comfort in this; for God is Father in the same way to the devils by creation; but he that made them will not save them.

(2) God is a Father by election, having chosen a certain number to be his children, upon whom he will entail heaven. 'He has chosen us in him' (Eph 1:4).

(3) God is a Father by special grace. He consecrates the elect by his Spirit and infuses a supernatural principle of holiness, therefore they are said to be 'born of God' (1 John 3:9). Such only as are sanctified can say, 'Our Father which art in heaven.'

What is the difference between God being the Father of Christ and the Father of the elect?

He is the Father of Christ in a more glorious and transcendent manner. Christ has the [first place]; he is the eldest Son, a Son by eternal generation; 'I was set up from everlasting, from the beginning, or ever the earth was' (Prov 8:23). 'Who shall declare his generation?' (Isa 53:8). Christ is a Son to the Father, as he is of the same nature with the Father, having all the incommunicable properties of the Godhead belonging to him; but we are sons of God by adoption and grace, 'That we might receive the adoption of sons' (Gal 4:5).

What is that which makes God our Father?

Faith. 'Ye are all the children of God by faith in Christ Jesus.' Gal 3:26. An unbeliever may call God his Creator, and his Judge, but not his Father. Faith legitimizes us and makes us of the blood-royal of heaven. 'Ye are the children of God by faith.' Baptism makes us church members, but faith makes us children. Without faith the devil can show as good a coat of arms as we can.

How does faith make God to be our Father?

As it is a uniting grace. By faith we have coalition and union with Christ, and so the kindred comes in; being united to Christ, the natural Son, we become adopted sons. God is the Father of Christ; faith makes us Christ's brethren, and so God comes to be our Father. Heb 2:11.

Wherein does it appear that God is the best Father?

(1) In that he is most ancient. 'The Ancient of days did sit.' Dan 7:9. A figurative representation of God, who was before all time, which may cause veneration.

(2) God is the best Father, because he is perfect. 'Your Father which is in heaven is perfect;' he is perfectly good. Matt 5:48. Earthly fathers are subject to infirmities; Elias, though a prophet, 'was a man subject to like passions' (James 5:17); but God is perfectly good. All the perfection we can arrive at in this life is sincerity. We may resemble God a little, but not equal him; he is infinitely perfect.

(3) God is the best Father in respect of wisdom. 'The only wise God.' 1 Tim 1:17. He has a perfect idea of wisdom in himself. He knows the fittest means to bring about his own designs. The angels light at his lamp. In particular, one branch of his wisdom is that he knows what is best for us. An earthly parent knows not, in some intricate cases, how to advise his child, or what may be best for him to do; but God is a most wise Father. He knows what is best for us; he knows what comfort is best for us: he keeps his cordials for fainting. 'God who comforts the downcast.' 2 Cor 7:6. He knows when affliction is best for us, and when it is fit to give a

bitter potion. 'If need be ye are in heaviness.' 1 Pet 1:6. He is the only wise God; he knows how to make evil things work for good to his children. Rom 8:28. He can make a sovereign treacle of poison. Thus he is the best Father for wisdom.

(4) He is the best Father because the most loving. 'God is love.' 1 John 4:16. He who causes bowels of affection in others, must needs have more bowels himself; [for he accomplishes the same]. The affections in parents are but marble and adamant in comparison of God's love to his children; he gives them the cream of his love — electing love, saving love. 'He will rejoice over you with joy; he will rest in his love; he will joy over you with singing.' Zeph 3:17. No father like God for love; if you are his child you cannot love your own soul so entirely as he loves you.

(5) He is the best Father for riches. He has land enough to give to all his children; he has unsearchable riches. Eph 3:8. He gives the hidden manna, the tree of life, rivers of joy. He has treasures that cannot be exhausted, gates of pearl, pleasures that cannot be ended. If earthly fathers should be ever giving, they would have nothing left to give; but God is ever giving to his children, and yet has not the less. His riches are imparted not impaired; like the sun that still shines, and yet has not less light. He cannot be poor who is infinite. Thus he is the best Father; he gives more to his children than any father or prince can bestow.

(6) God is the best Father because he can reform his children. When his son takes bad courses, a father knows not how to make him better; but God knows how to make the children of the election better. He can change their hearts. When Paul was breathing out persecution against the saints, God soon altered his course and set him praying. 'Behold, he prayeth.' Acts 9:11. None of those who belong to the election are so roughcast and un-hewn but God can polish them with his grace and make them fit for the inheritance.

(7) God is the best Father because he never dies. 'Who only has immortality.' 1 Tim. 6:16. Earthly fathers die, and their children are exposed to many injuries, but God lives forever. 'I am Alpha and Omega, the beginning and the ending.' Rev 1:8. God's crown has no successors.

Wherein lies the dignity of those who have God for their Father?

(1) They have greater honor than is conferred on the princes of the earth; they are precious in God's esteem. 'Because you are precious in my eyes, and honored...' Isa 43:4. The wicked are dross (Psa 119:119), and chaff (Psa 1:4); but God numbers his children among his jewels. Mal 3:17. He writes all his children's names in the book of life. 'Whose names are in the book of life.' Phil 4:3. Among the Romans the names of their senators were written down in a book. God enrolls the names of his children, and will not blot them out of the register. 'I will not blot his name out of the book of life.' Rev 3:5. God will not be ashamed of his children. 'God is not ashamed to be called their God.' Heb 11:16. One might think it were something below God to father such children as are dust and sin mingled; but he is not ashamed to be called our God. That we may see he is not ashamed of his children, he writes his own name upon them. 'I will write upon him the name of my God;' that is, I will openly acknowledge him before all the angels to be my child; I will write my name upon him, as the son bears his father's name. Rev 3:12. What an honor and dignity is this!

(2) God confers honorable titles upon his children. He calls them the excellent of the earth, or the magnificent, as Junius renders it. Psa 16:3. They must needs be excellent who are of the blood royal of heaven; they are the spiritual phoenixes of the world, the glory of the creation. God calls his children his glory. 'Israel, my glory.' Isa 46:13. He honors his people with the title of kings. 'And has made us kings.' Rev 1:6. All God's children are kings, though they have not earthly kingdoms. They carry a kingdom about them. 'The kingdom of God is within you. 'Grace is a kingdom set up in the hearts of God's children. Luke 17: 21. They are kings to rule over their sins, to bind those kings in chains. Psa 149:8. They are like kings. They have their insignia regalia, their ensigns of royalty and majesty. They have their crown. In this life they are kings in disguise; they are not known, therefore they are exposed to poverty and reproach. 'Now are we the sons of God, and it does not yet appear what we shall be.' 1 John 3:2. Why, what shall we be? Every son of God shall have his crown of glory, and white robes. 1 Pet 5:4; Rev. 6:2: Robes signify dignity, and white signifies sanctity.

(3) The honor of those who have God for their Father is, that they are all heirs; the youngest son is an heir. God's children are heirs to the things of this life. God being their Father, they have the best title to earthly things, they have a sanctified right to them. Though they have often the least share, they have the best right; and with what they have they have the blessing of God's love and favor. Others may have more of the venison, but God's children have more of the blessing. Thus they are heirs to the things of this life. They are heirs to the other world. 'Heirs of salvation' (Heb 1:14); 'Joint heirs with Christ' (Rom 8:17). They are co-sharers with Christ in glory. Among men the eldest son commonly carries away all; but God's children are all — joint-heirs with Christ, they have a co-partnership with him in his riches. Has Christ a place in the celestial mansions? So have the saints. 'In my Father's house are many mansions. I go to prepare a place for you.' John 14:2. Has he his Father's love? So have they. 'That the love with which thou hast loved me may be in them.' Psa 146:8; John 17:26. Does he sit upon a throne? So do God's children. Rev 3:21. What a high honor is this!

(4) God makes his children equal in honor to the angels. Luke 20:36. They are equal to the angels; nay, those saints who have God for their Father, are in some sense superior to the angels; for Jesus Christ having taken our nature, says Augustine, has ennobled and honored it above the angelic. Heb 2:16. God has made his children, by adoption, nearer to himself than the angels. The angels are the friends of Christ: believers are his members, and this honor have all the saints. What a comfort is this to God's children who are here despised, and loaded with calumnies and invectives! 'We are made as the filth of the world,' etc. 1 Cor 4:13. But God will put honor upon his children at the last day, and crown them with immortal bliss, to the envy of their adversaries.

How may we know that God is our Father? All cannot say, 'Our Father.' The Jews boasted that God was their Father. 'We have one Father, even God.' John 8:41. Christ tells them their true pedigree. 'Ye are of your father the devil;' ver. 44. They who are of Satanic spirits, and make use of their power to beat down the power of godliness, cannot say, God is their Father; they may say, 'Our father who art in hell.' How then may we know that God is our Father?

(1) By having a filial disposition, which is seen in four things. [1] To melt in tears for sin as a child weeps for offending his father: When Christ looked on Peter, and Peter remembered his sin in denying him, he fell to weeping. Clemens Alexandrinus reports of Peter that he never heard a cock crow but he wept. It is a sign that God is our Father when the heart of stone is taken away, and there is a gracious thaw in the heart; and it melts into tears for sin. He who has a childlike heart, mourns for sin in a spiritual manner, as it is sin he grieves for, as it is an act of pollution. Sin deflowers the virgin soul; it defaces God's image; it turns beauty into deformity; it is called the plague of the heart. 1 Kings 8:38. A child of God mourns for the defilement of sin; sin has to him a blacker aspect than hell.

He who has a childlike heart, grieves for sin, as it is an act of enmity. Sin is diametrically opposed to God. It is called walking contrary to God. 'If they shall confess their iniquity, and that they have walked contrary unto me.' Lev 26:40. It does all it can to spite God; if God be of one mind, sin will be of another; sin would not only enthrone God, but strike at his very being. If sin could help it, God would no longer be God. A childlike heart grieves for this; 'Oh!' say she, 'that I should have so much enmity in me, that my will should be no more subdued to the will of my heavenly Father!' This springs a leak of godly sorrow.

A childlike heart weeps for sin, as it is an act of ingratitude. It is an abuse of God's love; it is taking the jewels of his mercies, and making use of them to sin. God has done more for his children than others; he has planted his grace and given them some intimations of his favor; and to sin against kindness, dyes a sin in grain, and makes it crimson; like Absalom, who soon as his Father kissed him, and took him into favor, plotted treason against him. Nothing so melts a childlike heart in tears, as sins of unkindness. Oh, that I should sin against the blood of a Savior, and the bowels of a Father! I condemn ingratitude in my child, yet I am guilty of ingratitude against my heavenly Father. This opens a vein of godly sorrow, and makes the heart bleed afresh. Certainly it evidences God to be our Father, when he has given us a childlike frame of heart, to weep for sin as it is sin, an act of pollution, enmity and ingratitude. A wicked man may mourn for the bitter fruit of sin, but only a child of God can grieve for its odious nature.

[2] A filial disposition is to be full of sympathy. We lay to heart the dishonors reflected upon our heavenly Father. When we see his worship adulterated, and his truth mingled with the poison of error, it is as a sword in our bones, to see his glory suffer. 'I beheld the transgressors and was grieved. ' Psa 119:158. Homer describing Agamemnon's grief when forced to sacrifice his daughter Iphigenia, brings in all his friends weeping and condoling with him; so, when God is dishonored, we sympathize, and are as it were clad in mourning. A child that has any good nature, is cut to the heart to hear his father reproached; so an heir of heaven takes a dishonor done to God more heinous than a disgrace done to himself.

[3] A filial disposition, is to love our heavenly Father. He is unnatural that does not love his father. God who is crowned with excellency, is the proper object of delight; and every true child of God says as Peter, 'Lord, you know that I love you.' But who will not say he loves God? If ours be a true genuine love to our heavenly Father, it may be known by the effects. Then we have a holy fear. There is the fear which rises from love to God, of losing the visible tokens of his presence. Eli's 'heart trembled for the ark.' 1 Sam 4:13. It is not said his heart trembled for his two sons Hophni and Phinehas; but his heart trembled for the ark, because the ark was the special sign of God's presence; and if that were taken, the glory was departed. He who loves his heavenly Father, fears lest the tokens of his presence should be removed, lest profaneness should break in like a flood, lest Popery should get head, and God should go from his people. The presence of God in his ordinances is the glory and strength of a nation. The Trojans had the image of Dallas, and they had an opinion that as long as that image was preserved among them, they should never be conquered; so, as long as God's presence is with a people they are safe. Every true child of God fears lest God should go, and the glory depart. Let us try by this whether we have a filial disposition. Do we love God, and does this love cause fear and jealousy? Are we afraid lest we should lose God's presence, lest the Sun of Righteousness should remove out of our horizon? Many are afraid lest they should lose some of their worldly profits, but not lest they should lose the presence of God. If they may have peace and trading, they care not what becomes of the ark of God. A true child

of God fears nothing so much as the loss of his Father's presence. 'Woe to them when I depart from them.' Hos 9:12.

Love to our heavenly Father is seen by loving his day. 'If thou call the Sabbath a delight.' Isa 58:13. The ancients called this 'the queen of days.' If we love our Father in heaven, we spend this day in devotion, in reading, hearing, meditating; on this day manna falls double. God sanctified the Sabbath; he made all the other days in the week, but he has sanctified this day; this day he has crowned with a blessing. Love to our heavenly Father is seen by loving his children. 'Everyone who loves the Father loves whoever has been born of him.' 1 John 5:1. If we love God, the more we see of him in any, the more we love them. We love then though they are poor, as a child loves to see his father's picture, though hung in a mean frame. We love the children of our Father, though they are persecuted. 'Onesiphorus was not ashamed of my chain.' 2 Tim 1:16. Constantine kissed the hole of Paphnusius's eye, because he suffered the loss of his eye for Christ. They have no love to God, who have no love to his children; they care not for their company; they have a secret disgust and antipathy against them. Hypocrites pretend great reverence to departed saints; they canonize dead saints, but persecute living ones. I may say of these, as the apostle in Heb 12:8: they are 'bastards, not sons.'

If we love our heavenly Father, we shall be advocates for him, and stand up in the defense of his truth. He who loves his father will plead for him when he is traduced and wronged. He has no childlike heart, no love to God, who can hear his name dishonored and be silent. Does Christ appear for us in heaven, and are we afraid to appear for him on earth? Such as dare not own God and religion in times of danger, God will be ashamed to be called their God; it will be a reproach to him to have such children as will not own him. A childlike love to God is known by its degree. We love our Father in heaven above all other things; above estate, or relations, as oil runs above the water. Psa 73:25. A child of God seeing a supereminence of goodness and a constellation of all beauties in him, is carried out in love to him in the highest measure. As God gives his children electing love, such as he does not bestow upon the wicked, so his children give to him such love as they bestow upon none else. They give him the flower and spirits of their love; they love him with a love joined with worship; this spiced wine they keep only for their Father to drink of. Cant 8:2.

[4] A childlike disposition is seen in honoring our heavenly Father. 'A son honors his father.' Mal 1:6.

We show our honor to our Father in heaven, by having a reverential awe of him upon us. 'Thou shalt fear thy God.' Lev 25:17. This reverential fear of God, is when we dare do nothing that he has forbidden in his Word. 'How can I do this great wickedness, and sin against God?' Gen 39: 9. It is part of the honor a son gives to a father, that he fears to displease him. We show our honor to our heavenly Father, by doing all we can to exalt him and make his excellencies shine forth. Though we cannot lift him up higher in heaven, yet we may lift him higher in our hearts, and in the esteem of others. When we speak well of God, set forth his renown, display the trophies of his goodness; when we ascribe the glory of all we do to him; when we are the trumpeters of his praise; this is honoring our Father in heaven, and a sure sign of a childlike heart. 'He who offers praise, glorifies me.' Psa 123.

(2) We may know God is our Father by resembling him. The child is his father's picture. 'Each one resembled the children of a king', every child of God resembles the king of heaven. Judg 8: 18. Herein God's adopted children and man's differ. A man adopts one for his son and heir that does not at all resemble him; but whomsoever God adopts for his child is like him; he not only bears his heavenly Father's name, but his image. 'And have put on the new man, which is renewed after the image of him that created him.' Col 3:10. He who has God for his Father, resembles him in holiness, which is the glory of the Godhead. Exod 15:11. The holiness of God is the intrinsic purity of his essence. He who has God for his Father, partakes of the divine nature; though not of the divine essence, yet of the divine likeness; as the seal sets its print and likeness upon the wax, so he who has God for his Father, has the print and effigies of his holiness stamped upon him. 'Aaron, the saint of the Lord.' Psa 106:16. Wicked men desire to be like God hereafter in glory, but do not affect to be like him here in grace; they give it out to the world that God is their Father, yet have nothing of God to be seen in them; they are unclean: they are not only without his image, but hate it.

(3) We may know God is our Father by having his Spirit in us. [1] By having the intercession of the Spirit. It is a Spirit of prayer. 'Because ye are sons, God has sent forth the Spirit of his Son into your hearts, crying Abba, Father.' Gal 4:6. Prayer is the soul's breathing itself into the bosom of its heavenly Father. None of God's children are born dumb. The Holy Spirit fills his instrument, and the Spirit of God touches the hearts of the saints like the threads of harp-strings. Prosper. 'Behold, he prayeth.' Acts 9:11. But it is not every prayer that evidences God's Spirit in us. Such as have no grace may excel in gifts, and affect the hearts of others in prayer, when their own hearts are not affected; as the lute makes a sweet sound in the ears of others, but itself is not sensible.

How shall we know our prayers to be indicted by the Spirit, and so he is our Father?

When they are not only vocal, but mental; when they are not only gifts, but groans. Rom 8:26. The best music is in concert: the best prayer is when the heart and tongue join together in concert.

When they are zealous and fervent. 'The effectual fervent prayer of a righteous man availeth much.' James 5:16. The eyes melt in prayer, and the heart burns. Fervency is to prayer as fire to incense, which makes it ascend to heaven as a sweet perfume.

When prayer has faith mingled with it. Prayer is the key of heaven, and faith is the hand that turns it. 'We cry, Abba, Father.' Rom 8:15. 'We cry,' there is fervency in prayer; 'Abba, Father,' there is faith. Those prayers suffer shipwreck which dash upon the rock of unbelief. We may know God is our Father, by having his Spirit praying in us; as Christ intercedes above, so the Spirit intercedes within.

[2] By having the renewing of the Spirit, which is nothing else but regeneration, which is called a being born of the Spirit. John 3:5. This regenerating work of the Spirit is a transformation, or change of nature. 'Be ye transformed by the renewing of your mind.' Rom 12:2. He who is born of God has a new heart: new, not for substance, but for qualities. The strings of a viol may be the same, but the tune is altered. Before regeneration, there are spiritual pangs, much heart-breaking for sin. It is called a circumcision of the

heart. Col 2:11. In circumcision there was a pain in the flesh; so in spiritual circumcision there is pain in the heart; there is much sorrow arising from a sense of guilt and wrath. The jailor's trembling was a pang in the new birth. Acts 16:29. God's Spirit is a spirit of bondage before it is a spirit of adoption. This blessed work of regeneration spreads over the whole soul; it irradiates the mind; it consecrates the heart, and reforms the life; though regeneration be but in part, yet it is in every part. 1 Thess 5:23. Regeneration is the signature and engraving of the Holy Ghost upon the soul, the new-born Christian is bespangled with the jewels of the graces, which are the angels' glory. Regeneration is the spring of all true joy. At our first birth we come weeping into the world, but at our new birth there is cause of rejoicing; for now, God is our Father, and we are begotten to a lively hope of glory. 1 Pet 1:3. We may try by this our relation to God. Has a regenerating work of God's Spirit passed upon our souls? Are we made of another spirit, humble and heavenly? This is a good sign of sonship, and we may say, 'Our Father which art in heaven.'

[3] We know God is our Father by having the conduct of the Spirit. We are led by the Spirit. 'As many as are led by the Spirit of God, they are the sons of God.' Rom 8: 14. God's Spirit does not only quicken us in our regeneration, but leads us on till we come to the end of our faith. It is not enough that the child has life, but he must be led every step by the nurse. 'I taught Ephraim to go, taking them by their arms.' Hos 11:3. As the Israelites had the cloud and pillar of fire to go before them, and be a guide to them, so God's Spirit is a guide to go before us, and lead us into all truth, and counsel us in all our doubts, and influence us in all our actions. 'Thou shalt guide me with thy counsel.' Psa 73:24. None can call God Father but such as have the conduct of the Spirit. Try then what spirit you are led by. Such as are led by a spirit of envy, lust, and avarice, are not led by the Spirit of God; it were blasphemy for them to call God Father; they are led by the spirit of Satan, and may say, 'Our father which art in hell.'

[4] By having the witness of the Spirit. 'The Spirit itself bears witness with our spirit, that we are the children of God.' Rom 8:16. This witness of the Spirit, suggesting that God is our Father, is not a vocal witness or voice from heaven. The Spirit in the word witnesses: the Spirit in the word says, he who is qualified, who is a

hater of sin and a lover of holiness, is a child of God, and God is his Father. If I can find such qualifications wrought, it is the Spirit witnessing with my spirit that I am a child of God. Besides, we may carry it higher. The Spirit of God witnesses to our spirit by making more than ordinary impressions upon our hearts, and giving some secret hints and whispers that God has purposes of love to us, which is a concurrent witness of the Spirit with conscience, that we are heirs of heaven, and God is our Father. This witness is better felt than expressed; it scatters doubts and fears, and silences temptations. But what shall one do that has not this witness of the Spirit? If we lack the witness of the Spirit let us labor to find the work of the Spirit; if we have not the Spirit testifying, let us labor to have it sanctifying, and that will be a support to us.

(4) If God be our Father, we are of peaceable spirits. 'Blessed are the peacemakers: for they shall be called the children of God.' Matt 5:9. Grace infuses a sweet, amicable disposition; it files off the ruggedness of men's spirits; it turns the lion-like fierceness into a lamb-like gentleness. Isa 11:7. They who have God to be their Father follow peace as well as holiness. God the Father is called the 'God of peace,' Heb 13:20: God the Son, the 'Prince of Peace,' Isa 9:6:God the Holy Ghost, a Spirit of peace; 'the unity of the Spirit in the bond of peace.' Eph 4:3. The more peaceable, the more like God. God is not the Father of those who are fierce and cruel, as if, with Romulus, they had sucked the milk of a wolf 'The way of peace have they not known.' Rom 3:17. They sport in mischief, and are of a persecuting spirit, as Maximinus, Diocletian, Antiochus, who, as Eusebius says, took more tedious journeys, and ran more hazards in vexing and persecuting the Jews, than any of his predecessors had done in obtaining victories. These furies cannot call God Father. If they do, they will have as little comfort in saying Father, as Dives had in hell, when he said, 'Father Abraham.' Luke 16:24. Nor can those who are makers of division. 'Mark them which cause divisions, and avoid them.' Rom 16:17. Such as are born of God, are makers of peace. What shall we think of such as are makers of divisions? Will God father these? The devil made the first division in heaven. They may call the devil father; they may give the cloven foot in their coat of arms; their sweetest music is in discord; they unite to divide. Samson's fox tails were tied together only to set the Philistine' corn on fire. Judges 15:4. Papists unite

161

only to set the church's peace on fire. Satan's kingdom grows up by making divisions. Chrysostom observes of the church of Corinth, that when many converts were brought in, Satan knew no better way to dam up the current of religion than to throw in an apple of strife, and divide them into parties: one was for Paul, and another for Apollo, but few for Christ. Would Christ not have his coat rent, and can he endure to have his body rent? Surely, God will never father them who are not sons of peace. Of all those whom God hates, he is named for one who is a sower of discord among brethren. Prov 6:19.

(5) If God be our Father, we shall love to be near him, and to have converse with him. An ingenuous child delights to approach near to his father, and go into his presence. David envied the birds that built their nest near to God's altars, when he was debarred his Father's house. Psa 84:3. True saints love to get as near to God as they can. In the word they draw near to his holy oracle, in the sacrament they draw near to his table. A child of God delights to be in his Father's presence; he cannot stay away long from God; he sees a Sabbath-day approaching, and rejoices; his heart has been often melted and quickened in an ordinance; he has tasted that the Lord is good, therefore he loves to be in his Father's presence; he cannot keep away long from God. Such as care not for ordinances cannot say, 'Our Father which art in heaven.' Is God the Father of those who cannot endure to be in his presence?

Use 1. For instruction. See the amazing goodness of God that he is pleased to enter into the sweet relation of a Father to us. He needed not to adopt us, he did not need a Son, but we needed a Father. He showed power in being our Maker, but mercy in being our Father. That when we were enemies, and our hearts stood out as garrisons against God, he should conquer our stubbornness, and of enemies make us children, and write his name, and put his image upon us, and bestow a kingdom of glory; what a miracle of mercy is this! Every adopted child may say, 'Even so, Father, for so it seemed good in thy sight.' Matt 11:26.

If God be a Father, then I infer that whatever he does to his children, is in love.

(1) If he smiles upon them in prosperity, it is in love. They have the world not only with God's leave, but with his love. He says

to every child of his, as Naaman to Gehazi, 'Be content, take two talents.' 2 Kings 5:23. So God says to his child, 'I am thy Father, take two talents.' Take health, and take my love with it; take an estate, and take my love with it: take two talents. His love is a sweetening ingredient in every mercy.

How does it appear that a child of God has worldly things in love?

Because he has a good title to them. God is his father, therefore he has a good title. A wicked man has a civil title to the creature, but no more; he has it not from the hand of a father; he is like one that takes up cloth at the draper's, and it is not paid for; but a believer has a good title to every foot of land he has, for his Father has settled it upon him.

A child of God has worldly things in love, because they are sanctified to him. They make him better, and are loadstones to draw him nearer to God. He has his Father's blessing with them. A little that is blest is sweet. 'He shall bless thy bread and thy water.' Exod 23:25. Esau had the venison, but Jacob got the blessing. While the wicked have their meat sauced with God's wrath, believers have their comforts seasoned with a blessing. Psa 78:30, 31. It was a sacred blessing from God that made Daniel's pulse nourish him more, and made him look fairer than they that ate of the king's meat. Dan 1:15.

A child of God has worldly things in love, because whatever he has is an earnest of more; every bit of bread is a pledge and earnest of glory.

(2) God being a Father, if he frown, if he dip his pen in gall, and write bitter things, if he correct, it is in love. A father loves his child as well when he chastises and disciplines him, as when he settles his land on him. 'As many as I love, I rebuke.' Rev 3:19. Afflictions are sharp arrows, says Gregory Nazianzen, but they are shot from the hand of a loving Father. Correction is the school of character. God afflicts with love: he does it to humble and purify. Gentle correction is as necessary as daily bread; nay, as needful as ordinances, as word and sacraments. There is love in all: God smites that he may save.

(3) God being a Father, if he desert and hide his face from his child, it is in love. Desertion is sad in itself, a short hell. Job 6:9. When the light is withdrawn, the dew falls. Yet we may see a rainbow in the cloud — the love of a Father in all this. God hereby quickens grace. Perhaps grace lay dormant. Cant 5:2. It was as fire in the embers, and God withdrew comfort to invigorate and exercise it. Faith as a star sometimes shines brightest in the dark night of desertion. Jonah 2:4. When God hides his face from his child, he is still a Father, and his heart is towards his child. As when Joseph spoke roughly to his brethren, and made them believe he would take them for spies, his heart was full of love, and he was fain to go aside and weep; so God's bowels yearn towards his children when he seems to look strange. 'In a little wrath I hid my face from you, but with everlasting kindness will I have mercy on you.' Isa 54:8. Though God may have the look of an enemy, yet still he has the heart of a Father.

Learn hence the sad case of the wicked. They cannot say, 'Our Father in heaven;' they may say, 'Our Judge,' but not 'Our Father;' they fetch their pedigree from hell. 'Ye are of your father the devil.' John 8:44. Such as are unclean and profane, are the spurious brood of the old serpent, and it were blasphemy for them to call God Father. The case of the wicked is deplorable; if they are in misery, they have none to make their moan to. God is not their Father, he disclaims all kindred with them. 'I never knew you: depart from me, ye that work iniquity.' Matt 7:23. The wicked, dying in their sins, can expect no mercy from God as a Father. Many say, He that made them will save them; but 'It is a people of no understanding; therefore he that made them will not have mercy on them.' Isa 27:11. Though God was their Father by creation, yet because they were not his children by adoption, therefore He that made them would not save them.

Use 2. For invitation. Let all who are yet strangers to God, labor to come into this heavenly kindred; never cease till they can say, 'Our Father which art in heaven.'

But will God be a Father to me, who has profaned his name, and been a great sinner?

If thou wilt now at last seek God by prayer, and break off thy sins, he has the bowels of a Father for you, and will in nowise cast you out. When the prodigal arose and went to his father, 'his father had compassion, and ran and fell on his neck, and kissed him.' Luke 15:20. Though thou hast been a prodigal, and almost spent all upon thy lusts, yet if thou wilt give a bill of divorce to thy sins, and flee to God by repentance, know that he has the bowels of a Father; he will embrace you in the arms of his mercy, and seal thy pardon with a kiss. What though thy sins have been heinous? The wound is not so broad as the [plaster] of Christ's blood. The sea covers great rocks; the sea of God's compassion can drown thy great sins; therefore be not discouraged, go to God, resolve to cast thyself upon his Fatherly compassion. He may be entreated of you, as he was of Manasseh. 2 Chron 33:13.

Use 3. For comfort. Here is comfort for such as can, upon good grounds, call God Father. There is more sweetness in this word Father than if we had ten thousand worlds. David thought it a great matter to be son-in-law to a king. 'What is my father's family, that I should be son-in-law to the king?' 1 Sam 18:18. But what is it to be born of God, and have him for our Father?

Wherein lies the happiness of having God for our Father?

(1) If God be our Father he will teach us. What father will refuse to counsel his son? Does God command parents to instruct their children, and will not he instruct his? Deut 4:10. 'I am the Lord thy God, who teaches you to profit.' Isa 48:17. 'O God, thou hast taught me from my youth.' Psa 71:17. If God be our Father, he will give us the teachings of his Spirit. 'The natural man receives not the things of God, neither can he know them.' 1 Cor 2:14. The natural man may have excellent notions in divinity but God must teach us to know the mysteries of the gospel after a spiritual manner. A man may see the figures upon a dial, but he cannot tell how the day goes unless the sun shines; so we may read many truths in the Bible, but we cannot know them savingly, till God by his Spirit shines upon our soul. God teaches not only our ear, but our heart; he not only informs our mind, but inclines our will. We never learn aught till God teach us. If he be our Father, he will teach us how to order our affairs with discretion (Psa 112:5) and how to carry ourselves wisely. 'David behaved himself wisely.' 1 Sam 18:5. He will teach us what to answer when we are brought before governors; he will put words into our mouths. 'Ye shall be brought

before governors and kings for my sake; but take no thought how or what you shall speak; for it is not you who speaks, but the Spirit of your Father which speaks in you.' Matt 10:18, 19, 20.

(2) If God be our Father he has bowels of affection towards us. If it be so unnatural for a father not to love his child, can we think God can be defective in his love? All the affections of parents come from God, yet are they but a spark from his flame. He is the Father of mercies. 2 Cor 1:3. He begets all the mercies and bowels in the creature; his love to his children is a love which passes knowledge. Eph 3:19. It exceeds all dimensions; it is higher than heaven, it is broader than the sea. That you may see God's fatherly love to his children: Consider, God makes a precious valuation of them. 'Because you are precious in my sight...' Isa 43:4. A father prizes his child above his jewels. Their names are precious for they have God's own name written upon them. 'I will write upon him the name of my God.' Rev 3:12. Their prayers are a precious perfume; their tears he bottles. Psa 56:8. He esteems his children as a crown of glory in his hands. Isa 62:3. God loves the places where they were born in for their sakes. 'Of Zion it shall be said, This and that man was born in her'; this and that believer was born there. Psa 87:5. He loves the ground his children tread upon; hence, Judea, the seat of his children and chosen ones, he calls a delight some land. Mal 3:12. It was not only pleasant for situation and fruitfulness, but because his children, who were his Hephzibah, or delight, lived there. He charges the great ones of the world not to injure his children, because their persons are sacred. 'He suffered no man to do them wrong, yea, he reproved kings for their sakes, saying, Touch not mine anointed.' Psa 105:14,15. By anointed is meant the children of the high God, who have the unction of the Spirit, and are set apart for God. He delights in their company. He loves to see their countenance, and hear their voice. Cant 2:14. He cannot refrain long from their company; let but two or three of his children meet and pray together, he will be sure to be among them. 'Where two or three are gathered together in my name, there am I in the midst of them.' Matt 18:20. He bears his children in his bosom, as a nursing father does the sucking child. Numb 11:12; Isa 46:4. To be carried in God's bosom shows how near his children lie to his heart. He is full of solicitous care for them. 'He cares for you.' 1 Peter 5:7. His eye is still upon them, they are never out of his thoughts. A

father cannot always take care for his child, he sometimes is asleep; but God is a Father that never sleeps. 'He shall neither slumber nor sleep.' Psa 121:4. He thinks nothing too good to part with for his children; he gives them the kidneys of the wheat, and honey out of the rock, and 'wines on the lees well refined.' Isa 25:6. He gives them three jewels more worth than heaven — the blood of his Son, the grace of his Spirit, and the light of his countenance. Never was there such an indulgent, affectionate Father. If he has one love better than another, he bestows it upon them; they have the cream and quintessence of his love. 'He will rejoice over you, he will rest in his love.' Zeph 3:17. He loves his children with such a love as he loves Christ. John 17:26. It is the same love, for the unchangeableness of it. God will no more cease to love his adopted sons than he will to love his natural Son.

(3) If God be our Father, he will be full of sympathy. 'As a father pities his children, so the Lord pities them that fear him.' Psa 103:13. 'Is Ephraim my dear son? my bowels are troubled for him.' Jer 31:20. God pities his children in two cases.

[1] In case of infirmities. If the child be deformed, or has any bodily distemper, the father pities it; so, if God be our Father, he pities our weaknesses: and he so pities them as to heal them. 'I have seen his ways, and will heal him.' Isa 57:18. As he has bowels to pity, so he has balsam to heal.

[2] In case of injuries. Every blow of the child goes to the father's heart; so, when the saints suffer, God sympathizes. 'In all their affliction he was afflicted.' Isa 63:9. He did, as it were, bleed in their wounds. 'Saul, Saul, why persecutes thou me?' When the foot was trod on, the head cried out. God's soul was grieved for the children of Israel. Judges 10:16. As when one string in a lute is touched, all the rest sound; so when God's children are stricken, his bowels sound. 'He that touches you touches the apple of his eye.' Zech 2:8.

(4) If God be our Father, he will take notice of the least good he sees in us; if there be but a sigh for sin, he hears it. 'My groaning is not hid from you.' Psa 38:9. If but a penitential tear comes out of the eye he sees it. 'I have seen thy tears.' Isa 38:5. If there be but a good intention, he takes notice of it. 'Whereas it was in thine heart to build an house unto my name, thou didst well that

167

it was in thine heart.' 1 Kings 8:18. He punishes intentional wickedness, and crowns intentional goodness. 'Thou didst well that it was in thine heart,' He takes notice of the least scintilla, the least spark of grace in his children. 'Sara obeyed Abraham, calling him lord.' 1 Peter 3:6. The Holy Ghost does not mention Sara's unbelief, or laughing at the promise; he puts a finger upon the scar, winks at her failing, and only takes notice of the good that was in her, her obedience to her husband — she 'obeyed Abraham, calling him lord.' Nay, that good which the saints scarce take notice of in themselves, God in a special manner observes. 'I was hungry, and ye gave me meat; I was thirsty, and ye gave me drink. Then shall the righteous answer, Lord, when saw we you hungry and fed you?' Matt 25:35,37. They as it were overlooked and disclaimed their own works of charity, but Christ takes notice of them — 'I was hungry, and ye fed me.' What comfort is this! God spies the least good in his children; he can see a grain of corn hid under chaff, grace hid under corruption.

(5) If God be our Father, he will take all we do in good part. Those duties which we ourselves censure he will crown. When a child of God looks over his best duties, he sees so much sin cleaving to them that he is confounded. 'Lord,' he says, 'there is more sulphur than incense in my prayers.' But for your comfort, if God be your Father, he will crown those duties which you yourselves censure. He sees there is sincerity in the hearts of his children, and this gold, though light, shall have grains of allowance. Though there may be many defects in the services of his children, he will not cast away their offering. 'The Lord healed the people.' 2 Chron 30:20. The tribes of Israel, being straitened in time, wanted some legal purifications; yet because their hearts were right God healed them and pardoned them. He accepts of the good will. 2 Cor 8:12. A father takes a letter from his son kindly, though there are blots or bad English in it. What blotting are there in our holy things! Yet our Father in heaven accepts them. 'It is my child,' God says, 'and he will do better; I will look upon him, through Christ, with a merciful eye.'

(6) If God be our Father, he will correct us in measure. 'I will correct you in measure.' Jer 30:11. This he will do two ways. It shall be in measure for the kind. He will not lay upon us more than we are able to bear. 1 Cor 10:13. He knows our frame. Psa 103:14.

He knows we are not steel or marble, therefore will deal gently, he will not over-afflict. As the physician, who knows the temper of the body, will not give physic too strong for the body, nor give one drachma or scruple too much, so God, who has not only the title, but the bowels of a father, will not lay too heavy burdens on his children, lest their spirits fail before him. He will correct in measure, for duration; he will not let the affliction lie too long. 'The rod of the wicked shall not rest upon the lot of the righteous,' Psa 125:3. It may be there, but not rest. 'I will not contend forever.' Isa 57:16. Our heavenly Father will love forever, but he will not contend forever. The torments of the damned are forever. 'The smoke of their torment ascends up forever and ever.' Rev 14:11. The wicked shall drink a sea of wrath, but God's children only taste of the cup of affliction, and their heavenly Father will say, 'let this cup pass away from them.' Isa 35:10.

(7) If God be our Father, he will intermix mercy with all our afflictions. If he gives us wormwood to drink, he will mix it with honey. In the ark the rod was laid up and manna; so with our Father's rod there is always some manna. Asher's shoes were iron and brass, but his foot was dipped in oil. Deut 33:24,25. Affliction is the shoe of brass that pinches; but there is mercy in the affliction, there is the foot dipped in oil. When God afflicts the body, he gives peace of conscience; there is mercy in the affliction. An affliction comes to prevent falling into sin; there is mercy in an affliction. Jacob had his thigh hurt in wrestling; there was the affliction: but when he saw God's face, and received a blessing from the angel, there was mercy in the affliction. Gen 32:30. In every cloud a child of God may see a rainbow of mercy shining. As the painter mixes dark shadows and bright colors together, so our heavenly Father mingles the dark and bright together, crosses and blessings; and is not this a great happiness, for God thus to cheques his providence, and mingle goodness with severity?

(8) If God be our Father, the evil one shall not prevail against us. Satan is called the evil one, emphatically. He is the grand enemy of the saints; and that both in a military sense, as he fights against them with his temptations; and in a forensic or law sense, as he is an accuser, and pleads against them; yet neither way shall he prevail against God's children. As for shooting his fiery darts, God will bruise Satan shortly under the saints' feet. Rom 16:20. As for

his accusing, Christ is an advocate for the saints, and answers all bills of indictment brought against them. God will make all Satan's temptations promote the good of his children. [1] As they set them praying. 2 Cor 12:8. Temptation is a medicine for security. [2] As they are a means to humble them. 'Lest I should be exalted above measure, there was given to me a thorn in the flesh, the messenger of Satan.' 2 Cor 12:7. The thorn in the flesh was a temptation; it was to prick the bladder of pride. [3] As they establish them more in grace. A tree shaken by the wind is more settled and rooted; so the blowing of a temptation does but settle a child of God more in grace. Thus the evil one, Satan, shall not prevail against the children of God.

(9) If God be our Father, no real evil shall befall us. 'There shall no evil befall you.' Psa 91:10. It is not said, no trouble; but, no evil. God's children are privileged persons; they are privileged from being hurt of everything. 'Nothing shall by any means hurt you.' Luke 10:19. The hurt and malignity of the affliction is taken away. Affliction to a wicked man has evil in it; it makes him worse. 'Men were scorched with great heat and blasphemed the name of God.' Rev 16:9. But no evil befalls a child of God; he is bettered by affliction. 'That we might be made partakers of his holiness.' Heb 12:10. What hurt does the furnace to the gold? It only makes it purer. What hurt does affliction to grace? Only refine and purify it. What a great privilege it is to be freed, though not from the stroke, yet from the sting of affliction! No evil shall touch a saint. When the dragon, say they, has poisoned the water, the unicorn with his horn draws out the poison. Christ has drawn the poison out of every affliction, that it cannot injure a child of God. Again, no evil befalls a child of God, because no condemnation. 'No condemnation to them which are in Christ Jesus.' Rom 8:1. God does not condemn them, nor does conscience. When both jury and judge acquit, no evil befalls the accused; for nothing is really an evil but that which damns.

(10) If God be our Father, we may go with cheerfulness to the throne of grace. Were a man to petition his enemy, there were little hope; but when a child petitions his father, he may hope with confidence to succeed. The word 'Father' works upon God; it touches his very bowels. What can a father deny his child? 'If his son ask bread, will he give him a stone?' Matt 7:9. This may

embolden us to go to God for pardon of sin, and further degrees of sanctity. We pray to a Father of mercy sitting upon a throne of grace. 'If ye then, being evil, know how to give good gifts to your children, how much more shall your heavenly Father give the Holy Spirit to them that ask him?' Luke 11:13. This quickens the church, and adds wing to prayer. 'Look down from heaven.' Isa 63:15. 'Doubtless thou art our Father'; ver. 16. For whom does God keep his mercies but for his children? Three things may give boldness in prayer. We have a Father to pray to, and the Spirit to help us to pray, and an Advocate to present our prayers. God's children should in all their troubles run to their heavenly Father, as the sick child in 2 Kings 4:19: 'He said unto his father, My head, my head.' So pour out thy complaint to God in prayer. 'Father, my heart, my heart; my dead heart, quicken it; my hard heart, soften it in Christ's blood. Father, my heart, my heart.' Surely God, who hears the cry of ravens, will hear the cry of his children!

(11) If God be our Father, he will stand between us and danger. A father will keep off danger from his child. God calls himself Scutum, a shield. As a shield he defends the head, guards the vitals, and shields off dangers from his children. 'I am with you, and no man shall set on you to hurt you.' Acts 18:10. God is a hiding-place. Psa 27:5. He preserved Athanasius strangely; he put it into his mind to depart out of the house he was in, the night before the enemy came to search for him. As God has a breast to feed, so he has wings to cover his children. 'He shall cover you with his feathers, and under his wings shalt thou trust.' Psa 91:4. He appoints his holy angels to be a lifeguard about his children. Heb 1:14. Never was any prince so well guarded as a believer. The angels [1] are a numerous guard. 'The mountain was full of horses of fire round about Elisha.' 2 Kings 6:17. 'The horses and chariots of fire' were the angels of God to defend the prophet Elisha. [2] A strong guard. One angel, in a night, slew a hundred and fourscore and five thousand. 2 Kings 19:35. If one angel slew so many, what would an army of angels have done? [3] The angels are a swift guard; they are ready in an instant to help God's children. They are described with wings to show their swiftness: they fly to our help. 'At the beginning of thy supplications the commandment came forth, and I am come.' Dan 9:23. Here was swift motion for the angel, to come from heaven to earth between the beginning and ending of Daniel's

prayer. [4] The angels are a watchful guard; not like Saul's guard, asleep when their lord was in danger. 1 Sam 26:12. The angels are a vigilant guard; they watch over God's children to defend them. 'The angel of the Lord encamps round about them that fear him.' Psa 34:7. There is an invisible guardianship of angels about God's children.

(12) If God be our Father, we shall not lack anything that he sees to be good for us. 'They that seek the Lord shall not lack any good thing.' Psa 34:10. God is pleased sometimes to keep his children on hard commons, but it is good for them. As sheep thrive best on short pasture, so God sees too much may not be good for his people; plenty might breed surfeit. In prosperity men's characters run riot. God sees it good sometimes to diet his children, and keep them short, that they may run the heavenly race the better. It was good for Jacob that there was a famine in the land; it was the means of bringing him to his son Joseph; so God's children sometimes see the world's emptiness, that they may acquaint themselves more with Christ's fulness. If God sees it to be good for them to have more of the world, they shall have it. He will not let them lack any good thing.

(13) If God be our Father, all the promises of the Bible belong to us. His children are called 'heirs of promise.' Heb 6:17. A wicked man can lay claim to nothing in the Bible but the curses; he has no more to do absolutely with the promises than a ploughman has to do with the city charter. The promises are children's bread; they are the breasts of the gospel milking out consolations; and who are to suck these breasts but God's children? The promise of pardon is for them. 'I will pardon all their iniquities, whereby they have sinned against me.' Jer 33:8. The promise of healing is for them. Isa 57:19. The promise of salvation is for them. Jer 23:6. The promises are the supports of faith; they are God's sealed deed; they are a Christian's cordial. Oh, the heavenly comforts which are distilled from the promises! Chrysostom compares the Scripture to a garden: the promises are the fruit trees that grow in this garden. A child of God may go to any promise in the Bible, and pluck comfort from it; he is an heir of the promise.

(14) God makes all his children conquerors. They conquer themselves; he who conquers himself is stronger than he who

conquers the stoutest ramparts. The saints conquer their own lusts; they bind these princes in fetters of iron. Psa 149:8. Though the children of God may be sometimes foiled, and lose a single battle, yet not the victory. They conquer the world. The world holds forth her two breasts of profit and pleasure, and many are overcome by it; but the children of God have a world-conquering faith. 'This is the victory that overcomes the world, even our faith.' 1 John 5:4. They conquer their enemies. How can that be, when their enemies often take away their lives? They conquer, by not complying with them; as the three children would not fall down to the golden image. Dan 3:18. They would rather burn than bow. Thus they were conquerors. He who complies with another's lust, is a captive; he who refuses to comply, is a conqueror. God's children conquer their enemies by heroic patience. A patient Christian, like the anvil, bears all strokes invincibly. Thus the martyrs overcame their enemies by patience. God's children are more than conquerors. 'We are more than conquerors.' Rom 8:37. How are they more than conquerors? Because they conquer without loss, and because they are crowned after death, which other conquerors are not.

(15) If God be our Father, he will now and then send us some token of his love. His children live far from home, and meet sometimes with coarse usage from the unkind world; therefore, to encourage them, he sends them tokens and pledges of his love. What are these? He gives them an answer to prayer, which is a token of love; he quickens and enlarges their hearts in duty, which is a token of love; he gives them the first fruits of his Spirit, which are love tokens. Rom 8:23. As he gives the wicked the first fruits of hell, horror of conscience and despair, so he gives his children the first fruits of his Spirit, joy and peace, which are foretastes of glory. Some of his children, having received those tokens of love from him, have been so transported, that they have died for joy, as the glass often breaks with the strength of the wine put into it.

(16) If God be our Father, he will indulge and spare us. 'I will spare them, as a man spareth his own son that serveth him.' Mal 3:17. God's sparing his children, imports his clemency towards them. He does not punish them as he might. 'He has not dealt with us after our sins.' Psa 103:10. We often do that which merits wrath, grieve God's Spirit, and relapse into sin. God passes by much and spares us. He did not spare his natural Son, and yet he spares his

adopted sons. Rom 8:32. He threatened Ephraim to make him as the chaff driven with the whirlwind, but he soon repented. 'Yet I am the Lord thy God.' Hos 13:4. 'I will be thy king;' ver. 10. Here God spared him, as a father spares his son. Israel often provoked God with their complaints, but he used clemency towards them; he often answered their murmurings with mercies. Thus he spared them, as a father spares his son.

(17) If God be our Father, he will put honor and renown upon us at the last day. [1] He will clear the innocence of his children. His children in this life are strangely misrepresented. They are loaded with invectives — they are called factious, seditious; as Elijah, the troubler of Israel; and Luther, the trumpet of rebellion. Athanasius was accused to the Emperor Constantine as the raiser of tumults; and the primitive Christians were accused as 'killers of their children, guilty of incest.' Tertullus reported Paul to be a pestilent person. Acts 24:5. Famous Wycliffe was called the idol of the heretics, and reported to have died drunk. If Satan cannot defile God's children, he will disgrace then; if he cannot strike his fiery darts into their consciences he will put a dead fly to their names; but God will one day clear their innocence; he will roll away their reproach. As he will make a resurrection of bodies, so of names. 'The Lord God will wipe away tears from off all faces, and the rebuke of his people shall he take away.' Isa 25:8. He will be the saints' vindicator. 'He shall bring forth thy righteousness as the light.' Psa 37:6. The night casts its dark mantle upon the most beautiful flowers; but the light comes in the morning and dispels the darkness, and every flower appears in its orient brightness. So the wicked may by misreports darken the honor and repute of the saints; but God will dispel this darkness, and cause their names to shine forth. 'He shall bring forth thy righteousness as the light.' Thus God stood up for the honor of Moses when Aaron and Miriam sought to eclipse his fame. 'Wherefore then were ye not afraid to speak against my servant Moses?' Numb 12:8. So God will one day say to the wicked, 'Wherefore were ye not afraid to defame and traduce my children? Having my image upon them, how durst you abuse my picture?' At last his children shall come forth out of all their calumnies, as 'a dove covered with silver, and her feathers with yellow gold.' Psa 68:13. [2] God will make an open and honorable recital of all their good deeds. As the sins of the wicked

shall be openly mentioned, to their eternal infamy and confusion; so all the good deeds of the saints shall be openly mentioned, 'and then shall every man have praise of God.' 1 Cor 4:5. Every prayer made with melting eyes, every good service, every work of charity, shall be openly declared before men and angels. 'I was hungry, and ye gave me meat: thirsty, and ye gave me drink: naked, and ye clothed me.' Matt 25:35,36. Thus God will set a trophy of honor upon all his children at the last day. 'Then shall the righteous shine forth as the sun in the kingdom of their Father.' Matt 13:43.

(18) If God be our Father, he will settle a good inheritance upon us. 'Blessed be the God and Father of our Lord Jesus, which has begotten us again unto a lively hope, to an inheritance incorruptible, and undefiled.' I Pet 1:3,4. A father may have lost his goods, and have nothing to leave his son but his blessing; but God will settle an inheritance on his children, and an inheritance no less than a kingdom. 'It is your Father's good pleasure to give you the kingdom.' Luke 12:32. This kingdom is more glorious and magnificent than any earthly kingdom; it is set out by pearls, precious stones, and the richest jewels. Rev 21:19. What are all the rarities of the world, the coasts of pearl, the islands of spices, the rocks of diamonds, to this kingdom? In this heavenly kingdom is satisfying, unparalleled beauty, rivers of pleasure, and that forever. 'At thy right hand are pleasures forevermore.' Psa 16:2. Heaven's eminence is its permanence; and this kingdom God's children enter into immediately after death. There is a sudden transition and passage from death to glory. 'Absent from the body, present with the Lord.' 2 Cor 5:8. God's children shall not wait long for their inheritance; it is but winking, and they shall see God. How should this comfort those of God's children who are low in the world! Your Father in heaven will settle a kingdom upon you at death, such a kingdom as eye has not seen; he will give you a crown not of gold, but glory; he will give you white robes lined with immortality. 'It is your Father's good pleasure to give you the kingdom.'

(19) If God be our Father, it is a comfort in case of the loss of relations. Hast thou lost a father? If thou art a believer, thou art no orphan, thou hast a heavenly Father, a Father that never dies. 'Who only has immortality.' 1 Tim 6:16. It is comfort in case of your own death. God is thy Father, and death is but going to thy Father. Well might Paul say death is yours. 1 Cor 3:22. It is your

friend that will carry you home to your Father. How glad are children when they are going home! It was Christ's comfort at death that he was going to his Father. 'I leave the world, and go to the Father.' John 16:28. 'I ascend unto my Father.' John 20:17. If God be our Father, we may with comfort, at the day of death, resign our souls into his hand. Thus did Christ. 'Father, into thy hands I commend my spirit.' Luke 23:46. If a child has any jewel, he will in time of danger put it into his father's hands, where he thinks it will be kept most safe; so the soul, which is our richest jewel, we may resign at death into God's hands, where it will be safer than in our own keeping. 'Father, into thy hands I commend my spirit.' What a comfort it is that death carries a believer to his Father's house, where are delights unspeakable and full of glory! How glad was old Jacob when he saw the wagons and chariots to carry him to his son Joseph! 'The spirit of Jacob revived.' Gen 45:27. Death is a triumphant chariot, to carry every child of God to his Father's mansion-house.

(20) If God be our Father he will not disinherit us. He may for a time desert his children, but will not disinherit them. The sons of kings have sometimes been disinherited by the cruelty of usurpers; as the son of Alexander the Great was put out of his just right, through the violence and ambition of his father's captains; but what power on earth can hinder the heirs of the promise from their inheritance? Men cannot, and God will not cut off the entail. The Armenians hold falling away from grace, so that a child of God may be deprived of his inheritance, but God's children can never be degraded or disinherited, and their heavenly Father will not cast them off from being children. It is evident that God's children cannot be finally disinherited, by virtue of the eternal decree of heaven. God's decree is the very pillar and basis on which the saints' perseverance depends. That decree ties the knot of adoption so fast, that neither sin, death, nor hell, can break it asunder. 'Whom he did predestinate, them he also called,' &c. Rom 8:30. Predestination is nothing else but God's decreeing a certain number to be heirs of glory, on whom he will settle the crown; for whom he predestinates, he glorifies. What shall hinder God's electing love, or make his decree null and void? Besides God's decree, he has engaged himself by promise, that the heirs of heaven shall never be put out of their inheritance. His promises are not like blanks in a

lottery, but as a sealed deed which cannot be reversed; they are the saints' royal charter; and one promise is that their heavenly Father will not disinherit them. 'I will make an everlasting covenant with them, that I will not turn away from them; but I will put my fear in their hearts, that they shall not depart from me.' Jer 32:40. God's fidelity, which is the richest pearl of his crown, is engaged in this promise for his children's perseverance. 'I will not turn away from them.' A child of God cannot fall away while he is held fast in these two arms of God — his love, and his faithfulness. Jesus Christ undertakes that all God's children by adoption shall be preserved in a state of grace till they inherit glory. The heathens feigned of Atlas that he bore up the heavens from falling; but Jesus Christ is that blessed Atlas that bears up the saints from falling away.

How does Christ preserve the saints' graces, till they come to heaven?

(1) By the influence of the Spirit. He carries on grace in the souls of the elect, by the influence and co-operation of his Spirit. He continually excites and quickens grace in the godly; he by his Spirit blows up the sparks of grace into a holy flame. The Spirit is Christ's vicar on earth, his proxy, his executor, to see that all that he has purchased for the saints be made good. Christ has obtained for them an inheritance incorruptible, and the Spirit is his executor, to see that the inheritance be settled upon them. 1 Pet 1:4,5. (2) He carries on his work perseveringly in the souls of the elect, by the prevalence of his intercession. 'He ever lives to make intercession for them.' Heb 7:25. He prays that every saint may hold out in grace till he comes to heaven. Can the children of such prayers perish? If the heirs of heaven should be disinherited, and fall short of glory, then God's decree must be reversed, his promise broken, and Christ's prayer frustrated, which would be blasphemy to imagine.

(3) That God's children cannot be disinherited, or put out of their right to the crown of heaven, is evident from their mystic union with Christ. Believers are incorporated into him; they are knit to him as members to the head, by the nerves and ligaments of faith, so that they cannot be broken off. 'The church, which is his body.' Eph 1:22, 23. What was once said of Christ's natural body, is as true of his mystic body. 'A bone of it shall not be broken.' As it is impossible to sever the leaven and the dough when they are once

mingled and kneaded together, so it is impossible, when Christ and believers are once united, that they should ever, by the power of death or hell, be separated. Christ and his spiritual members make one Christ. Is it possible that any part of Christ should perish? How can Christ want any member of his mystic body and be perfect? Every member is an ornament to the body, and adds to the honor of it. How can Christ part with any mystic member, and not part with some of his glory too? By all this it is evident that God's children must needs persevere in grace, and cannot be disinherited. If they could be disinherited, the Scripture could not be fulfilled, which tells us of glorious rewards for the heirs of promise. 'Verily there is a reward for the righteous.' Psa 58:11. If God's adopted children should fall away finally from grace, and miss of heaven, what reward would there be for the righteous? Moses indiscreetly looked for the recompense of the reward, and a door would be opened to despair.

But the doctrine of final perseverance, and the certainty of the heavenly inheritance may lead to carnal security, and unholy walking.

Corrupt nature may suck poison from this flower; but he who has felt the efficacy of grace upon his heart, dares not abuse this doctrine. He knows that perseverance is attained in the use of means, and walks homily, that in the use of the means he may arrive at perseverance. Paul knew that he should not be disinherited, and that nothing could separate him from the love of Christ; but who more holy and watchful than he was? 'I keep under my body.' 1 Cor 9:27. 'I press toward the mark.' Phil 3:14. God's children have a holy fear which keeps them from self-security and wantonness; they believe the promise, therefore they rejoice in hope; they fear their hearts, therefore they watch and pray.

Thus you see what strong consolation there is for all the heirs of the promise. Such as have God for their Father are the happiest persons on earth; they are in such a condition that nothing can hurt them; they have their Father's blessing, all things conspire for their good; they have a kingdom settled on them, and the entail can never be cut off. How comforted should they be in all conditions, let the times be what they will! Their Father who is in heaven rules over all. If troubles arise, they carry them sooner to their Father. The more violently the wind beats against the sails of a ship, the sooner it is brought to the haven; and the more fiercely God's children are assaulted, the sooner they come to their Father's house. 'Wherefore comfort one another with these words.' 1 Thess 4:18.

Use 4. For exhortation. Let us behave ourselves as the children of such a Father.

(1) Let us depend upon him in all our straits and exigencies; let us believe that he will provide for all our needs. Children rely upon their parents for the supply of their needs. If we trust God for salvation, shall we not trust him for a livelihood? There is a lawful and prudent care to be used. But beware of being distrustful. 'Consider the ravens: for they neither sow nor reap; and God feeds them.' Luke 12:24. Does God feed the birds of the air, and will he not feed his children? 'Consider the lilies how they grow: they spin not; yet Solomon in all his glory was not arrayed like one of these;' ver. 27. Does God clothe the lilies, and will he not clothe his lambs? Even the wicked taste of his bounty. 'Their eyes stand out with fatness.' Psa 73:7. Does God feed his slaves, and will he not feed his family? His children may not have a liberal share in the things of this life; they may have but little meal in the barrel; they may be drawn low, and almost dry; but they shall have as much as God sees to be good for them. 'They that seek the Lord shall not lack any good thing.' Psa 34:10. If God gives them not what they need, he will give what is good for them; if he gives them not always what they crave, he will give them what they need; if he gives them not a feast, he will give them a bait by the way. Let them depend upon his fatherly providence; let them not give way to distrustful thoughts, distracting cares, or indirect means. 'Casting all your care upon him; for he cares for you.' I Pet 5:7. An earthly parent may have affection for his child, and would gladly provide for him, but may not be able; but God is never at a loss to provide for his children, and he has promised an adequate supply. 'Verily thou shalt be fed.' Psa 37:3. Will God give his children heaven, and will he not give them enough to bear their charges thither? Will he give them a kingdom, and deny them daily bread? O put your trust in him, for he has said, 'I will never leave you, nor forsake you.' Heb 13:5.

(2) If God be our Father, let us imitate him. The child not only bears his father's image, but imitates him in his speech, gesture and behavior. If God be our Father, let us imitate him. 'Be ye followers of God, as dear children.' Eph 5:1. Imitate God in forgiving injuries. 'I have blotted out, as a thick cloud, thy transgressions.' Isa 44:22. As the sun scatters not only thin mists, but thick clouds, so God pardons great offenses. Imitate him in this. 'Forgiving one another.' Eph 4:32. Cranmer was a man of a forgiving spirit: he buried injuries and requited good for evil. He who has God for his Father, will have him for his pattern. Imitate God in works of mercy. 'The Lord looseth the prisoners.' Psa 146:7. He opens his hand and satisfies the desire of every living thing. Psa 145:16. He drops his sweet dew upon the thistle as well as the rose. Imitate God in works of mercy; relieve the needs of others; be rich in good works. 'Be merciful, as your Father also is merciful.' Luke 6:36. Be not so hard hearted as to shut out the poor from all communication. Dives denied Lazarus a crumb of bread, and Dives was denied a drop of water.

(3) If God be our Father, let us submit patiently to his will. If he lay his strokes on us, they are the corrections of a Father, not the punishments of a judge. This made Christ himself patient. 'The cup which my Father has given me, shall I not drink it?' John 18:11. He sees we need affliction. 1 Pet 1:6. He appoints it as a diet drink, to purge and sanctify us. Isa 27:9. Therefore dispute not, but submit. 'We have had fathers of our flesh which corrected us, and we gave them reverence.' Heb 12:9. They might correct out of ill humor, but God does it for our profit. Heb 12:10. Therefore say as Eli, 'It is the Lord: let him do what seems him good'. 1 Sam 3:18. What does the child get by struggling, but more blows? What got Israel by their murmuring and rebelling, but a longer and more tedious march, till, at last, their carcass fell in the wilderness?

(4) If God be our Father, let it cause in us a childlike reverence. 'If I be a father, where is mine honor?' Mal 1:6. It is part of the honor we give to God to reverence and adore him; if we have not always a childlike confidence, let us always preserve a childlike reverence. How ready are we to run into extremes, either to despond or to grow wanton! Because God is a Father, do not think you may take liberty to sin, if you do, he may act as if he were no Father, and throw hell into your conscience. When David

presumed upon God's paternal affection, and began to wax wanton under mercy, God made him pay dear for it by withdrawing the sense of his love; and, though he had the heart of a Father, yet he had the look of an enemy. David prayed, 'Make me to hear joy and gladness.' Psa 51:8. He lay several months in desertion, and it is thought never recovered his full joy to the day of his death. O keep alive holy fear! With childlike confidence, preserve an humble reverence. The Lord is a Father, therefore love to serve him, he is the mighty God, therefore fear to offend him.

(5) If God be our Father, let us walk obediently. 'As obedient children.' I Pet 1:14. When God bids you be humble and self-denying, deny yourselves; part with your bosom sin. Be sober in your attire, savory in your speech, grave in your deportment; obey your Father's voice; open to him as the flower to the sun. If you expect your Father's blessing, obey him in whatever he commands, both in first and second table duties. When a musician would make sweet music, he touches upon every string of the lute. The ten commandments are like a ten-stringed instrument, and we must touch every string, obey every commandment, or we cannot make sweet melody in religion. Obey your heavenly Father, though he commands things contrary to flesh and blood; when he commands to mortify sin, the sin which has been most dear: pluck out a right eye, that you may see better to go to heaven; when he commands you to suffer for sin. Acts 21:13. Every good Christian has a spirit of martyrdom in him, and is ready to suffer for the truth rather than the truth should suffer. Luther said he had rather be a martyr than a monarch. Peter was crucified with his head downwards, as Eusebius relates. Ignatius called his chains his spiritual pearls, and wore his fetters as a bracelet of diamonds. We act as God's children, when we obey his voice, and count not our lives dear, so that we may show our love to him. 'They loved not their lives unto the death.' Rev 12:11.

(6) If God be our Father, let us show by our cheerful looks that we are the children of such a Father. Too much drooping and despondency disparages the relation in which we stand to him. What though we meet with hard usage in the world! We are now in a strange land, far from home, it will be shortly better with us when we are in our own country, and our Father has us in his arms. Does not the heir rejoice in hope? Shall the sons of a king walk dejected?

'Why art thou, being the king's son, lean?' 2 Samuel 13:4. Is God an unkind Father? Are his commands grievous? Has he no land to give his heirs? Why, then, do his children walk so sad? Never had children such privileges as they who are of the seed-royal of heaven, and have God for their Father. They should rejoice who are within a few hours of being crowned with glory.

(7) If God be our Father, let us honor him by walking very homily. 'Be ye holy; for I am holy.' I Pet 1:16. A young prince, having asked a philosopher how he should behave himself, the philosopher said, 'Remember thou art a king's son; do nothing but what becomes the son of a king.' So let us remember we are the adopted sons and daughters of the high God, and do nothing unworthy of such a relation. A debauched child is the disgrace of his father. 'Is this thy son's coat?' said they to Jacob, when they brought it home dipped in blood. So, when we see a person defiled with malice, passion, drunkenness, we may say, Is this the coat of God's adopted son? Does he look like an heir of glory? It is blaspheming the name of God to call him Father, and yet live in sin. Such as profess God to be their Father and live unholily, slander and defraud; they are as bad to God as the heathen. 'Are ye not as children of the Ethiopians to me, O children of Israel? saith the Lord.' Amos 9:7. When Israel grew wicked, they were no better to God than Ethiopians, who were uncircumcised, a base and ill-bred people. Loose, scandalous livers under the gospel are no better in God's esteem than Pagans; nay, they shall have a hotter place in hell. Oh! let all who profess God to be their Father, honor him by their unspotted lives. Scipio abhorred the embraces of a harlot, because he was the general of an army. Abstain from all sin, because you are born of God, and have God for your Father. 'Abstain from all appearance of evil.' 1 Thess 5:22. It was a saying of Augustus, that 'an emperor should not only be free from crimes, but from the suspicion of them.' By a holy life you should bring glory to your heavenly Father, and cause others to become his children. The fragrance of virtue is seductive. Causinus, in his hieroglyphics, speaks of a dove, whose wings being perfumed with sweet ointments, drew the other doves after her; so the holy lives of God's children are a sweet perfume to draw others to religion, and make them to be of the family of God. Justin Martyr says, that

which converted him to Christianity was beholding the blameless lives of the Christians.

(8) If God be our Father, let us love all that are his children. 'How pleasant it is for brethren to dwell together in unity!' Psa 133:1. It is compared to ointment for its sweet fragrance. 'Love the brotherhood.' 1 Peter 2:17. The motion of the soul is the same towards the image and the reality. The saints are the walking pictures of God. If God be our Father, we shall love to see his picture of holiness in believers; shall pity them for their infirmities, but love them for their graces; we shall prize their company above others. Psa 119:63. It may justly be suspected that God is not Father of those who love not his children. Though they retain the communion of saints in their creed, they banish the communion of saints out of their company.

(9) If God be our Father, let us show heavenly-mindedness. They who are born of God, set their affections on things that are above. Col 3:2. O ye children of the high God! do not disgrace your high birth by sordid covetousness. What, a son of God, and a slave to the world! What, sprung from heaven, and buried in the earth! For a Christian, who pretends to derive his pedigree from heaven, wholly to mind earthly things is to debase himself; as if a king should leave his throne to follow the slough. 'Do you seek great things for thyself?' Jer 45:5. As if the Lord had said, 'What thou Barak, thou who art born of God, akin to angels, and by thy office a Levite dost thou debase thyself, and spot the silver wings of thy grace by beliming them with earth! Seekest thou great things? Seek them not.' The earth chokes the fire; so earthliness chokes the fire of good affections.

(10) If God be our Father, let us own him as such in the worst times, stand up in his cause, and defend his truths. Athanasius owned God when most of the world turned Asians. If suffering come, do not deny God. He is a bad son who denies his father. Such as are ashamed to own God in times of danger, he will be ashamed to own for his children. 'Whosoever therefore shall be ashamed of me and of my words in this adulterous generation, of him also shall the Son of man be ashamed, when he comes in the glory of his Father, with the holy angels.' Mark 8:38.

II. The second part of the preface is, 'Which art in heaven.' God is said to be in heaven, not because he is so included there as if he were nowhere else; for 'the heaven of heavens cannot contain you.' 1 Kings 8:27. But the meaning is, that he is chiefly resident in what the apostle calls 'the third heaven,' where he reveals his glory most to saints and angels. 2 Cor 12:2.

What may we learn from God being in heaven?

(1) That we are to raise our minds in prayer above the earth. God is nowhere to be spoken with but in heaven. He never denied that soul its suit that went as far as heaven to ask it.

(2) We learn his sovereign power. "By this word we learn that all things are under his rule". Calvin. 'Our God is in the heavens: he has done whatsoever he has pleased.' Psa 115:3. In heaven he governs the universe, and orders all occurrences here below for the good of his children. When the saints are in straits and dangers, and see no way of relief, he sends from heaven and helps them. 'He shall send from heaven, and save me.' Psa 57:3.

(3) We learn his glory and majesty. He is in heaven; therefore he is covered with light. Psa 104:2. He is 'clothed with honor.' Psa 104:1: He is far above all worldly princes, as heaven is above earth.

(4) We learn his omniscience. All things are naked and unmasked to his eye. Heb 4:13. Men plot and contrive against the church; but God is in heaven, and they do nothing but what he sees. If a man were on the top of a tower or theatre, he might see all the people below; God in heaven, as on a high tower or theatre, sees all the transactions of men. The wicked make wounds in the backs of the righteous, and then pour in vinegar; but God writes down their cruelty. 'I have surely seen the affliction of my people.' Exod 3:7. God can thunder out of heaven upon his enemies. 'The Lord thundered in the heavens; yea, he sent out his arrows, and scattered them; and he shot out lightnings, and discomfited them.' Psa 18:13,14.

(5) We learn comfort for the children of God. When they pray to their Father, the way to heaven cannot be blocked up. One may have a father living in foreign parts, but the way, both by sea and land, may be so blocked up, that there is no coming to him; but

thou, saint of God, when you pray to your Father, he is in heaven; and though you are ever so confined, you may have access to him. A prison cannot keep you from your God; the way to heaven can never be blocked up.

III. I shall next speak of the pronoun 'our.' There is an appropriation of the appellation, 'Father.' 'Our Father.' Christ, by the word 'our,' would teach us thus much: that in all our prayers to God, we should exercise faith. Father denotes reverence: Our Father, denotes faith. In all our prayers to God we should exercise faith. Faith baptizes prayer, and gives it a name; it is called 'the prayer of faith.' James 5:15. Without faith, it is speaking, not praying. Faith is the breath of prayer; prayer is dead unless faith breathe in it. Faith is a necessary requisite in prayer. The oil of the sanctuary was made up of several sweet spices, pure myrrh, cassia, cinnamon. Exod 30:23, 24. Faith is the chief spice or ingredient in prayer, which makes it go up to the Lord as sweet incense. 'Let him ask in faith.' James 1:6. 'Whatsoever ye shall ask in prayer, believing, ye shall receive.' Matt 21:22. 'Lord,' said Cruciger, 'I pray, though with a weak faith, yet with faith.' Prayer is the gun we shoot with, fervency is the fire that discharges it, and faith is the bullet which pierces the throne of grace. Prayer is the key of heaven, faith is the hand that turns it. Pray in faith, 'Our Father.' Faith must take prayer by the hand, or there is no coming near to God. Prayer without faith is unsuccessful. If a poor handicraftsman, who lives by his labor, has spoiled his tools so that he cannot work, how shall he subsist? Prayer is the tool we work with, which procures all good for us; but unbelief spoils and blunts our prayers, and then we get no blessing from God. A faithless prayer is fruitless. As Joseph said, 'Ye shall not see my face, except your brother be with you' (Gen 43:3); so prayer cannot see God's face unless it bring its brother faith with it. What is said of Israel, 'They could not enter in because of unbelief,' is as true of prayer; it cannot enter into heaven because of unbelief. Heb 3:19. Prayer often suffers shipwreck because it dashes upon the rock of unbelief. O mingle faith with prayer! We must say, 'Our Father.'

What does praying in faith imply?

Praying in faith implies having faith, and the act implies the habit. To walk implies a principle of life; so to pray in faith implies a habit of grace. None can pray in faith but believers.

What is it to pray in faith?

(1) It is to pray for that which God has promised. Where there is no promise, we cannot pray in faith.

(2) It is to pray in Christ's meritorious name. 'Whatsoever ye shall ask in my name, that will I do.' John 14:13. To pray in Christ's name, is to pray with confidence in Christ's merit. When we present Christ to God in prayer; when we carry the Lamb slain in our arms; when we say, 'Lord, we are sinners, but here is our surety; for Christ's sake be propitious,' we come to God in Christ's name; and this is to pray in faith.

(3) It is to fix our faith in prayer on God's faithfulness, believing that he hears and will help. This is taking hold of God. Isa 64:7. By prayer we draw near to God, by faith we take hold of him. 'They cried unto the Lord;' and this was the crying of faith. 2 Chron 13:14. They 'prevailed, because they relied upon the Lord God of their fathers;' ver. 18. Making supplication to God, and staying the soul on God, is praying in faith. To pray, and not rely on God to grant our petitions, says Pelican; 'it is to abuse and put a scorn on God.' By praying we seem to honor God; by not believing we affront him. In prayer we say, 'Almighty, merciful Father;' by not believing, we blot out all his titles again.

How may we know that we truly pray in faith?

(1) When faith in prayer is humble. A presumptuous person hopes to be heard for some inherent worthiness in himself; he is so qualified, and has done God good service, therefore he is confident God will hear him. See an instance in Luke 18:11, 12: 'The Pharisee stood and prayed thus, God, I thank you, that I am not as other men are, extortioners, unjust. I fast twice in the week; I give tithes of all that I possess.' This was a presumptuous prayer; but a sincere heart evinces humility in prayer as well as faith. 'The publican, standing afar off, would not lift up so much as his eyes unto heaven, but smote upon his breast, saying, God be merciful to me a sinner.' 'God be merciful,' there was faith; 'to me a sinner,' there was humility and a sense of unworthiness. Luke 18:13.

(2) We may know we pray in faith, when, though we have not the thing we pray for, we believe God will grant it, and are willing to stay his leisure. A Christian having a command to pray, and a promise, is resolved to follow God with prayer, and not give over; as Peter knocked, and when the door was not opened, continued knocking until at last it was opened. Acts 12:16. So when a Christian prays, and prays, and has no answer, he continues to knock at heaven's door, knowing an answer will come. 'Thou wilt answer me.' Psa 86:7. Here is one that prays in faith. Christ says, 'Pray, and faint not.' Luke 18:1. A believer, at Christ's word, lets down the net of prayer, and though he catch nothing, he will cast the net again, believing that mercy will come. Patience in prayer is nothing but faith spun out.

Use 1. For reproof of those who pray in formality, not in faith; they who question whether God hears or will grant. 'Ye ask, and receive not, because ye ask amiss.' James 4:3. He does not say, ye ask that which is unlawful; but ye ask amiss, and therefore ye receive not. Unbelief clips the wings of prayer, that it will not fly to the throne of grace; the rubbish of unbelief stops the current of prayer.

Use 2. For exhortation. Let us set faith to work in prayer. The husband man sows in hope; prayer is the seed we sow, and when the hand of faith scatters this seed, it brings forth a fruitful crop of blessing. Prayer is the ship we send out to heaven; when faith makes an adventure in this ship, it brings home large returns of mercy. O pray in faith; say, 'Our Father.' That we may exercise faith in prayer, consider:

(1) God's readiness to hear prayer. Did God forbid all addresses to him, it would put a damp upon the trade of prayer; but his ear is open to prayer. One of the names by which he is known, is, 'O you who hear prayer.' Psa 65:2. The aediles among the Romans had their doors always open, that all who had petitions might have free access to them. God is both ready to hear and grant prayer, which should encourage faith in prayer. Some may say, they have prayed, but have had no answer. God may hear prayer, though he does not immediately answer it. We write a letter to a friend, he may have received it, though we have yet had no answer to it. Perhaps you pray for the light of God's face; he may lend you an

ear, though he does not show you his face. God may give an answer to prayer, when we do not perceive it. His giving a heart to pray, and inflaming the affections in prayer, is an answer to prayer. 'In the day when I cried you answered me, and strengthened me with strength in my soul.' Psa 138:3. David's inward strength was an answer to prayer. Therefore let God's readiness to hear prayer encourage faith in prayer.

(2) That we may exercise faith in prayer, let us consider that we do not pray alone. Christ prays our prayers over again. His prayer is the ground why our prayer is heard. He takes the dross out of our prayer, and presents nothing to his Father but pure gold. He mingles his sweet odors with the prayers of the saints. Rev 5:8. Think of the dignity of his person, he is God; and the sweetness of his relation, he is a Son. Oh, what encouragement is here, to pray in faith! Our prayers are put into the hand of a Mediator. Christ's prayer is mighty and powerful.

(3) We pray to God for nothing but what is pleasing to him, and he has a mind to grant. If a son asks nothing but what his father is willing to bestow, it will make him go to him with confidence. When we pray to God for holy hearts, there is nothing more pleasing to him. 'This is the will of God, even your sanctification.' 1 Thess 4:3. We pray that God would give us hearts to love him, and there is nothing he more desires than our love. How should it make us pray in faith, when we pray for nothing but what is acceptable to God, and which he delights to bestow!

(4) To encourage faith in prayer, let us consider the many sweet promises that God has made to prayer. The cork keeps the net from sinking, so the promises are the cork to keep faith from sinking in prayer. God has bound himself to us by his promises. The Bible is bespangled with promises made to prayer. 'He will be very gracious unto you at the voice of thy cry.' Isa 30:19. 'The Lord is rich unto all that call upon him.' Rom 10:12. 'Ye shall find me, when ye shall search for me with all your heart.' Jer 29:13. 'He will fulfill the desire of them that fear him.' Psa 145:19. The Syrians tied their god Hercules with a golden chain that he should not remove; God has tied himself fast to us by his promises. How should these animate and spirit faith in prayer! Faith gets strength in prayer by sucking from the breast of a promise.

(5) That we may exercise faith in prayer, consider that Jesus Christ has purchased that which we pray for. We may think the things we ask for in prayer too great for us to obtain, but they are not too great for Christ to purchase. We pray for pardon. Christ has purchased it with his blood. We pray for the Spirit to animate and inspire us. The sending down of the Holy Ghost into our hearts, is the fruit of Christ's death. It should put life into our prayers, and make us pray in faith, to reflect that the things we ask, though more than we deserve, yet they are not more than Christ has purchased for us.

(6) To pray in faith, consider there is such bountifulness in God, that he often exceeds the prayers of his people. He gives them more than they ask! Hannah asked a son, and God not only gave her a son, but a prophet. Solomon asked wisdom, and God gave him not only wisdom, but riches and honor besides. Jacob prayed that God would give him food and raiment, and he increased his pilgrim's staff into two bands. Gen 32:10. God is often better to us than our prayers, as when Gehazi asked but one talent, Naaman would needs force two upon him. 2 Kings 5:23. We ask one talent, and God gives two. The woman of Canaan asked but a crumb, namely, to have the life of her child; and Christ gave her more, he sent her home with the life of her soul.

(7) The great success which the prayer of faith has found. Like Jonathan's bow, it has not returned empty. The little word 'father' spoken in the heart, says Luther. The little word father, pronounced in faith, has overcome God. 'Deliver me, I pray you.' Gen 32:11. This was mixed with faith in the promise. 'You said, I will surely do you good;' ver. 12. This prayer had power with God, and prevailed. Hos 12:4. The prayer of faith has opened prison doors, stopped the chariot of the sun, locked and unlocked heaven. James 5:17. The prayer of faith has strangled the plots of enemies in their birth, and has routed their forces. Moses' prayer against Amalek did more than Joshua's sword; and should not this hearten and corroborate faith in prayer?

(8) If all this will not prevail, consider how heartless and comfortless it is not to pray in faith! The heart misgives secretly that God does not hear, nor will he grant. Faithless praying must needs be comfortless; for there is no promise made to unbelieving prayer.

It is sad sailing where there is no anchoring, and sad praying where there is no promise to anchor upon. James 1:7. The disciples toiled all night and caught nothing; so the unbeliever toils in prayer and catches nothing; he receives not any spiritual blessings, pardon of sin, or grace. As for the temporal mercies which the unbeliever has, he cannot look upon them as the fruit of prayer, but as the overflowing of God's bounty. Oh, therefore labor to exert and put forth faith in prayer!

But so much sin cleaves to my prayer, that I fear it is not the prayer of faith, and God will not hear it.

If you mourn for this, it hinders nothing but that your prayer may be in faith, and God may hear it. Weakness shall not make void the saint's prayers. 'I said in my haste, I am cut off.' Psa 31:22. There was much unbelief in that prayer: 'I said in my haste:' in the Hebrew, 'in my trembling,' David's faith trembled and fainted, yet God heard his prayer. The saints' passions do not hinder their prayers. James 5:17. Therefore be not discouraged, for though sin will cleave to thy holy offering, yea, these two things may comfort, that thou mayest pray with faith, though with weakness; and God sees the sincerity, and will pass by the infirmity.

How shall we pray in faith?

Implore the Spirit of God. We cannot say, 'Our Father,' but by the Holy Ghost. God's Spirit helps us, not only to pray with sighs and groans, but with faith. The Spirit carries us to God, not only as to a Creator, but a Father. 'God has sent forth the Spirit of his Son into your hearts, crying, Abba, Father.' Gal 4:6. 'Crying:' there the Spirit causes us to pray with fervency. 'Abba, Father:' there the Spirit helps us to pray with faith. The Spirit helps faith to turn the key of prayer, and then it unlocks heaven.

Chapter 16 - Alexander Whyte on the Lord's Prayer

(Alexander Whyte, 1836 – 1921)

Taken from 'An Exposition on The Shorter Catechism'

Q. 99. What rule has God given for our direction in prayer?

A. The whole word of God is of use to direct us in prayer; but the special rule of direction is that form of prayer which Christ taught his disciples, commonly called The Lord's Prayer.

The whole word of God - It is a most interesting and instructive study to trace how one psalm or prayer is incorporated with another, and how the matter and language of prayer thus grow as Scripture and the life of the Church grow. Our Lord Himself, in this lesson He taught His disciples, only gathers into a short and memorable form certain petitions that are scattered up and down the whole of the Old Testament. The whole word of God is of use to direct us in prayer, and the better that any man knows the word of God, the less will he need to depend on any special rule of direction. "Let the word of Christ dwell in you richly."

the special rule of direction – "How is the Lord's Prayer to be used? The Lord's Prayer is not only for direction, as a pattern, according to which we are to make other prayers; but may also be used as a prayer, so that it be done with understanding, faith, reverence, and other graces necessary to the right performance of the duty of prayer." The student of Church history will trace in this statement an echo of the Puritan contendings against the abuse of liturgical forms in public worship.

which Christ taught his disciples -"One of His disciples said unto Him, Lord, teach us to pray, as John also taught his disciples. And He said unto them, When ye pray, say, Our Father," etc. The disciples of John the Baptist and the disciples of Christ waited on their respective masters for instructions how to pray. It was in vain that the duty of repentance was preached to the one, and of faith to the other; they knew the truth, but they could not use it. So different a thing is it to be instructed in religion, and to have so mastered it in practice that it is altogether our own' (Newman, i. 257).

Commonly called The Lord's Prayer. Commonly, but somewhat improperly. This is properly the disciples' prayer. The prayer recorded in the seventeenth of John is with more propriety called THE LORD'S PRAYER. (See Robert Traill on The Lord's Prayer•, p. 1.)

Q. 100. What doth the preface of the Lord's prayer teach us?

A. The preface of the Lord's prayer (which is, Our Father which art in heaven b) teaches us to draw near to God with all holy reverence and confidence, as children to a father, able and ready to help us; and that we should pray with and for others.

Our Father which art in heaven - "God lovingly invites us, in this little preface, truly to believe in Him, that He is our true Father, and that we are truly His children, so that full of confidence we may more boldly call upon His name, even as we see children with a kind of confidence ask anything of their parents" (Luther's Catechism). "God has not taken the name of a Father, nor Christ of an Elder Brother for nought, but because these names import more nearly than any other the nature of the affection which they bear us." (Edward Irving On the Lord's Prayer).

"Our Father which art in heaven" is the Christian child's first prayer, just as "The Lord's my Shepherd" is his first psalm. From the very beginning of the Christian Church this prayer has been in constant use. It has been offered daily among the disciples of Jesus Christ ever since that fruitful day when one of the twelve came to Him, saying, "Lord, teach me to pray." But though it was first taught in the childhood of the Church, and is still taught to the children of every Christian home, it is not for all that to be taken as only a child's prayer. It is true the shortest memory may retain it, and the busiest life may utter it; the weakest understanding may sufficiently grasp it, and the most childlike faith may feel at home in it; but while all that is true, yet men of God who have their senses best exercised among divine things will feel that this prayer grows with their growing experience, and gradually gathers unto itself the whole fulness of the Word of God and the need of man.

God is named Father in several senses in the Bible. He is sometimes called Father simply as the Creator of all things. Again, He is called the Father of mankind, because they were made in His image, and made to be His spiritual children, But in a higher sense still He is called the Father of regenerate sons, because by their new birth, union to Christ, and adoption into His family, they have become in more than a metaphorical sense the sons of God and He their Father. "They have been received into the number, and have a right to all the privileges, of the sons of God. " (See Answer 14.) But all this leaves unmentioned the real and true sense, the eternal and divine sense, in which God is the Father of His Only Begotten Son. (For this see Answers 6 and 21.)

At every step of our exposition we shall have occasion to remark on the mistake of calling this series of petitions the Lord's Prayer. The very preface compels us to distinguish between the Paternity of the Father toward Jesus Christ and toward us. And all our Lord's utterances in this direction observe this distinction. He never once says, "Our Father," including Himself with us as a son. He says, "Father," "Holy Father," "Righteous Father," and "My Father" but never Our Father. Once He says, "My Father and your Father," but He distinguishes in so saying. "God is the Father of Him and of us, but not of us as of Him" (Pearson). Heaven is the dwelling-place of God; it is our Father's house. And though it is not to be limited and localized as a place in our most spiritual conceptions, yet it is right and necessary for us to think of heaven as above us. Thus we read that Jesus Himself, when He prayed, "lifted up His eyes to heaven." Heaven is not about or above the stars; it is high above us as God is high above man; and as good is above evil, and us blessedness is above condemnation and misery. There is a spiritual world as well as a material; and there is a spiritual geometry, with its various directions, as well as a material. "But as it is only half of our reliance that is founded on the goodness of God. in the next clause, which art in heaven, He gives us a lofty idea of the power of God" (Calvin).

Section 6 - Early Church Fathers

Chapter 17 – Chrysostom on the Lord's Prayer

(John Chrysostom, c. 347–407)

Taken from 'Homilies on the Gospel of St. Matthew'

"After this manner, therefore, pray ye," says He: "Our Father, which art in heaven."

See how He straightway stirred up the hearer, and reminded him of all God's bounty in the beginning. For he who calls God Father, by him both remission of sins, and taking away of punishment, and righteousness, and sanctification, and redemption, and adoption, and inheritance, and brotherhood with the Only-Begotten, and the supply of the Spirit, are acknowledged in this single title. For one cannot call God Father without having attained to all those blessings. Doubly, therefore, does He awaken their spirit, both by the dignity of Him who is called on, and by the greatness of the benefits which they have enjoyed. But when He says, "in Heaven," He speaks not this as shutting up God there, but as withdrawing him who is praying from earth, and fixing him in the high places and in the dwellings above.

He teaches, moreover, to make our prayer common in behalf of our brethren also. For He says not, "my Father, which art in Heaven," but, "our Father," offering up his supplications for the body in common, and nowhere looking to his own, but everywhere to his neighbor's good. And by this He at once takes away hatred, and quells pride, and casts out envy, and brings in the mother of all good things, even charity, and exterminates the inequality of human things, and shows how far the equality reaches between the king and the poor man, if at least in those things which are greatest and most indispensable we are all of us fellows. For what harm comes of our kindred below, when in that which is on high we are all of us knit together, and no one has anything more than another; neither the rich more than the poor, nor the master than the servant, neither the ruler than the subject, nor the king than the common soldier, nor the philosopher than the barbarian, nor the skillful than the unlearned? For to all has He given one nobility, having condescended to be called the Father of all alike.

When therefore He has reminded us of this nobility, and of the gift from above, and of our equality with our brethren, and of charity; and when He has removed us from earth, and fixed us in Heaven; let us see what He commands us to ask after this. Not but, in the first place, even that saying alone is sufficient to implant instruction in all virtue. For he who has called God Father, and a common Father, would be justly bound to show forth such a conversation, as not to appear unworthy of this nobility, and to exhibit a diligence proportionate to the gift. Yet is He not satisfied with this, but adds, also another clause, thus saying,

"Hallowed be your name."

Worthy of him who calls God Father, is the prayer to ask nothing before the glory of His Father, but to account all things secondary to the work of praising Him. For "hallowed" is glorified. For His own glory He has complete, and ever continuing the same, but He commands him who prays to seek that He may be glorified also by our life. Which very thing He had said before likewise, "Let your light so shine before men, that they may see your good works, and glorify your Father which is in heaven." Yea, and the seraphim too, giving glory, said on this wise, "Holy, holy, holy." So that "hallowed" means this, viz. "glorified." That is, "grant," says he, "that we may live so purely, that through us all may glorify You." Which thing again appertains unto perfect self-control, to present to all a life so irreprehensible, that every one of the beholders may offer to the Lord the praise due to Him for this.

"Thy kingdom come."

And this again is the language of a right-minded child, not to be riveted to things that are seen, neither to account things present some great matter; but to hasten unto our Father, and to long for the things to come. And this springs out of a good conscience, and a soul set free from things that are on earth. This, for instance, Paul himself was longing after every day: wherefore he also said, that "even we ourselves, who have the first-fruits of the Spirit, groan, waiting for an adoption, the redemption of our body."

For he who has this fondness can neither be puffed up by the good things of this life, nor abashed by its sorrows; but as though dwelling in the very heavens, is freed from each sort of irregularity.

"Thy will be done in earth, as it is in Heaven."

Behold a most excellent train of thought, in that He bade us indeed long for the things to come, and hasten towards that sojourn; and, till that may be, even while we abide here, so long to be earnest in showing forth the same conversation as those above. For you must long, says He, for heaven, and the things in heaven; however, even before heaven, He has bidden us make the earth a heaven and do and say all things, even while we are continuing in it, as having our conversation there; insomuch that these too should be objects of our prayer to the Lord. For there is nothing to hinder our reaching the perfection of the powers above, because we inhabit the earth; but it is possible even while abiding here, to do all, as though already placed on high. What He says therefore is this: "As there all things are done without hindrance, and the angels are not partly obedient and partly disobedient, but in all things yield and obey (for He says, 'Mighty in strength, performing His word'); so grant that we men may not do your will by halves, but perform all things as You desire."

Do you see how He has taught us also to be modest, by making it clear that virtue is not of our endeavors only, but also of the grace from above? And again, He has enjoined each one of us, who pray, to take upon himself the care of the whole world. For He did not at all say, "Thy will be done" in me, or in us, but everywhere on the earth; so that error may be destroyed, and truth implanted, and all wickedness cast out, and virtue return, and no difference in this respect be henceforth between heaven and earth. "For if this come to pass," says He, "there will be no difference between things below and above, separated as they are in nature; the earth exhibiting to us another set of angels."

"Give us this day our daily bread."

What is "daily bread"? That for one day.

For because He had said thus, "Thy will be done in earth as it is in heaven," but was discoursing to men encompassed with flesh, and subject to the necessities of nature, and incapable of the same impassibility with the angels:--while He enjoins the commands to be practiced by us also, even as they perform them; He condescends likewise, in what follows, to the infirmity of our nature. Thus, "perfection of conduct," says He, "I require as great, not however freedom from passions; no, for the tyranny of nature permits it not: for it requires necessary food." But mark, I pray you, how even in things that are bodily, that which is spiritual abounds. For it is neither for riches, nor for delicate living, nor for costly raiment, nor for any other such thing, but for bread only, that He has commanded us to make our prayer. And for "daily bread," so as not to "take thought for the morrow." Because of this He added, "daily bread," that is, bread for one day.

And not even with this expression is He satisfied, but adds another too afterwards, saying, "Give us this day;" so that we may not, beyond this, wear ourselves out with the care of the following day. For that day, the intervals before which you know not whether you shall see, wherefore do you submit to its cares?

This, as He proceeded, he enjoined also more fully, saying, "Take no thought for the morrow." He would have us be on every hand unencumbered and winged for flight, yielding just so much to nature as the compulsion of necessity requires of us.

Then forasmuch as it comes to pass that we sin even after the washing of regeneration, He, showing His love to man to be great even in this case, commands us for the remission of our sins to come unto God who loves man, and thus to say,

"Forgive us our debts, as we also forgive our debtors."

Do you see surpassing mercy? After taking away so great evils, and after the unspeakable greatness of His gift, if men sin again, He counts them such as may be forgiven. For that this prayer belongs to believers, is taught us both by the laws of the church, and by the beginning of the prayer. For the uninitiated could not call God Father. If then the prayer belongs to believers, and they pray, entreating that sins may be forgiven them, it is clear that not even after the layer is the profit of repentance taken away. Since, had He not meant to signify this, He would not have made a law that we should so pray. Now He who both brings sins to remembrance, and bids us ask forgiveness, and teaches how we may obtain remission and so makes the way easy; it is perfectly clear that He introduced this rule of supplication, as knowing, and signifying, that it is possible even after the font to wash ourselves from our offenses; by reminding us of our sins, persuading us to be modest; by the command to forgive others, setting us free from all revengeful passion; while by promising in return for this to pardon us also, He holds out good hopes, and instructs us to have high views concerning the unspeakable mercy of God toward man.

But what we should most observe is this, that whereas in each of the clauses He had made mention of the whole of virtue, and in this way had included also the forgetfulness of injuries (for so, that "His name be hallowed," is the exactness of a perfect conversation; and that "His will be done," declares the same thing again: and to be able to call God "Father," is the profession of a blameless life; in all which things had been comprehended also the duty of remitting our anger against them that have transgressed): still He was not satisfied with these, but meaning to signify how earnest He is in the matter, He sets it down also in particular, and after the prayer, He makes mention of no other commandment than this, saying thus:

"For if you forgive men their trespasses, your heavenly Father also will forgive you."

So that the beginning is of us, and we ourselves have control over the judgment that is to be passed upon us. For in order that no one, even of the senseless, might have any complaint to make, either great or small, when brought to judgment; on you, who art to give account, He causes the sentence to depend; and "in what way soever you have judged for thyself, in the same," says He, "do I also judge you." And if you forgive your fellow servant, you shall obtain the same favor from me; though indeed the one be not equal to the other. For you forgives in your need, but God, having need of none: you, your fellow slave; God, His slave: you liable to unnumbered charges; God, being without sin. But yet even thus does He show forth His lovingkindness towards man.

Since He might indeed, even without this, forgive you all your offenses; but He wills you hereby also to receive a benefit; affording you on all sides innumerable occasions of gentleness and love to man, casting out what is brutish in you, and quenching wrath, and in all ways cementing you to him who is your own member.

For what can you have to say? that you have wrongfully endured some ill of your neighbor? (For these only are trespasses, since if it be done with justice, the act is not a trespass.) But you too are drawing near to receive forgiveness for such things, and for much greater. And even before the forgiveness, you have received no small gift, in being taught to have a human soul, and in being trained to all gentleness. And with this a great reward shall also be laid up for you elsewhere, even to be called to account for none of your offenses.

What sort of punishment then do we not deserve, when after having received the privilege, we betray our salvation? And how shall we claim to be heard in the rest of our matters, if we will not, in those which depend on us, spare our own selves?

"And lead us not into temptation; but deliver us from the evil one: for Your is the kingdom, and the power, and the glory, forever. Amen."

Here He teaches us plainly our own vileness, and quells our pride, instructing us to deprecate all conflicts, instead of rushing upon them. For so both our victory will be more glorious, and the devil's overthrow more to be derided. I mean, that as when we are dragged forth, we must stand nobly; so when we are not summoned, we should be quiet, and wait for the time of conflict; that we may show both freedom from vainglory, and nobleness of spirit.

And He here calls the devil "the wicked one," commanding us to wage against him a war that knows no truce, and implying that he is not such by nature. For wickedness is not of those things that are from nature, but of them that are added by our own choice. And he is so called pre-eminently, by reason of the excess of his wickedness, and because he, in no respect injured by us, wages against us implacable war. Wherefore neither said He, "deliver us from the wicked ones," but, "from the wicked one;" instructing us in no case to entertain displeasure against our neighbors, for what wrongs soever we may suffer at their hands, but to transfer our enmity from these to him, as being himself the cause of all our wrongs.

Having then made us anxious as before conflict, by putting us in mind of the enemy, and having cut away from us all our remissness; He again encourages and raises our spirits, by bringing to our remembrance the King under whom we are arrayed, and signifying Him to be more powerful than all. "For Thine," says He, "is the kingdom, and the power, and the glory."

Does it not then follow, that if His be the kingdom, we should fear no one, since there can be none to withstand, and divide the empire with him. For when He says, "Yours is the kingdom," He sets before us even him who is warring against us, brought into subjection, though he seem to oppose, [with] God for a while permitting it. For in truth he too is among God's servants, though of the degraded class, and those guilty of offense; and he would not dare set upon any of his fellow servants, had he not first received license from above. And why say I, "his fellow servants?" Not even against swine did he venture any outrage, until He Himself allowed him; nor against flocks, nor herds, until he had received permission from above.

"And the power," says He. Therefore, manifold as your weakness may be, you may of right be confident, having such a one to reign over you, who is able fully to accomplish all, and that with ease, even by you.

"And the glory, forever. Amen." Thus He not only frees you from the dangers that are approaching you, but can make you also glorious and illustrious. For as His power is great, so also is His glory unspeakable, and they are all boundless, and no end of them. Do you see how He has by every means anointed His Champion and has framed Him to be full of confidence?

Chapter 18 - Augustine on the Lord's Prayer

(Augustine of Hippo, 354 - 430)

Taken from 'Homilies on the Gospels'

Ye then who have found a Father in heaven, be loath to cleave to the things of earth. For ye are about to say, **"Our Father, which art in heaven."** You have begun to belong to a great family. Under this Father the lord and the slave are brethren; under this Father the general and the common soldier are brethren; under this Father the rich man and the poor are brethren. All Christian believers have divers fathers in earth, some noble, some obscure; but they all call upon one Father which is in heaven. If our Father be there, there is the inheritance prepared for us. But He is such a Father, that we can possess with Him what He gives. For He gives an inheritance; but He doth not leave it to us by dying. For He doth not depart Himself, but He abides ever, that we may come to Him. Seeing then we have heard of Whom we are to ask, let us know also what to ask for, lest haply we offend such a Father by asking amiss.

3. What then has the Lord Jesus Christ taught us to ask of the Father which is in heaven? **"Hallowed be Thy Name."** What kind of blessing is this that we ask of God, that His Name may be hallowed? The Name of God is always Holy; why then do we pray that it may be hallowed, except that we may be hallowed by it? We pray then that that which is Holy always, may be hallowed in us. The Name of God is hallowed in you when ye are baptized. Why will ye offer this prayer after ye have been baptized, but that that which ye shall then receive may abide ever in you?

4. Another petition follows, **"Thy kingdom come."** God's kingdom will come, whether we ask it or not. Why then do we ask it, but that that which will come to all saints may also come to us; that God may count us also in the number of His saints, to whom His kingdom is to come?

5. We say in the third petition, **"Thy will be done as in heaven, so in earth."** What is this? That as the Angels serve Thee

in heaven, so we may serve Thee in earth. For His holy Angels obey Him; they do not offend Him; they do His commands through the love of Him. This we pray for then, that we too may do the commands of God in love. Again, these words are understood in another way, "Thy will be done as in heaven, so in earth." Heaven in us is the soul, earth in us is the body. What then is, "Thy will be done as in heaven, so in earth"? As we hear Thy precepts, so may our flesh consent unto us; lest, while flesh and spirit strive together, we be not able to fulfill the commands of God.

6. **"Give us this day our daily bread,"** comes next in the Prayer. Whether we ask here of the Father support necessary for the body, by "bread" signifying whatever is needful for us; or whether we understand that daily Bread, which ye are soon to receive from the Altar; well it is that we pray that He would give it us. For what is it we pray for, but that we may commit no evil, for which we should be separated from that holy Bread. And the word of God which is preached daily is daily bread. For because it is not bread for the body, it is not on that account not bread for the soul. But when this life shall have passed away, we shall neither seek that bread which hunger seeks; nor shall we have to receive the Sacrament of the Altar, because we shall be there with Christ, whose Body we do now receive; nor will those words which we are now speaking, need to be said to you, nor the sacred volume to be read, when we shall see Him who is Himself the Word of God, by whom all things were made, by whom the Angels are fed, by whom the Angels are enlightened, by whom the Angels become wise; not requiring words of circuitous discourse; but drinking in the Only Word, filled with whom they burst forth and never fail in praise. For, "Blessed," saith the Psalm, "are they who dwell in Thy house; they will be always praising Thee."

7. Therefore in this present life, do we ask what comes next, **"Forgive us our debts, as we also forgive our debtors."** In Baptism, all debts, that is, all sins, are entirely forgiven us. But because no one can live without sin here below, and if without any great crime which entails separation from the Altar, yet altogether without sins can no one live on this earth, and we can only receive the one Baptism once for all; in this Prayer we hear how we may day by day be washed, that our sins may day by day be forgiven us; but only if we do what follows, "As we also forgive our debtors."

Accordingly, my Brethren, I advise you, who are in the grace of God my sons, yet my Brethren under that heavenly Father; I advise you, whenever anyone offends and sins against you, and comes, and confesses, and asks your pardon, that ye do pardon him, and immediately from the heart forgive him; lest ye keep off from your own selves that pardon, which comes from God. For if ye forgive not, neither will He forgive you. Therefore it is in this life that we make this petition, for that it is in this life that sins can be forgiven, where they can be done. But in the life to come they are not forgiven, because they are not done.

8. Next after this we pray, saying, **"Lead us not into temptation, but deliver us from evil."** This also, that we be not led into temptation, it is necessary for us to ask in this life, because in this life there are temptations; and that "we may be delivered from evil," because there is evil here. And thus of all these seven petitions, three have respect to the life eternal, and four to the present life. "Hallowed be Thy name." This will be forever. "Thy kingdom come." This kingdom will be forever. "Thy will be done as in heaven, so in earth." This will be forever. "Give us this day our daily bread." This will not be forever. "Forgive us our debts." This will not be forever. "Lead us not into temptation." This will not be forever. "But deliver us from evil." This will not be forever: but where there is temptation, and where there is evil, there is it necessary that we make this petition.

Chapter 19 - Cyprian on the Lord's Prayer

(Cyprian, bishop of Carthage, c. 200 - 258)

Taken from Treatise IV, On the Lord's Prayer

1. The evangelical precepts, beloved brethren, are nothing else than divine teachings,—foundations on which hope is to be built, supports to strengthen faith, nourishments for cheering the heart, rudders for guiding our way, guards for obtaining salvation,—which, while they instruct the docile minds of believers on the earth, lead them to heavenly kingdoms. God, moreover, willed many things to be said and to be heard by means of the prophets His servants; but how much greater are those which the Son speaks, which the Word of God who was in the prophets testifies with His own voice; not now bidding to prepare the way for His coming, but Himself coming and opening and showing to us the way, so that we who have before been wandering in the darkness of death, without forethought and blind, being enlightened by the light of grace, might keep the way of life, with the Lord for our ruler and guide!

2. He, among the rest of His salutary admonitions and divine precepts with which He counsels His people for their salvation, Himself also gave a form of praying—Himself advised and instructed us what we should pray for. He who made us to live, taught us also to pray, with that same benignity, [that is to say], with which He has condescended to give and confer all things else; in order that while we speak to the Father in that prayer and supplication which the Son has taught us, we may be the more easily heard. Already He had foretold that the hour was coming "when the true worshippers should worship the Father in spirit and in truth;" and He thus fulfilled what He before promised, so that we who by His sanctification have received the Spirit and truth, may also by His teaching worship truly and spiritually. For what can be a more spiritual prayer than that which was given to us by Christ, by whom also the Holy Spirit was given to us? What praying to the Father can be more truthful than that which was delivered to us by

the Son who is the Truth, out of His own mouth? So that to pray otherwise than He taught is not ignorance alone, but also sin; since He Himself has established, and said, "Ye reject the commandments of God, that ye may keep your own traditions."

3. Let us therefore, brethren beloved, pray as God our Teacher has taught us. It is a loving and friendly prayer to beseech God with His own word, to come up to His ears in the prayer of Christ. Let the Father acknowledge the words of His Son when we make our prayer, and let Him also who dwells within in our breast Himself dwell in our voice. And since we have Him as an Advocate with the Father for our sins, let us, when as sinners we petition on behalf of our sins, put forward the words of our Advocate. For since He says, that "whatsoever we shall ask of the Father in His name, He will give us," how much more effectually do we obtain what we ask in Christ's name, if we ask for it in His own prayer!

4. But let our speech and petition when we pray be under discipline, observing quietness and modesty. Let us consider that we are standing in God's sight. We must please the divine eyes both with the habit of body and with the measure of voice. For as it is characteristic of a shameless man to be noisy with his cries, so, on the other hand, it is fitting to the modest man to pray with moderated petitions. Moreover, in His teaching the Lord has bidden us to pray in secret—in hidden and remote places, in our very bed-chambers—which is best suited to faith, that we may know that God is everywhere present, and hears and sees all, and in the plenitude of His majesty penetrates even into hidden and secret places, as it is written, "I am a God at hand, and not a God afar off. If a man shall hide himself in secret places, shall I not then see him? Do not I fill heaven and earth?" And again: "The eyes of the Lord are in every place, beholding the evil and the good." And when we meet together with the brethren in one place, and celebrate divine sacrifices with God's priest, we ought to be mindful of modesty and discipline—not to throw abroad our prayers indiscriminately, with un-subdued voices, nor to cast to God with tumultuous wordiness a petition that ought to be commended to God by modesty; for God is the hearer, not of the voice, but of the heart. Nor need He be clamorously reminded, since He sees men's thoughts, as the Lord proves to us when He says, "Why think ye evil in your hearts?" And

in another place: "And all the churches shall know that I am He who searches the hearts and reins."

5. And this Hannah in the first book of Kings, who was a type of the Church, maintains and observes, in that she prayed to God not with clamorous petition, but silently and modestly, within the very recesses of her heart. She spoke with hidden prayer, but with manifest faith. She spoke not with her voice, but with her heart, because she knew that thus God hears; and she effectually obtained what she sought, because she asked it with belief. Divine Scripture asserts this, when it says, "She spoke in her heart, and her lips moved, and her voice was not heard; and God did hear her." We read also in the Psalms, "Speak in your hearts, and in your beds, and be ye pierced." The Holy Spirit, moreover, suggests these same things by Jeremiah, and teaches, saying, "But in the heart ought God to be adored by thee."

6. And let not the worshipper, beloved brethren, be ignorant in what manner the publican prayed with the Pharisee in the temple. Not with eyes lifted up boldly to heaven, nor with hands proudly raised; but beating his breast, and testifying to the sins shut up within, he implored the help of the divine mercy. And while the Pharisee was pleased with himself, this man who thus asked, the rather deserved to be sanctified, since he placed the hope of salvation not in the confidence of his innocence, because there is none who is innocent; but confessing his sinfulness he humbly prayed, and He who pardons the humble heard the petitioner. And these things the Lord records in His Gospel, saying, "Two men went up into the temple to pray; the one a Pharisee, and the other a publican. The Pharisee stood, and prayed thus with himself: God, I thank Thee that I am not as other men are, unjust, extortioners, adulterers, even as this publican. I fast twice in the week, I give tithes of all that I possess. But the publican stood afar off, and would not so much as lift up his eyes unto heaven, but smote upon his breast, saying, God, be merciful to me a sinner. I say unto you, this man went down to his house justified rather than the Pharisee: for every one that exalts himself shall be abased; and whosoever humbles himself shall be exalted."

7. These things, beloved brethren, when we have learned from the sacred reading, and have gathered in what way we ought

to approach to prayer, let us know also from the Lord's teaching what we should pray. "Thus," says He, "pray ye:—

"Our Father, which art in heaven, Hallowed be Thy name. Thy kingdom come. Thy will be done, as in heaven so in earth. Give us this day our daily bread. And forgive us our debts, as we forgive our debtors. And suffer us not to be led into temptation; but deliver us from evil. Amen."

8. Before all things, the Teacher of peace and the Master of unity would not have prayer to be made singly and individually, as for one who prays to pray for himself alone. For we say not "My Father, which art in heaven," nor "Give me this day my daily bread;" nor does each one ask that only his own debt should be forgiven him; nor does he request for himself alone that he may not be led into temptation, and delivered from evil. Our prayer is public and common; and when we pray, we pray not for one, but for the whole people, because we the whole people are one. The God of peace and the Teacher of concord, who taught unity, willed that one should thus pray for all, even as He Himself bore us all in one. This law of prayer the three children observed when they were shut up in the fiery furnace, speaking together in prayer, and being of one heart in the agreement of the spirit; and this the faith of the sacred Scripture assures us, and in telling us how such as these prayed, gives an example which we ought to follow in our prayers, in order that we may be such as they were: "Then these three," it says, "as if from one mouth sang an hymn, and blessed the Lord." They spoke as if from one mouth, although Christ had not yet taught them how to pray. And therefore, as they prayed, their speech was availing and effectual, because a peaceful, and sincere, and spiritual prayer deserved well of the Lord. Thus also we find that the apostles, with the disciples, prayed after the Lord's ascension: "They all," says the Scripture, "continued with one accord in prayer, with the women, and Mary who was the mother of Jesus, and with His brethren." They continued with one accord in prayer, declaring both by the urgency and by the agreement of their praying, that God, "who makes men to dwell of one mind in a house," only admits into the divine and eternal home those among whom prayer is unanimous.

9. But what matters of deep importance are contained in the Lord's prayer! How many and! How great, briefly collected in the words, but spiritually abundant in virtue! so that there is 'absolutely nothing passed over that is not comprehended in these our prayers and petitions, as in a compendium of heavenly doctrine. "After this manner," says He, "pray ye: Our Father, which art in heaven." The new man, born again and restored to his God by His grace, says "Father," in the first place because he has now begun to be a son. "He came," He says, "to His own, and His own received Him not. But as many as received Him, to them gave the power to become the sons of God, even to them that believe in His name." The man, therefore, who has believed in His name, and has become God's son, ought from this point to begin both to give thanks and to profess himself God's son, by declaring that God is his Father in heaven; and also to bear witness, among the very first words of his new birth, that he has renounced an earthly and carnal father, and that he has begun to know as well as to have as a father Him only who is in heaven, as it is written: "They who say unto their father and their mother, I have not known thee, and who have not acknowledged their own children these have observed Thy precepts and have kept Thy covenant. Also the Lord in His Gospel has bidden us to call "no man our father upon earth, because there is to us one Father, who is in heaven." And to the disciple who had made mention of his dead father, He replied, "Let the dead bury their dead;" for he had said that his father was dead, while the Father of believers is living.

10. Nor ought we, beloved brethren, only to observe and understand that we should call Him Father who is in heaven; but we add to it, and say our Father, that is, the Father of those who believe—of those who, being sanctified by Him, and restored by the nativity of spiritual grace, have begun to be sons of God. A word this, moreover, which rebukes and condemns the Jews, who not only unbelievingly despised Christ, who had been announced to them by the prophets, and sent first to them, but also cruelly put Him to death; and these cannot now call God their Father, since the Lord confounds and confutes them, saying, "Ye are born of your father the devil, and the lusts of your father ye will do. For he was a murderer from the beginning, and abode not in the truth, because there is no truth in him." And by Isaiah the prophet God cries in

wrath, "I have begotten and brought up children; but they have despised me. The ox knows his owner, and the ass his master's crib; but Israel hath not known me, and my people hath not understood me. Ah sinful nation, a people laden with sins, a wicked seed, corrupt children! Ye have forsaken the Lord; ye have provoked the Holy One of Israel to anger." In repudiation of these, we Christians, when we pray, say Our Father; because He has begun to be ours, and has ceased to be the Father of the Jews, who have forsaken Him. Nor can a sinful people be a son; but the name of sons is attributed to those to whom remission of sins is granted, and to them immortality is promised anew, in the words of our Lord Himself: "Whoever commits sin is the servant of sin. And the servant abides not in the house forever, but the son abides forever."

11. But how great is the Lord's indulgence! how great His condescension and plenteousness of goodness towards us, seeing that He has wished us to pray in the sight of God in such a way as to call God Father, and to call ourselves sons of God, even as Christ is the Son of God, a name which none of us would dare to venture on in prayer, unless He Himself had allowed us thus to pray! We ought then, beloved brethren, to remember and to know, that when we call God Father, we ought to act as God's children; so that in the measure in which we find pleasure in considering God as a Father, He might also be able to find pleasure in us. Let us converse as temples of God that it may be plain that God dwells in us. Let not our doings be degenerate from the Spirit; so that we who have begun to be heavenly and spiritual, may consider and do nothing but spiritual and heavenly things; since the Lord God Himself has said, "Them that honor me I will honor; and he who despises me shall be despised." The blessed apostle also has laid down in his epistle: "Ye are not your own; for ye are bought with a great price. Glorify and bear about God in your body."

12. After this we say, "Hallowed be Thy name;" not that we wish for God that He may be hallowed by our prayers, but that we beseech of Him that His name may be hallowed in us. But by whom is God sanctified, since He Himself sanctifies? Well, because He says, "Be ye holy, even as I am holy," we ask and entreat, that we who were sanctified in baptism may continue in that which we have begun to be. And this we daily pray for; for we have need of daily sanctification that we who daily fall away may wash out our

sins by continual sanctification. And what the sanctification is which is conferred upon us by the condescension of God, the apostle declares, when he says, "neither fornicators, nor idolaters, nor adulterers, nor effeminate, nor abusers of themselves with mankind, nor thieves, nor deceivers, nor drunkards, nor revilers, nor extortioners, shall inherit the kingdom of God. And such indeed were you; but ye are washed; but ye are justified; but ye are sanctified in the name of our Lord Jesus Christ, and by the Spirit of our God." He says that we are sanctified in the name of our Lord Jesus Christ, and by the Spirit of our God. We pray that this sanctification may abide in us and because our Lord and Judge warns the man that was healed and quickened by Him, to sin no more lest a worse thing happen unto him, we make this supplication in our constant prayers, we ask this day and night, that the sanctification and quickening which is received from the grace of God may be preserved by His protection.

13. There follows in the prayer, Thy kingdom come. We ask that the kingdom of God may be set forth to us, even as we also ask that His name may be sanctified in us. For when does God not reign, or when does that begin with Him which both always has been, and never ceases to be? We pray that our kingdom, which has been promised us by God, may come, which was acquired by the blood and passion of Christ; that we who first are His subjects in the world, may hereafter reign with Christ when He reigns, as He Himself promises and says, "Come, ye blessed of my Father, receive the kingdom which has been prepared for you from the beginning of the world." Christ Himself, dearest brethren, however, may be the kingdom of God, whom we day by day desire to come, whose advent we crave to be quickly manifested to us. For since He is Himself the Resurrection, since in Him we rise again, so also the kingdom of God may be understood to be Himself, since in Him we shall reign. But we do well in seeking the kingdom of God, that is, the heavenly kingdom, because there is also an earthly kingdom. But he who has already renounced the world, is moreover greater than its honors and its kingdom. And therefore he who dedicates himself to God and Christ, desires not earthly, but heavenly kingdoms. But there is need of continual prayer and supplication, that we fall not away from the heavenly kingdom, as the Jews, to whom this promise had first been given, fell away; even as the Lord

sets forth and proves: "Many," says He, "shall come from the east and from the west, and shall recline with Abraham, and Isaac, and Jacob in the kingdom of heaven. But the children of the kingdom shall be cast out into outer darkness: there shall be weeping and gnashing of teeth." He shows that the Jews were previously children of the kingdom, so long as they continued also to be children of God; but after the name of Father ceased to be recognized among them, the kingdom also ceased; and therefore we Christians, who in our prayer begin to call God our Father, pray also that God's kingdom may come to us.

14. We add, also, and say, "Thy will be done, as in heaven so in earth;" not that God should do what He wills, but that we may be able to do what God wills. For who resists God, that He may not do what He wills? But since we are hindered by the devil from obeying with our thought and deed God's will in all things, we pray and ask that God's will may be done in us; and that it may be done in us we have need of God's good will, that is, of His help and protection, since no one is strong in his own strength, but he is safe by the grace and mercy of God. And further, the Lord, setting forth the infirmity of the humanity which He bore, says, "Father, if it be possible, let this cup pass from me'" and affording an example to His disciples that they should do not their own will, but God's, He went on to say, "Nevertheless not as I will, but as Thou wilt." And in another place He says, "I came down from heaven not to do my own will, but the will of Him that sent me." Now if the Son was obedient to do His Father's will, how much more should the servant be obedient to do his Master's will! as in his epistle John also exhorts and instructs us to do the will of God, saying, "Love not the world, neither the things that are in the world. If any man love the world, the love of the Father is not in him. For all that is in the world is the lust of the flesh, and the lust of the eyes, and the ambition of life, which is not of the Father, but of the lust of the world. And the world shall pass away, and the lust thereof: but he that doeth the will of God abides forever, even as God also abides forever." We who desire to abide forever should do the will of God, who is everlasting.

15. Now that is the will of God which Christ both did and taught. Humility in conversation; steadfastness in faith; modesty in words; justice in deeds; mercifulness in works; discipline in morals;

to be unable to do a wrong, and to be able to bear a wrong when done; to keep peace with the brethren; to love God with all one's heart; to love Him in that He is a Father; to fear Him in that He is God; to prefer nothing whatever to Christ, because He did not prefer anything to us; to adhere inseparably to His love; to stand by His cross bravely and faithfully; when there is any contest on behalf of His name and honor, to exhibit in discourse that constancy with which we make confession; in torture, that confidence with which we do battle; in death, that patience by which we are crowned;— this is to desire to be fellow-heirs with Christ; this is to do the commandment of God; this is to fulfill the will of the Father.

16. Moreover, we ask that the will of God may be done both in heaven and in earth, each of which things pertains to the fulfillment of our safety and salvation. For since we possess the body from the earth and the spirit from heaven, we ourselves are earth and heaven; and in both—that is, both in body and spirit—we pray that God's will may be done. For between the flesh and spirit there is a struggle; and there is a daily strife as they disagree one with the other, so that we cannot do those very things that we would, in that the spirit seeks heavenly and divine things, while the flesh lusts after earthly and temporal things; and therefore we ask that, by the help and assistance of God, agreement may be made between these two natures, so that while the will of God is done both in the spirit and in the flesh, the soul which is new-born by Him may be preserved. This is what the Apostle Paul openly and manifestly declares by his words: "The flesh," says he, "lusts against the spirit, and the spirit against the flesh: for these are contrary the one to the other; so that ye cannot do the things that ye would. Now the works of the flesh are manifest, which are these; adulteries, fornications, uncleanness, lasciviousness, idolatry, witchcraft, murders, hatred, variance, emulations, wraths, strife, seditions, dissensions, heresies, envyings, drunkenness, revellings, and such like: of the which I tell you before, as I have also told you in times past, that they which do such things shall not inherit the kingdom of God. But the fruit of the spirit is love, joy, peace, magnanimity, goodness, faith, gentleness, continence, chastity." And therefore we make it our prayer in daily, yea, in continual supplications that the will of God concerning us should be done both in heaven and in earth; because this is the will of God, that

earthly things should give place to heavenly, and that spiritual and divine things should prevail.

17. And it may be thus understood, beloved brethren, that since the Lord commands and admonishes us even to love our enemies, and to pray even for those who persecute us, we should ask, moreover, for those who are still earth, and have not yet begun to be heavenly, that even in respect of these God's will should be done, which Christ accomplished in preserving and renewing humanity. For since the disciples are not now called by Him earth, but the salt of the earth, and the apostle designates the first man as being from the dust of the earth, but the second from heaven, we reasonably, who ought to be like God our Father, who makes His sun to rise upon the good and bad, and sends rain upon the just and the unjust, so pray and ask by the admonition of Christ as to make our prayer for the salvation of all men; that as in heaven—that is, in us by our faith—the will of God has been done, so that we might be of heaven; so also in earth—that is, in those who believe not—God's will may be done, that they who as yet are by their first birth of earth, may, being born of water and of the Spirit, begin to be of heaven.

18. As the prayer goes forward, we ask and say, "Give us this day our daily bread." And this may be understood both spiritually and literally, because either way of understanding it is rich in divine usefulness to our salvation. For Christ is the bread of life; and this bread does not belong to all men, but it is ours. And according as we say, "Our Father," because He is the Father of those who understand and believe; so also we call it "our bread," because Christ is the bread of those who are in union with His body. And we ask that this bread should be given to us daily, that we who are in Christ, and daily receive the Eucharist for the food of salvation, may not, by the interposition of some heinous sin, by being prevented, as withheld and not communicating, from partaking of the heavenly bread, be separated from Christ's body, as He Himself predicts, and warns, "I am the bread of life which came down from heaven. If any man eat of my bread, he shall live forever: and the bread which I will give is my flesh, for the life of the world." When, therefore, He says, that whoever shall eat of His bread shall live forever; as it is manifest that those who partake of His body and receive the Eucharist by the right of communion are

living, so, on the other hand, we must fear and pray lest anyone who, being withheld from communion, is separate from Christ's body should remain at a distance from salvation; as He Himself threatens, and says, "Unless ye eat the flesh of the Son of man, and drink His blood, ye shall have no life in you." And therefore we ask that our bread—that is, Christ—may be given to us daily, that we who abide and live in Christ may not depart from His sanctification and body.

19. But it may also be understood this way, that we who have renounced the world, and have cast away its riches and pomps in the faith of spiritual grace, should only ask for ourselves food and support, since the Lord instructs us, and says, "Whosoever forsakes not all that he has, cannot be my disciple." But he who has begun to be Christ's disciple, renouncing all things according to the word of his Master, ought to ask for his daily food, and not to extend the desires of his petition to a long period, as the Lord again prescribes, and says, "'Take no thought for the morrow, for the morrow itself shall take thought for itself. Sufficient for the day is the evil thereof." With reason, then, does Christ's disciple ask food for himself for the day, since he is prohibited from thinking of the morrow; because it becomes a contradiction and a repugnant thing for us to seek to live long in this world, since we ask that the kingdom of God should come quickly. Thus also the blessed apostle admonishes us, giving substance and strength to the steadfastness of our hope and faith: "We brought nothing into this world," he says, "nor indeed can we carry anything out. Having therefore food and raiment, let us be with this content. But they that will be rich fall into temptation and a snare, and into many and hurtful lusts, which drown men in perdition and destruction. For the love of money is the root of all evil; which while some coveted after, they have made shipwreck from the faith, and have pierced themselves through with many sorrows."

20. He teaches us that riches are not only to be despised, but that they are also full of peril; that in them is the root of seducing evils, that deceive the blindness of the human mind by a hidden deception. From that principle also God rebukes the rich fool, who thinks of his earthly wealth, and boasts himself in the abundance of his overflowing harvests, saying, "Thou fool, this night thy soul shall be required of thee; then whose shall those

things be which thou hast provided?" The fool who was to die that very night was rejoicing in his stores, and he to whom life already was failing, was thinking of the abundance of his food. But, on the other hand, the Lord tells us that he becomes perfect and complete who sells all his goods, and distributes them for the use of the poor, and so lays up for himself treasure in heaven. He says that that man is able to follow Him, and to imitate the glory of the Lord's passion, who, free from hindrance, and with his loins girded, is involved in no entanglements of worldly estate, but, at large and free himself, accompanies his possessions, which before have been sent to God. For which result, that every one of us may be able to prepare himself, let him thus learn to pray, and know, from the character of the prayer, what he ought to be.

21. For daily bread cannot be lacking to the righteous man, since it is written, "The Lord will not slay the soul of the righteous by hunger" and again "I have been young and now am old, yet have I not seen the righteous forsaken, nor his seed begging their bread." And the Lord moreover promises and says, "Take no thought, saying, "What shall we eat, or what shall we drink, or with what shall we be clothed? For after all these things do the nations seek. And your Father knows that you have need of all these things. Seek first the kingdom of God and His righteousness, and all these things shall be added unto you." To those who seek God's kingdom and righteousness, He promises that all things shall be added. For since all things are God's, nothing will be lacking to him who possesses God, if God Himself be not lacking to him. Thus a meal was divinely provided for Daniel: when he was shut up by the king's command in the den of lions, and in the midst of wild beasts who were hungry, and yet spared him, the man of God was fed. Thus Elijah in his flight was nourished both by ravens ministering to him in his solitude, and by birds bringing him food in his persecution. And—oh detestable cruelty of the malice of man!—the wild beasts spare, the birds feed, while men lay snares, and rage!

22. After this we also entreat for our sins, saying, "And forgive us our debts, as we also forgive our debtors." After the supply of food, pardon of sin is also asked for, that he who is fed by God may live in God, and that not only the present and temporal life may be provided for, but the eternal also, to which we may come if our sins are forgiven; and these the Lord calls debts, as He

says in His Gospel, " I forgave you all that debt because you pleaded with me." And how necessarily, how providently and salutarily are we admonished that we are sinners, since we are compelled to entreat for our sins, and while pardon is asked for from God, the soul recalls its own consciousness of sin! Lest anyone should flatter himself that he is innocent, and by exalting himself should more deeply perish, he is instructed and taught that he sins daily, in that he is bidden to entreat daily for his sins. Thus, moreover, John also in his epistle warns us, and says, "If we say that we have no sin, we deceive ourselves, and the truth is not in us; but if we confess our sins, the Lord is faithful and just to forgive us our sins." In his epistle he has combined both, that we should entreat for our sins, and that we should obtain pardon when we ask. Therefore he said that the Lord was faithful to forgive sins, keeping the faith of His promise; because He who taught us to pray for our debts and sins, has promised that His fatherly mercy and pardon shall follow.

23. He has clearly joined with this and added the law, and has bound us by a certain condition anti engagement, that we should ask that our debts be forgiven us in such a manner as we ourselves forgive our debtors, knowing that that which we seek for our sins cannot be obtained unless we ourselves have acted in a similar way in respect of our debtors. Therefore also He says in another place, "With what measure ye mete, it shall be measured to you again." And the servant who, after having had all his debt forgiven him by his master, would not forgive his fellow-servant, is cast back into prison; because he would not forgive his fellow-servant, he lost the indulgence that had been shown to himself by his lord. And these things Christ still more urgently sets forth in His precepts with yet greater power of His rebuke. "When ye stand praying," says He, "forgive if ye have aught against any, that your Father which is in heaven may forgive you your trespasses. But if ye do not forgive, neither will your Father which is in heaven forgive you your trespasses." There remains no ground of excuse in the day of judgment when you will be judged according to your own sentence; and whatever you have done, that you also will suffer. For God commands us to be peacemakers, and in agreement, and of one mind in His house; and such as He makes us by a second birth, such He wishes us when new-born to continue, that we who have

begun to be sons of God may abide in God's peace, and that, having one spirit, we should also have one heart and one mind. Thus God does not receive the sacrifice of a person who is in disagreement, but commands him to go back from the altar and first be reconciled to his brother, that so God also may be appeased by the prayers of a peace-maker. Our peace and brotherly agreement is the greater sacrifice to God,—and a people united in one in the unity of the Father, and of the Son, and of the Holy Spirit.

24. For even in the sacrifices which Abel and Cain first offered, God looked not at their gifts, but at their hearts, so that he was acceptable in his gift who was acceptable in his heart. Abel, peaceable and righteous in sacrificing in innocence to God, taught others also, when they bring their gift to the altar, thus to come with the fear of God, with a simple heart, with the law of righteousness, with the peace of concord. With reason did he, who was such in respect of God's sacrifice, become subsequently himself a sacrifice to God; so that he who first set forth martyrdom, and initiated the Lord's passion by the glory of his blood, had both the Lord's righteousness and His peace. Finally, such are crowned by the Lord, such will be avenged with the Lord in the day of judgment; but the quarrelsome and disunited, and he who has not peace with his brethren, in accordance with what the blessed apostle and the Holy Scripture testifies, even if he have been slain for the name of Christ, shall not be able to escape the crime of fraternal dissension, because, as it is written, "He who hates his brother is a murderer " and no murderer attains to the kingdom of heaven, nor does he live with God. He cannot be with Christ, who had rather be an imitator of Judas than of Christ. How great is the sin which cannot even be washed away by a baptism of blood— how heinous the crime which cannot be expiated by martyrdom!

25. Moreover, the Lord of necessity admonishes us to say in prayer, "And suffer us not to be led into temptation." In which words it is shown that the adversary can do nothing against us except God shall have previously permitted it; so that all our fear, and devotion, and obedience may be turned towards God, since in our temptations nothing is permitted to evil unless power is given from Him. This is proved by divine Scripture, which says, "Nebuchadnezzar king of Babylon came to Jerusalem, and besieged

it; and the Lord delivered it into his hand." But power is given to evil against us according to our sins, as it is written, "Who gave Jacob for a spoil, and Israel to those who make a prey of Him? Did not the Lord, against whom they sinned, and would not walk in His ways, nor hear His law? and He has brought upon them the anger of His wrath." And again, when Solomon sinned, and departed from the Lord's commandments and ways, it is recorded, "And the Lord stirred up Satan against Solomon himself."

26. Now power is given against us in two modes: either for punishment when we sin, or for glory when we are proved, as we see was done with respect to Job; as God Himself sets forth, saying, "Behold, all that he hath I give unto thy hands; but be careful not to touch himself." And the Lord in His Gospel says, in the time of His passion, "You would have no power over me unless it were given you from above." But when we ask that we may not come into temptation, we are reminded of our infirmity and weakness in that we thus ask, lest any should insolently vaunt himself, lest any should proudly and arrogantly assume anything to himself, lest any should take to himself the glory either of confession or of suffering as his own, when the Lord Himself, teaching humility, said, "Watch and pray, that ye enter not into temptation; the spirit indeed is willing, but the flesh is weak," so that while a humble and submissive confession comes first, and all is attributed to God, whatever is sought for suppliantly with fear and honor of God, may be granted by His own lovingkindness.

27. After all these things, in the conclusion of the prayer comes a brief clause, which shortly and comprehensively sums up all our petitions and our prayers. For we conclude by saying, "But deliver us from evil," comprehending all adverse things which the enemy attempts against us in this world, from which there may be a faithful and sure protection if God deliver us, if He afford His help to us who pray for and implore it. And when we say, Deliver us from evil, there remains nothing further which ought to be asked. When we have once asked for God's protection against evil, and have obtained it, then against everything which the devil and the world work against us we stand secure and safe. For what fear is there in this life to the man whose guardian in this life is God?

28. What wonder is it, beloved brethren, if such is the prayer which God taught, seeing that He condensed in His teaching all our prayer in one saving sentence? This had already been before foretold by Isaiah the prophet, when, being filled with the Holy Spirit, he spoke of the majesty and lovingkindness of God, "consummating and shortening His word," He says, "in righteousness, because a shortened word will the Lord make in the whole earth." For when the Word of God, our Lord Jesus Christ, came unto all, and gathering alike the learned and unlearned, published to every sex and every age the precepts of salvation He made a large compendium of His precepts, that the memory of the scholars might not be burdened in the celestial learning, but might quickly learn what was necessary to a simple faith. Thus, when He taught what is life eternal He embraced the sacrament of life in a large and divine brevity, saying, "And this is life eternal that they might know Thee, the only and true God, and Jesus Christ, whom Thou hast sent." Also, when He would gather from the law and the prophets the first and greatest commandments, He said, "Hear, O Israel; the Lord thy God is one God: and thou shall love the Lord thy God with all thy heart, and with all thy mind, and with all thy strength. This is the first commandment. And the second is like unto it, Thou shalt love thy neighbor as thyself." "On these two commandments hang all the law and the prophets." And again: "Whatsoever good things ye would that men should do unto you, do ye even so to them. For this is the law and the prophets."

29. Nor was it only in words, but in deeds also, that the Lord taught us to pray, Himself praying frequently and beseeching, and thus showing us, by the testimony of His example, what it behooved us to do, as it is written, "But Himself departed into a solitary place, and there prayed." And again: "He went out into a mountain to pray, and continued all night in prayer to God." But if He prayed who was without sin, how much more ought sinners to pray; and if He prayed continually, watching through the whole night in uninterrupted petitions, how much more ought we to watch nightly in constantly repeated prayer!

30. But the Lord prayed and besought not for Himself—for why should He who was guiltless pray on His own behalf?—but for our sins, as He Himself declared, when He said to Peter, "Behold, Satan hath desired that he might sift you as wheat. But I have

prayed for thee, that thy faith fail not." And subsequently He beseeches the Father for all, saying, "Neither pray I for these alone, but for them also which shall believe on me through their word; that they all may be one; as Thou, Father, art in me, and I in Thee, that they also may be one in us." The Lord's lovingkindness, no less than His mercy, is great in respect of our salvation, in that, not content to redeem us with His blood, He in addition also prayed for us. Behold now what was the desire of His petition, that like as the Father and Son are one, so also we should abide in absolute unity; so that from this it may be understood how greatly he sins who divides unity and peace, since for this same thing even the Lord besought, desirous doubtless that His people should thus be saved and live in peace, since He knew that discord cannot come into the kingdom of God.

31. Moreover, when we stand praying, beloved brethren, we ought to be watchful and earnest with our whole heart, intent on our prayers. Let all carnal and worldly thoughts pass away, nor let the soul at that time think on anything but the object only of its prayer. For this reason also the priest, by way of preface before his prayer, prepares the minds of the brethren by saying, "Lift up your hearts," that so upon the people's response, "We lift them up unto the Lord," he may be reminded that he himself ought to think of nothing but the Lord. Let the breast be closed against the adversary, and be open to God alone; nor let it suffer God's enemy to approach to it at the time of prayer. For frequently he steals upon us, and penetrates within, and by crafty deceit calls away our prayers from God, that we may have one thing in our heart and another in our voice, when not the sound of the voice, but the soul and mind, ought to be praying to the Lord with a simple intention. But what carelessness it is, to be distracted and carried away by foolish and profane thoughts when you are praying to the Lord, as if there were anything which you should rather be thinking of than that you are speaking with God! How can you ask to be heard of God, when you yourself do not hear yourself? Do you wish that God should remember you when you ask, if you yourself do not remember yourself? This is absolutely to take no precaution against the enemy; this is, when you pray to God, to offend the majesty of God by the carelessness of your prayer; this is to be watchful with your eyes, and to be asleep with your heart, while the Christian, even though

he is asleep with his eyes, ought to be awake with his heart, as it is written in the person of the Church speaking in the Song of Songs," I sleep, yet my heart awakes." Wherefore the apostle anxiously and carefully warns us, saying, "Continue in prayer, and watch in the same;" teaching, that is, and showing that those are able to obtain from God what they ask, whom God sees to be watchful in their prayer.

32. Moreover, those who pray should not come to God with fruitless or naked prayers. Petition is ineffectual when it is a barren entreaty that beseeches God. For as every tree that does not bring forth fruit is cut down and cast into the fire; assuredly also, words that do not bear fruit cannot deserve anything of God, because they are fruitful in no result. And thus Holy Scripture instructs us, saying, "Prayer is good with fasting and almsgiving." For He who will give us in the day of judgment a reward for our labors and alms, is even in this life a merciful hearer of one who comes to Him in prayer associated with good works. Thus, for instance, Cornelius the centurion, when he prayed, had a claim to be heard. For he was in the habit of doing many alms-deeds towards the people, and of ever praying to God. To this man, when he prayed about the ninth hour, appeared an angel bearing testimony to his labors, and saying, "Cornelius, thy prayers and thine alms are gone up in remembrance before God."

33. Those prayers quickly ascend to God which the merits of our labors urge upon God. Thus also Raphael the angel was a witness to the constant prayer and the constant good works of Tobias, saying, "It is honorable to reveal and confess the works of God. For when thou didst pray, and Sarah, I did bring the remembrance of your prayers before the holiness of God. And when thou didst bury the dead in simplicity, and because thou didst not delay to rise up and to leave thy dinner, but didst go out and cover the dead, I was sent to prove thee; and again God has sent me to heal thee, and Sarah thy daughter-in-law. For I am Raphael, one of the seven holy angels which stand and go in and out before the glory of God." By Isaiah also the Lord reminds us, and teaches similar things, saying, "Loosen every knot of iniquity, release the oppressions of contracts which have no power, let the troubled go into peace, and break every unjust engagement. Break thy bread to the hungry, and bring the poor that are without shelter into thy

house. When you see the naked, clothe him; and despise not those of the same family and race as thyself. Then shall thy light break forth in season, and thy raiment shall spring forth speedily; and righteousness shall go before thee, and the glory of God shall surround thee. Then shalt thou call, and God shall hear thee; and while thou shalt yet speak, He shall say, Here I am." He promises that He will be at hand, and says that He will hear and protect those who, loosening the knots of unrighteousness from their heart, and giving alms among the members of God's household according to His commands, even in hearing what God commands to be done, do themselves also deserve to be heard by God. The blessed Apostle Paul, when aided in the necessity of affliction by his brethren, said that good works which are performed are sacrifices to God. "I am full," saith he, "having received of Epaphroditus the things which were sent from you, an odor of a sweet smell, a sacrifice acceptable, well pleasing to God." For when one has pity on the poor, he lends to God; and he who gives to the least gives to God—sacrifices spiritually to God an odor of a sweet smell.

34. And in discharging the duties of prayer, we find that the three children with Daniel, being strong in faith and victorious in captivity, observed the third, sixth, and ninth hour, as it were, for a sacrament of the Trinity, which in the last times had to be manifested. For both the first hour in its progress to the third shows forth the consummated number of the Trinity, and also the fourth proceeding to the sixth declares another Trinity; and when from the seventh the ninth is completed, the perfect Trinity is numbered every three hours, which spaces of hours the worshippers of God in time past having spiritually decided on, made use of for determined and lawful times for prayer. And subsequently the thing was manifested, that these things were of old Sacraments, in that anciently righteous men prayed in this manner. For upon the disciples at the third hour the Holy Spirit descended, who fulfilled the grace of the Lord's promise. Moreover, at the sixth hour, Peter, going up unto the house-top, was instructed as well by the sign as by the word of God admonishing him to receive all to the grace of salvation, whereas he was previously doubtful of the receiving of the Gentiles to baptism. And from the sixth hour to the ninth, the Lord, being crucified, washed away our sins by His

blood; and that He might redeem and quicken us, He then accomplished His victory by His passion.

35. But for us, beloved brethren, besides the hours of prayer observed of old, both the times and the sacraments have now increased in number. For we must also pray in the morning, that the Lord's resurrection may be celebrated by morning prayer. And this formerly the Holy Spirit pointed out in the Psalms, saying, "My King, and my God, because unto Thee will I cry; O Lord, in the morning shalt Thou hear my voice; in the morning will I stand before Thee, and will look up to Thee." And again, the Lord speaks by the mouth of the prophet: "Early in the morning shall they watch for me, saying, Let us go, and return unto the Lord our God." Also at the sunsetting and at the decline of day, of necessity we must pray again. For since Christ is the true sun and the true day, as the worldly sun and worldly day depart, when we pray and ask that light may return to us again, we pray for the advent of Christ, which shall give us the grace of everlasting light. Moreover, the Holy Spirit in the Psalms manifests that Christ is called the day. "The stone," says He, "which the builders rejected, is become the head of the corner. This is the Lord's doing; and it is marvelous in our eyes. This is the day which the Lord has made; let us walk and rejoice in it." Also the prophet Malachi testifies that He is called the Sun, when he says, "But to you that fear the name of the Lord shall the Sun of righteousness arise, and there is healing in His wings." But if in the Holy Scriptures the true sun and the true day is Christ, there is no hour excepted for Christians wherein God ought not frequently and always to be worshipped; so that we who are in Christ—that is, in the true Sun and the true Day—should be instant throughout the entire day in petitions, and should pray; and when, by the law of the world, the revolving night, recurring in its alternate changes, succeeds, there can be no harm arising from the darkness of night to those who pray, because the children of light have the day even in the night. For when is he without light who has light in his heart? or when has not he the sun and the day, whose Sun and Day is Christ?

36. Let not us, then, who are in Christ—that is, always in the lights cease from praying even during night. Thus the widow Anna, without intermission praying and watching, persevered in deserving well of God, as it is written in the I Gospel: "She

departed not," it says, "from the temple, serving with fastings and prayers night and day." Let the Gentiles look to this, who! are not yet enlightened, or the Jews who have remained in darkness by having forsaken the light. Let us, beloved brethren, who are always in the light of the Lord, who remember and hold fast what by grace received we have begun to be, reckon night for day; let us believe that we always walk in the light, and let us not be hindered by the darkness which we have escaped. Let there be no failure of prayers in the hours of night—no idle and reckless waste of the occasions of prayer. New-created and newborn of the Spirit by the mercy of God, let us imitate what we shall one day be. Since in the kingdom we shall possess day alone, without intervention of night, let us so watch in the night as if in the daylight. Since we are to pray and give thanks to God forever, let us not cease in this life also to pray and give thanks.

Sources Used For Original Material

Christian Classics Ethereal Library

Westminster Shorter Catechism -
http://www.ccel.org/ccel/anonymous/westminster1.txt

The Small Catechism – Martin Luther -
http://www.ccel.org/ccel/luther/smallcat.txt

The Heidelberg Catechism -
http://www.ccel.org/creeds/heidelberg-cat-ext.txt

J.C. Ryle Expository Thoughts on Matthew -
http://www.ccel.org/ccel/ryle/matthew.txt

John Calvin – Institutes of the Christian Religion -
http://www.ccel.org/ccel/calvin/institutes.v.xxi.html

John Wesley's Notes on the Whole Bible -
http://www.ccel.org/ccel/wesley/notes.txt

Charles Spurgeon – Sermons, Volume 24 –
http://www.ccel.org/ccel/spurgeon/sermons24.xii.html

E.M. Bounds – The Reality of Prayer –
http://www.ccel.org/ccel/bounds/reality.txt

Thomas Watson – The Lord's Prayer -
http://www.ccel.org/ccel/watson/prayer.txt

Chrysostom - Homilies on the Gospel of St. Matthew –

http://www.ccel.org/ccel/schaff/npnf110.txt

Augustine – Sermon on the Mount -
http://www.ccel.org/ccel/schaff/npnf106.txt

e-Sword Resources - http://www.e-sword.net/index.html

Matthew Henry - Commentary on the Whole Bible

G. Campbell Morgan – Commentary on Matthew

Charles Simeon – Horae Homileticae (Biblesupport.com)

Andrew Murray – With Christ in the School of Prayer

Cyprian – Treatise IV, On the Lord's Prayer (Biblesupport.com)

Sermon Index - www.SermonIndex.Net

John Broadus - Text Sermons

http://www.sermonindex.net/modules/articles/index.php?view=article&aid=2429

Archive.org – www.archive.org

John Henry Jowett – Bringing Heaven to Earth

OChristian.com – www.ochristian.com

George H. Morrison – Devotional Sermons –

http://devotionals.ochristian.com/George-H.-Morrison-Devotional-Sermons/1208.shtml

Shorter Catechism Project – www.shortercatechism.com

Alexander Whyte – A Commentary on the Shorter Catechism –

http://www.shortercatechism.com/resources/whyte/wsc_whyte_006.html

Afterword

About reNEW Publications

reNEW Publications is a publishing company that promotes love for God by promoting writings from the pre-20th century and renewing them for the modern reader. reNEW Publications seeks to create an interest among today's readers in some of the most significant authors of the past by using creative design layouts and modernized language.

About Curtis Rose

Curtis Rose is a Bible teacher and author. Curtis works as a software consultant in the Denver area. His passion is to explore the Bible, to explain it, and then to exhort others to follow it. He has also authored two books entitled *Transformed Into His Image* and *Lord, Teach Us to Pray.*

He and his wife, Jeane, live in Castle Rock, CO. They have three children and fourteen grandchildren.

Curtis Rose can be reached by e-mail at: curtis@seetheroses.com.

Made in the USA
Las Vegas, NV
30 October 2020